MIND SCULPTURE

MIND SCULPTURE

UNLOCKING YOUR BRAIN'S UNTAPPED POTENTIAL

IAN H. ROBERTSON

FROMM INTERNATIONAL
NEW YORK

To you, Fiona, my love and gratitude . . .
. . . and to you Deirdre, Ruairi and Niall – the same

Contents

Author's Note

The introduction to Chapter 5 was originally part of an article by the author published in *The Times*, London, 25 July 1995. The introduction to Chapter 6 is also part of an article first published by the author in *The Times* on 8 March 1994. The author would like to thank *The Times* for permission to reprint these sections of the articles.

Acknowledgements

To my friends and colleagues at the Medical Research Council Cognition and Brain Sciences Unit in Cambridge, thanks for your indulgence and patient reading of draft chapters: Dorothy Bishop, Tim Dalgleish, Tom Manly, Joost Heutink. Thanks also to Peter Halligan in Oxford, and to Gordon Winocur at the Rotman Research Institute in Toronto. To these and all my other colleagues and collaborators in Cambridge, Toronto and London, thanks for giving me all the brain stimulation a man can cope with. Special thanks to Alan Baddeley for his inspiration and to Don Stuss for these exhausting, exhilarating discussions.

To my brother Jim, in celebration of our trips to Knoydart, Rum, Carnmore, Loch Scionascaig and other places where the trout eluded him. To my friend Geoff for his enthusiasm and for his violent, if erratic, tennis. To Tony for improving his saxophone playing and Tom Shipsey for his hip-flask. To Dave for putting me on to the Wellcome Trust's popular-science writing competition while thrashing me at snooker. Sincere thanks for everything to my agent Felicity Bryan, and to my editor at Transworld, Ursula Mackenzie, a revelation to a man accustomed only to the neglect of academic editors.

To my parents, John and Anne Robertson, my love and thanks for staying young at heart.

Finally, to Fiona, without whose support I could not have done this.

1

The Electric *YOU*

Listen. Can you hear an aircraft passing overhead? A dog barking? The twittering of birds? In straining to listen, you have just sent a surge of electrical activity through millions of brain cells. In choosing to do this, you have changed your brain – you have made brain cells fire, at the side of your head, above the right eye.

As you come back to reading these words, a quite different part of the brain pulses with the electricity of you. At this precise moment, your brain is sending extra blood to the left side of your brain and to the back of your brain. This is fuel for the electricity needed for a different kind of mental effort – the act of transforming these squiggles on the paper into thought.

By the time you have read this far, you will have changed your brain permanently. These words will leave a faint trace in the woven electricity of you. For 'you' exists in the trembling web of connected brain cells. This web is in flux, continually remoulded, sculpted by the restless energy of the world. That energy is transformed at your senses into that utterly unique weave of brain connections that is 'you'.

Your brain takes up a fifth of all the energy generated by your body in its resting state. It is like a 20-watt lightbulb, continuously glowing. This energy is needed to drive activity in the vast trembling web of connected cells that is your brain. And you – the captain of this amazing ship – can direct this activity, as you have just done.

That you can read these strange, arbitrary lines on the page is because people have changed your brain. Just as I am moulding the electricity of your brain connections at the moment you read this, so your parents and teachers physically sculpted your brain by what they taught you. Without this mind sculpture you would be illiterate. You were taught to read because it isn't something your brain does naturally. Had you not been taught to read, you would not be 'you'. For who 'you' are arises from the restless murmuring and urging of the world at the gates of your senses.

Through your senses, and in the trembling weave of your brain, this energy is transmuted into the electricity of you. And you, in turn, give this energy back to the universe by what you choose to do and say. Thus you are locked into an intimate embrace with the universe, the universe transforming you and you changing it.

Escape from the shackles of biology

Your brain is changed physically by the conversations you have, the events you witness and the love you receive. This is true all through your life, not just when you are an infant. Until very recently, scientists were pessimistic about the possibility of sculpting the brain through experience. This is understandable because of a stark fact which has been known for over half a century: unlike almost all the other cells in the body, brain and spinal cord cells in the main do not replace themselves. Once dead, most brain cells stay dead, although recent research has found new brain cells being produced in adults, in a part of the brain known as the hippocampus. But assuming that cells mostly can't grow, how can our brains be sculpted and our abilities enhanced by experience? We will discover the answer to this question in this book.

It is often argued that the brain is 'hard-wired', meaning that if the wiring is broken, or indeed if a brain never gets wired in the first place, then change is impossible. It is true that the brain *is* hard-wired to a great extent, but research over the last ten years has proved dramatically that in fact its wiring can be much less 'hard' than was once thought.

With the sparkling advances in the science of genetics it has become widely accepted that much of what 'you' are as a human being is pre-ordained in your genes. Of course to a considerable extent this is true, but the pendulum has swung too far away from the idea of what 'you' can *become*.

In human evolution, the last part of the brain to develop was the frontal lobes, right behind the forehead, above the eyes. These make up more than 40 per cent of the brain's volume. This is also the last area in the brain to connect up in the child – in fact, it really only wires up fully in the late teens or early twenties. It is this part of the brain that makes us truly human.

In the frontal lobes you hold an image of yourself, and it is according to this image that you go out to meet the world. How you behave in that world will depend on the frontal lobes regulating the older parts of the brain. In the frontal lobes you project yourself into a future and steer yourself through life by plans and goals set in that future. The electric 'you', born of love and experience, soothes your inherited biology, trimming its sails for the soft winds of human relationships and civilization.

It is in the frontal lobes that you conceive of the minds of other people, with all that that entails for morals, trust, faith and love. Without the frontal lobes, you are no longer 'you'. Without the frontal lobes, there can be no conscience, will or civilized humanity. Of all the parts of the brain, the frontal lobes are the least hard-wired, the most adaptable to the world's restless tugging and murmuring at our senses. The frontal lobes are evolution's gift to us – or its curse. Here reside our self-awareness and our loss of innocence. We were cast out of the Garden of Eden when this part of the brain became fully evolved, for with it came choice, will and conscience.

We are unique because evolution has endowed us with the ability to shape our own destinies – and to shape our own brains. As a species, we have succeeded because of this 40 per cent of the brain with its capacity for near-infinite adaptability. So let's cast off the notion that we

3

are pre-programmed clusters of brain modules doomed to behave according to ancient plans while deluded by the notion that we act through free will! On the contrary: while much of our behaviour is genetically influenced, we can – through our civilization and culture – mould the human brain. In so doing we can have some escape from the shackles of biology.

2

The Trembling Web

Take a moment to glance at the picture on page 6, then bring your eyes back here and read on. Do you recognize what the picture shows? Random dots? In a moment I will ask you to look again, but this time, when you are scanning the picture, try to be aware of your eyes as they search it for meaning. At the moment you scan the picture, your brain will send electrochemical impulses through chains of nerve cells to your eyes, commanding them back and forth across the page, trying to make sense of the pattern. As this happens, your eyes will be transmitting the patterns of the figure through the nerve cells to the vision centres at the back of your brain, just above the nape of your neck. From there, signals will be sent forward again through more and more advanced decoding centres of the brain's visual system.

Now look at the picture again briefly, before bringing your eyes back to this line of print. Try to imagine this electrical to-ing and fro-ing along the bundles of long white fibres that connect the brain's nerve cells. If pick-ups were attached to your scalp at the moment of looking, the electrical activity would be displayed as a continuously moving wave on a screen. The microvoltage could even be amplified to light an electric bulb or move a toy electric train.

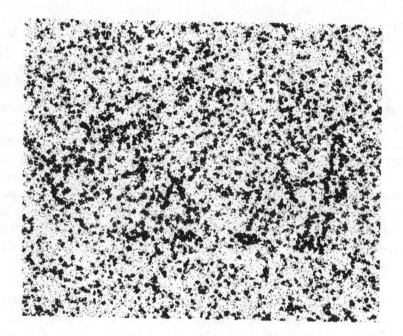

Now glance once more at the picture. What is it? Could you sense the brain's decoders trying to make guesses about what it is you were looking at? Could it be a flower? A piece of furniture? Just above your ears – in the temporal cortex – the brain's centres for decoding and recognizing objects were working overtime trying to match the pattern of dots with real objects it has learned and stored in memory.

Each time your eyes moved to another position on the picture, a new set of signals passed from the eye, to the back of the brain and forward again to the decoders. New guesses were made, but they drew a blank. The eyes were instructed to move again, to search further for meaning. More electrical current, more brain activity – but the decoders still drew a blank.

Turn now to the picture on page 232 and glance at it before turning back here. You should have seen the picture of a rhinoceros. Now peep again at the picture opposite. Do you see the animal there that you didn't recognize before? You should see it now. If not, hold the book at arm's length. These dots should have form and meaning now. Neurones – brain cells – specialized for detecting objects are now firing in the temporal lobes of your brain. A few seconds ago the pictures were meaningless dots and the object-recognition brain cells were not reponding strongly. Now these cells spark into life as they suddenly discern a meaning that was missing before.

You have just changed your brain. A week from now, if you look at the same dotty puzzle, you will see the rhino in it because the object-recognition brain cells have been primed to fire to such images. They learned through just one fragment of experience – a glance at the picture on page 232 – which prepared them to fire. Thus readied, when the blobs reached them again these cells had a sort of 'ah-ha' experience and fired to the tiny clues almost hidden in the jumble of dots.

This fragment of experience changed the connections between neurones in your brain. This was brain sculpture in action – the moulding like soft plastic of nerve tissue by the murmuring and flickering of the world on your senses. Thus a fragment of the energy present in the universe impinges upon you and changes you for ever. You, in turn, transform and return that energy to the universe in many ways: by what you say, do, think and feel; by the flickering millivoltages spreading at this very moment from your brain out into the cosmos.

The trembling web

Everything which makes up 'you' – memories and hopes, pain and pleasure, morals and malevolence – is embroidered in a trembling web of 100 billion brain cells. On average, each cell is connected 1,000 times with other neurones, making a total of 100,000 billion connections. There are more cell meeting-points in a human brain than there are stars in our galaxy.

A meeting-point between two cells is called a 'synapse' and was first described by the Oxford physiologist Sir Charles Sherrington at the turn of the century. A brain cell is shaped a bit like an onion, with a roundish middle, a single long shoot at one end and lots of thinner root-like fibres sticking out at the other. An onion sucks up nutrients from the ground, processes them in the onion bulb and sends the results up into the sprouting shoot. Brain cells work a bit like this.

The cluster of thin fibres converging on the brain cell corresponding to the onion's roots are called 'dendrites'. These, like the roots of the onion, suck nutrition into the brain cell. The particular 'nutrition' which they bring consists of electrochemical impulses from other brain cells. The tendrils from these other cells itch and nag at our cell's surface, trying to annoy it into action. Or at least some of them do: others try to nag the cell into 'silence' – to inhibit it.

Whether or not a brain cell fires therefore depends upon the final arithmetic of the combined hectoring of all these inputs – all the 'Go, go!' inputs minus all the 'Stop, stop!' inputs. Once this arithmetic exceeds a particular level, then the brain cell fires, sending an electro-chemical impulse shooting up the equivalent of the onion's single green shoot.

This green shoot on the brain cell is called its 'axon'. A cell has a single axon, which is its only channel into the rest of the brain. Axons can range in length from a tenth of a millimetre to 2 metres! When the brain cell is coaxed into sending a signal up its axon, it does so in a single blurting pulse rather than in a constant trickle. This pulse lasts about a thousandth of a second and travels at a speed of anything between 2 and 200 miles per hour.

Having travelled up the axon, the pulse causes an itch at the point of contact with the dendrites of another brain cell. That point of contact is the synapse. This reaction continues through the trembling web of neurones, connected by synapses, and so a chain reaction occurs, with cells firing off in their hundreds, thousands or millions across the three-dimensional net. Some of these cells are triggered by the impulses reaching their dendrite roots, others are silenced and inhibited.

At this very moment, as you read this sentence, exactly this cascade of brain-cell firings is happening in your brain, across these all-important junctions – the synapses. At the beginning of the chapter, when you recognized the rhinoceros emerging out of the blobs, it was changes at the synapses in the object-recognition areas of your brain that made you see the familiar pattern of the animal. At first you didn't see the rhino because the dots were not clear enough to trigger activity in the brain cells which are specialized for recognizing objects. Shown a more recognizable object, however, these cells *did* spring into life.

The dots in the first figure did, of course, have some similarity to the face in the second picture and these similarities were strong enough to fire the object-decoding cells when you looked at the blobs again. So isn't this just the same as when you eat a piece of garlic and then for a while everything tastes of garlic? There's nothing very surprising about that. The object-recognition cells get some exercise by being shown the clear picture and so are just a bit more limbered up when given the blobs. What has this got to do with brain sculpture?

While there is certainly something in the garlic analogy, it is far from being the whole story. The rest of the story takes us to the brain's central trick – and this trick is the reason that our brains are such a wonderful medium for sculpture. We have seen that a brain cell fires when it gets enough of a push from the axons of other brain cells itching and nagging at its surface. When you saw the clear animal, this sent impulses cascading down thousands of dendrites into the cell. In response, the neurone spat a pulse up its axon, which in turn helped trigger another cell into action.

As all this happens, cells that don't have much to do with each other end up firing off at more or less the same time. This is not because they are close buddies, but simply because both happened to be triggered by the same cascade of activity in the brain – the surge of electrical activity generated by seeing the animal. It's a bit like being stuck in a delayed plane with someone: at first you don't have anything to do with the person beside you, but after an hour or two you will be groaning and complaining together. A similar thing happens to brain cells. After a few repetitions of firing together, they tend to team up. When two connected neurones have been triggered at the same time on several occasions, the cells and synapses between them change chemically so that when one now fires, it will be a stronger trigger to the other. In other words, they become partners and in future will fire off in tandem much more readily than before. This is called 'Hebbian learning', after the Canadian psychologist Donald Hebb, and the chemical change in cells and synapses is called 'long-term potentiation' (LTP).

In the case of the dotted figure you stared at earlier, only when the easy-to-recognize rhino had activated the relevant cells did they fire. Once this has happened a few times, however, the brain activity caused by the blobs becomes linked with the 'oh there's a . . .' action in the object-decoding cells. In other words, through Hebbian learning, the brain activity associated with the unclear dots becomes linked with the object-decoding cell activity.

Look at the unclear figure again. You see the animal easily now, probably, not everyone does. This is because the synapses between key neurones in your brain have been changed by the experience of seeing the clearer picture of the rhinoceros. So the very act of reading this chapter has remoulded connections between nerve cells in your brain. Whereas the term 'Hebbian learning' would have triggered no particular response in your brain before, these words will in future evoke some flicker of recognition.

As we live our lives, experience gradually remoulds us. Connections are made in the brain, and connections are broken. We learn and we forget. Anger transmutes to forgiveness, love to indifference, resignation to hope. You sign up for Spanish classes and embark on remoulding a few million synapses as you wrestle with the grammar, vocabulary and pronunciation. Then you become too busy to continue and the connections wither. Go to Spain on holiday next year, however, and you surprise yourself with what emerges from your lips as you relax over a glass of perfumed Rioja. Words and phrases you thought you had forgotten slip out. You even understand snatches of conversation between the two Spaniards at the next table. Traces of your evening classes have lingered in your brain, filigreed in the trembling web of connections between cells, and, just as the prince's kiss woke Sleeping Beauty, the sound of the Spanish language on your holiday has woken those dormant connections. There, in the synapses' chemistry, lingers the memory of the changes which experience and learning have wrought.

Some experience stamps itself on your brain so firmly that even dementia does not dislodge it. Alzheimer's Disease, in its last stages, can make you forget your loved ones and lose track of time, place and personality. Yet when Margaret Thatcher was British Prime Minister, it was common for Alzheimer's patients who could remember little else to be able to recognize her face and recall her name.

Nor do you forget the smell of new-baked bread from the bakery in the small French town where you had that wonderful holiday; the feeling of holding your child for the first time; the moment you heard some terrible news ... Some experiences echo so widely and strongly through our brains that the changes they cause in the synapses will never be undone. This is particularly true when these events activate the emotional centres of the brain, for then the experience becomes woven into an even wider fabric of nerve tissue – and is hence much less easily unravelled.

Experience, in short, is sculpted into the *pattern* of connections between neurones, not necessarily into specific connections between particular pairs of neurones. This is not only good news but is also utterly essential for our survival, as our brain connections are in flux throughout our life. If all our experience, memories and personality depended on very specific connections between particular neurones, then memory and personality would degrade far more dramatically and unpredictably than they actually do under normal circumstances. This brings us on to the subject of dance and death.

The death of cells and the synaptic dance.

The connections between cells are constantly changing. In certain parts of the brain with particularly rapidly changing connections, it has been estimated that the average life of any one synaptic connection may be as short as eight hours. Neurones have been filmed, showing a continual, restless flux in their connections with other neurones.

It is just as well, therefore, that our sculptured brains do not lose their shape when some synapses disappear: if they did, we would all be like newborn babies, having to relearn each day the basics of living. In principle, however, the way the brain functions is little different from the way in which human organizations – companies, clubs or universities – work. These social groupings do not – unless they are very badly organized – collapse if a particular individual becomes sick or leaves. If an individual – even a very senior person – does go, the organization continues doing its job. It goes on because what it does is defined largely by the *relationships* between the employees, and these exist through roles and rules. Hence if the bookkeeper runs off with the postroom supervisor, the organization will not grind to a halt. Other employees can be drafted in to help out in these roles. To the outsider, the organization will continue working as if nothing had happened.

So it is in your brain. Today the connections between brain cells will change, yet tomorrow your family and workmates will not notice anything different about you. This is because the billions of connections which make you 'you' preserve the *patterns* which store your experience and memory, even when some of the individual connections in these patterns disappear.

That is one of the key principles behind this book: the whole is more than the sum of its parts. And the whole can survive when some of the parts disappear. But why is there such restlessness in the synapses? Why are they continually in flux, touching, letting go, touching again? That brings us to our second key principle.

Cells that fire together, wire together

Does 'Hebbian learning' ring any bells for you? If so, it is because reading this book has moulded the synapses in the language centres of your brain so that these words now have some sort of meaning – no matter how vague or confused – linked to them. As we saw a few pages back, when several brain cells are triggered at roughly the same time, they team up. The synapses linking these cells develop a sort of hair-trigger, so that when one fires, they all tend to fire.

This neural trade unionism is one major reason for the restless ebbing and flowing of the brain's connections. Every second of every day, you experience events which trigger different sets of neurones in your brain. The billboard you glimpse on your way to work shows a car driven by a beautiful woman racing through a brush fire in an exotic, tropical location. These images fire off neurones in the emotional centres of your brain. At the same moment, the language and visual neurones of your brain register the logo and brand name of the car. Bingo! Two sets of neurones in distinct areas of the brain are switched on at the same time. Pass that billboard every morning for a few weeks, see similar images on television in the evening, and you have a complex of interconnected neurones wired together because they fired together. And what happens? You see the car in a showroom window and some fragment of the emotion which has been connected to it gets triggered – or so the marketing team hopes!

Advertising agents spend their lives trying to mould your synapses through Hebbian learning. Their constant battle is to try to link the products they are pushing with emotional circuits in the brain. Such methods are so successful in sculpting brains that regulatory codes for advertisers have had to be imposed. For instance, one such code in the UK forbids alcohol advertisers from using sexual images. However, linking anything with the sexual circuits of the brain through Hebbian learning is so effective in boosting sales that advertisers sail very close to the wind with, and at times flout, this regulation.

Marketing men and women want to link their products to the neurones in the emotional centres of your brain because such synaptic connections are much harder to dissolve than connections between other sets of neurones. Just try to remember what you learned in that Spanish class for confirmation of this!

Binding the body in the brain

Take a moment to look at the back of your left hand. Now take the fore-finger of your right hand and slowly stroke the back of the left hand's middle finger. Close your eyes and do that several times, noticing the sensations in the middle finger.

Even with your eyes closed, there is no doubt which finger is being touched. As your forefinger moves down its length, the light pressure on each part of the finger triggers a separate set of neurones. It is the fact that each part of your finger is uniquely wired to a particular set of neurones in the brain that allows you to know where on your middle finger the touch is.

In fact, the whole surface of your body is precisely mapped on to a thin strip of tissue on the outer surface of your brain (the cortex). Known as the 'somato-sensory strip', it runs from approximately halfway along the top of your head down to just above each ear.

When your middle finger is touched, sensory neurones fire, sending electrochemical impulses up your arm and into the back of the spinal cord. The current passes along thin white nerve fibres – the axons – until it reaches the first synapse in the spinal cord. The electrochemical discharge caused by the touch then triggers the synapse in the spinal cord, which in turn fires. Its discharge travels up the spine through the long, uninterrupted, gossamer-thin axons, until it reaches a second synapse at the lowest part of your brain – the 'medulla'.

The incoming current arriving at this tiny synaptic canyon fires the neurone across to the other side of the valley. This is only the second such synapse that the touch-induced current has had to cross in the long journey between your left hand and the outer boundaries of your brain. The nerve fibres now cross to the right side of the brain.

The third stretch of axonal thread travels up from the very bottom of your brain, to a message-centre structure deep in the middle of the brain called the 'thalamus'. Here your touch-current reaches its third synapse, in the right half of the thalamus. The message jumps the synaptic hurdle and finishes the last leg of its journey – the few centimetres between the thalamus and the somato-sensory strip on the cortex.

Because sensation on the right side of the body is registered on the left side of the brain, it was the right cortex that detected the touch on your left middle finger. Remember too that in its travels between your hand and brain, the electrochemical current crossed only three synapses.

Now another small exercise. Close your eyes again and run the fore-finger of your right hand down your cheek. As you do so, try to pay attention to the fine sensations over the part of your face touched by the finger. Now, still with your eyes closed, run your finger down your calf. Again, be aware of the feelings in the touched skin.

How did the two sensations compare? You should have felt a much more delicate and precise sensation in your face than in your calf. One reason for this is that the number of brain cells devoted to each square centimetre of face is greater than for the calf.

The whole surface of the body is connected to the brain in an orderly fashion, with a so-called one-to-one mapping. In other words, all the fibres from the hand cluster together on the somato-sensory strip on the brain surface, and indeed each finger has its own block-booked season ticket of neurones clustered together on the cortex. Even the 5–6-foot wires from toe to brain finally hug together at the cortex, like refugees reunited after a long journey. There is no democracy for the refugees, however. The big hitters – face, hands, genitals – get allocated far more brain space than humbler parts of the body such as feet, legs and chest. One could blame corrupt immigration officials, but evolutionary pressure probably has more to do with it.

On the sensory strip, however, the different areas of the body are arranged in a slightly peculiar way. For instance, the hand season-ticket holders sit next to the face season-ticket holders in the stadium. This can have ghostly consequences if you lose part of your body – more of this later.

So, there we have it. Our nerve cells have wired up by the time we are toddlers and, like small-town accountants with loyal customers, the sensory cortex cells settle securely into a lifetime of blameless service to their client body part. Or do they?

As privileged members of the body, each finger has a big chunk of brain tissue at its disposal. There is, however, a rare congenital disorder known as 'webbed-finger syndrome', or 'syndactyly'. Some people are born with a hand which is more like a fist: though you can discern the outlines of fingers, they are webbed together so that they never move independently, but always together as a group.

What does the sensory map of the brain look like for the hands of these individuals? Well, the answer is that the brain space allocated to one finger is pretty well merged into the space devoted to another. In other words, the brain hasn't bothered to treat the fingers as individuals but deals with them largely as a single group, allocating one chunk of brain space to the whole hand.

Why is this? Maybe the same congenital factors that caused the webbed hand were also responsible for the unusual brain organization? Perhaps – but there is one dramatic way to test this. Surgeons have developed techniques for separating the webbed fingers so that they can be moved independently. When this happens, what happens to the brain? If the brain organization is set in stone by genetic factors, then nothing should happen.

Well, something quite dramatic does happen. Before surgery, the fingers have a single blob of cortex allocated to them *en masse*. Less than a month after surgery, however, the brain has given each finger its own personal patch of neurones. In short, brain organization has altered because the shape of the hand has changed.

Why? Remember the slogan of this section: 'cells that fire together, wire together'. When the fingers of the hand were joined up, each time one finger moved, every other finger also moved. On the principle of Hebbian learning, this meant that the neurones responding to these individual fingers became synaptically connected with each other. In other words, when one fired, they all tended to fire.

When a group of neurones all fire in response to different stimuli, then the brain can't distinguish these different stimuli. If, for instance, the neurones responding to different types of fruit all joined together in a Hebbian fashion in your brain, then you would lose the ability to distinguish a banana from a plum. Each would register in your brain as being much the same thing.

So it was for the fingers of the webbed hand. It was as if the block-booked season tickets in the stadium for four different groups of fans had become mixed up. When the fingers were surgically separated, however, the 'fire together, wire together' rule began to break down. When the forefinger moved, the little finger did not necessarily move with it. As a result, the synaptic connections between the areas representing the two fingers began to weaken, so that when one set was triggered the other set did not necessarily fire in solidarity. In consequence, each finger developed a more independent and specialized region of the brain.

We know now, therefore, that in the normal hand and brain each finger has its own neat allocation of neurones. This is in part because the brain cells representing each finger have become wired together through continually firing together in infancy. If this is true, then it would follow that if your mother had forced you to wear tight-fitting mitts for a long time, your brain would have developed a mitt-shaped map of your hand, without giving separate cells to separate fingers.

Indeed the brain can be trained in this kind of way to change its maps of the body surface. In one American study, for instance, monkeys were given harmless vibrating stimulation *across* the fingers over a long period. For many thousands of trials, the tip of each finger was touched at the same time by a vibrating bar. In normal life, the brain cells representing one finger all tend to fire together as that finger moves and touches something, but now, artificially, the brain cells for equivalent segments of *different* fingers were made to fire together again and again by the vibrating bar. The result was that the neurones representing the tips of each finger merged together in a Hebbian way. In effect, this meant creating in the brain a new *horizontal* finger across the hand – as well as, of course, 'dissolving' the old fingers! This happened because these neurones fired together repeatedly over a long period.

These maps, however, could easily be returned to normal after the training ended. As soon as the fingers stopped always getting the same horizontal touch at the same time, then normal stimulation of the fingers resumed. With each finger tending to move individually, this meant returning to the old situation where brain cells on the same finger were usually triggered together. This is brain sculpture in action, with neurones rewiring in line with experiences provided by the outside world.

Suppose one brain cell is made to fire by a touch on the skin. Then suppose that another cell close by which is *not* switched on by that outside trigger is made to fire repeatedly at the same time. Then, according to Hebbian learning, these two cells should become wired up together. Now, the touch-neutral cell should begin to fire when the skin is touched, because it has teamed up with the other touch-sensitive cell.

This is fine in theory, but how can you contrive to make cells fire together in this way? Well, one way is to stimulate the surface of the brain with tiny electric currents. When you do this, you trigger a whole bunch of cells into firing together, even though they might not normally do so in response to stimulation from the outside world. If you do this for long enough – over several hours in fact – sure enough, you find that you have created new sensory body maps in the stimulated part of the brain.

You changed your brain by looking at the rhinoceros picture at the beginning of this chapter. Thoughts and experience change the way your brain is wired up, but so can passing tiny electrical currents through your brain. These two totally different methods for changing the brain are, however, based on the one principle – Hebbian learning.

When cells fire apart, wires depart

As we have seen, the monkeys whose fingers had been stimulated, so changing their finger brain maps, didn't stay permanently altered by the experience: the artificial horizontal finger maps in the brain quickly dissolved once the monkeys resumed normal life. Holiday romances and friendships tend not to survive the return to normal workaday life. In the same way, clusters of cells that have wired together through common experience tend to stop being buddies once that experience ends.

This makes good sense. If such wiring were permanent, then a lifetime of brain moulding would lead to massive mental traffic jams. After all, if we remained close friends with everyone we got on well with on holiday, we would have to work full time at keeping up the hundreds of resulting friendships accumulating throughout our lives. The brain has evolved rules to avoid such traffic jams.

Not only do cells that fire together wire together, but cells that don't fire together suffer a weakening of the synapses connecting them. If a signal arrives at the synapse canyon, but a signal is not triggered at the other side of the valley, then that particular synapse weakens and the hair-trigger between it and the cell which usually fires it also weakens.

In essence, this is a sort of free-market competition between active and inactive synapses. In other words, if you want to make your name as a big-time synapse in a particular syndicate, then you'd better make sure you keep visible by firing when the others do. If you start to get lax and don't snap into action with the rest of the team, then your days in the mob are numbered.

Why do brain cells sometimes break ranks and stop firing together? Well, a single brain cell can have as many as 10,000 different synapses bearing down on it. Some of these will help the neurone fire, but others strive to suppress or inhibit it. When signals are triggered at these inhibitory synapses, this tends to hold back the neurone at the other side of the synaptic valley from being triggered.

Whether or not that neurone fires at any one time depends on the combined signals of thousands of triggering and thousands of suppressing neurones all screaming in its ears. This is a little like the stockmarket: whether a particular equity rises or falls depends on the end result of thousands of selling and buying transactions of that particular share. If the buying exceeds the selling, then the share price goes up; if the selling exceeds the buying, the share price falls.

In other words, a neurone can stop working with the rest of the gang if the combined firing of inhibitory synapses on that neurone exceeds the combined input of all the positive, excitatory synapses. A neurone may, however, also drop out of the team if it gets better offers from other brain cells to which it is connected.

Take Beethoven's Ninth Symphony, for instance. Over many years of my life, this work of musical genius moulded an exquisite assembly of synaptically connected cells in my brain. Apart from the obvious emotional brain centres affected, the piece aroused vivid visual images of wood-panelled concert halls in which grey-headed cellists hunched over heartrending chords and massed choirs exulted in a noble hymn to universal brotherhood. A year spent living in Italy, however, shredded that delicious neural assembly more completely than psychosurgery. This was because Italy's classical radio station used as a jingle a few ruined chords of the 'Alle Menschen werden Brüdern' climax of the piece. Heard a dozen times a day for weeks, the neuronal assemblies associated with brushing teeth and making breakfast quickly displaced the old, more romantic clusters. The sheer frequency and intrusion of the jingle was too much for the delicate synapses of the old assemblies, which disintegrated, leaving only the scummy residue of a ravaged masterpiece strewn across my brain tissue.

Fame and extinction

If you are famous, you will be famous for some activity or characteristic. When people think of that activity or characteristic, the more famous you are, the more likely it is that you will be the example they think of. Dancer-actor? John Travolta. Tenor? Luciano Pavarotti. Female politician? Margaret Thatcher. And so on. But finding the right answer means discarding all other plausible answers to the question. To get to John Travolta, we did not select another possible candidate like Rudolph Nureyev. Similarly, recalling Pavarotti meant not remembering Placido Domingo.

There is, however, a particularly painful truth for the famous. When the public remember someone, not only do they boost that person's memory-trace, but they also suppress the memories of other people in the same category. For instance, remembering Margaret Thatcher both boosts her already strong memory-trace in your mind, and also depresses the memory-traces of other female politicians. How many of you, for instance, can remember the name of Turkey's first woman Prime Minister?

Applied to the world of glitz and fame, these results make painful reading if you are a rock musician whose career is in decline. For if the public is encouraged to remember the name and image of another rock star again and again, then they will find it harder to remember your name. This amnesia can be quite longlasting, as any forgotten rock star will ruefully tell you.

Advertisers intuitively hit on this principle many years ago. The best adverts are those which do not thrust the name of the product on to you. Rather, sophisticated advertisers try to make you pull out their product from memory on the basis of hints and clues. Hence the sight on billboards of apparently bizarre and surreal images which make you puzzle and stare at them, until you suddenly notice some fragment of a logo to which you cry 'Aha!' in recognition.

Being challenged and teased makes you pay more attention to the product. What's more, you are being coaxed into actively remembering (rather than passively recognizing) the product: so at a stroke the advertisers make it easier for you to remember their product *and* make it harder to recall their competitor's.

This is all a long way from a single inhibitory synapse discouraging a brain cell from firing. Also, it is not yet known whether the inhibition in memory retrieval rests on exactly the same processes as inhibition at the single-cell level. We can get closer to the single cell, however, in studying a phenomenon known as 'ocular dominance'.

If you hold a finger 3 inches in front of your eye, you will see two images of it. Closing each eye in turn will give a view of the single finger from a different angle. In everyday life, however, our brain does not allow us to see two of everything. The two slightly different images of every object we look at are merged in the brain to give us a single view: this is why you see only one full stop at the end of this sentence, not two.

The binocular view of the world that gives us single rather than double vision arises because cells in the visual part of the brain are arranged in what are known as 'ocular-dominance columns'. Input from each eye is divided between a series of alternating columns in the visual part of the brain – left, right, left, right, etc. Early in the brain's development, however, some fibres from the left eye also feed into the right-eye columns and vice versa.

These cluttered, mixed-up columns begin to sort themselves out as the visual world impinges on the brain through the eyes. The fibres from the left eye ending in a particular column tend to fire together when something flickers across the eye. Because of the Hebbian 'fire together, wire together' principle, this joint activity strengthens the connections between the synapses from the left eye at this particular column.

But what happens to the right-eye fibres that wire into this column? Remember the two different views of your finger from your two eyes? This shows that the input arriving in the brain from each eye is slightly different. In other words, in the mixed-up ocular-dominance columns, while the left-eye synapses will fire together, the right-eye fibres will not be triggered in precisely the same way because the view of the right eye is slightly different from that of the left.

Given the principle 'when cells fire apart, wires depart', this out-of-kilter firing leads to a gradual pruning of the right-eye fibres in the mainly left-eye columns and vice versa. In this way, experience and learning cultivate the brain garden, weeding out the left-eye dahlias from the right-eye rosebeds and the other way round. As the gardening progresses, so the right-eye rosebeds flourish under their Hebbian fertilizer, as do the dahlias in their own, segregated flowerbeds.

One important constituent of the fertilizer is 'neural-growth factor'. When released from the far side of the synaptic canyon, neural-growth factor fosters the growth of extra terminals on the other bank of the synaptic canyon, thus building stronger and bigger bridges across the chasm. Growth factor leaks out only when enough cells fire together, thus producing a large enough burst of current in the far side of the synapse.

22

Stores of growth factor are, however, limited, and the ruthless economics of the brain is such that gangs of terminals firing together will suck up the growth factor and gain new synaptic recruits. Terminals of cells which do not fire at exactly the same time will be starved of this growth factor and will wither. So, in the young brain, the minority right-eye fibres innocently branching into predominantly left-eye columns are starved out, like victims of ethnic cleansing. The result is a series of 'ethnically pure' left- and right-eye columns.

What happens, however, if one eye becomes damaged and input to the columns of cells for that eye is cut off? Connections between cells are in constant competition with each other, forging alliances when cells fire together and breaking them when they fire apart. The synapses starved of stimulus from the damaged eye weaken and the victorious army-columns representing the healthy eye expand their territory in the brain. So the brain adjusts itself to the input that the world provides.

Some children are born with an eye disorder known as 'strabismus' – a squint – where the eyes are out of alignment. Doctors used to wait until children had reached the age of eight or nine before operating on the squinting eye to bring it into alignment with the other eye. When they realized how experience sculpted the brain, though, they rapidly changed their practice. Squints are now corrected at a much younger age because of the way in which the brain responds to the input coming from two out-of-kilter eyes. Initially, these children have good vision in each eye, but because the eyes are out of alignment the brain cannot fuse the images in the two eyes. As a result, the child often favours one eye and the brain centres serving the other eye are slowly starved of stimulation. If this continues uncorrected, the child may lose useful vision in the neglected eye. An early operation will prevent this loss of vision, whereas an operation at eight or nine is much less likely to do so. This is because this particular type of brain plasticity has a 'critical period' during which experience can change brain structure. Beyond this age range, the loss of effective vision in the neglected eye cannot be reversed by the vision available in eyes newly aligned by corrective surgery.

Ultimately, all that we think, see, learn and do depends on the firing of brain cells and the transmission of electrochemical impulses down a vast, trembling web. Our mental processes are constantly moulding and reshaping the connections between these networks of brain cells. Let's now see some of these processes at work in the mental gym.

3

Pumping Iron in the Mental Gym

The hurdler is hunched over the starting blocks, his mind aware of nothing but his body's crescent of taut muscle. The gun explodes. He bursts on to the track as if a leash has been cut, high-stepping the straight towards the first hurdle. His arms are precision blades, machine-tooling the air. He lifts and clears the hurdle, grounding to a crisp reunion of spike and track. He flies the first 200 metres. But suddenly the angels of energy desert him and he is abandoned, leaden-legged, at that bleak cross-roads of speed and stamina where 400-metre hurdlers are crucified. On his own now, each step willed, every jump a theorem to be proved, the air a cloying paste on his blunted hands. He falls across the line, eyes turned from straining sockets to catch the clock. Damn! Damn! Two seconds slower than his best!

Slowly he walks his heart to calmness, fists clenched in frustration – two seconds might as well be two years so close to a championship. Nothing else for it. Has to run again. Legs have stopped trembling, fingers are loose, head lifting. One more time. He finds the blocks again and slowly drops to the ready. He and the gun erupt as one and he takes the first hurdles like a hunted deer with half a mile to live. Two hundred metres and his body tells him the time is good. But suddenly – what's happening? He's slowing. His legs have turned to rubber, arms wind-milling far above his head. He slews off the track and falls vomiting to the turf.

The athlete barely makes it to the bathroom from the chair where he has run two races against the clock. As he throws up he knows at once his error. Two back-to-back 400-metre races are simply not possible for the body – would never be attempted by an athlete on a track without a decent break. No more are they possible for the mind in its mental gym. For the mental race run from the armchair is a precise facsimile of its real-world brother, right down to the split-second timing. The difference is only really obvious to the watcher, who sees nothing of the mental race run by the stock-still athlete. But to the runner it is all there – even to the point of the retching exhaustion of over-exertion.

The British javelin-thrower and Olympic medallist Steve Backley, in his book The Winning Mind, *gives the example of such a hurdler, whose mental training was so lifelike that it produced this dramatic effect. It is very common for world-class athletes to train on the mental track or in the mental gym. On one occasion, Backley himself sprained his ankle just four weeks before the competition season began. For two weeks he was immobile – normally a crippling disadvantage for an athlete at this stage in the season. From his chair during those two weeks, however, he mentally threw the javelin a thousand times in every major stadium in the world. At first it was difficult for him to visualize the mental throws without his sprained ankle forcing him to limp! He found, however, that if he concentrated his mental imagery on the undamaged side of his body, he could visualize the minutiae of fluent, often perfect throws. As a result, at the end of the two weeks he was able to resume real practice, carrying on from where he had left off before the injury.*

Neuroscientists are now studying this phenomenon, which athletes have practised intuitively for decades. We will see in this chapter how, in the mental gym, brain connections are sculpted to build strength and skill. We will discover too how idleness in the mental gym can also have dramatic effects on the brain.

The body in your brain

Hold your left palm up towards you. Mentally number the fingers: fore-finger 1, middle finger 2, ring finger 3 and little finger 4. Now look away from your hand and touch the fingers with your thumb in the sequence 4-1-3-2-4. Practise this several times, without looking at your hand and always in this order: little finger, forefinger, ring finger, middle finger, little finger and so on.

The moment you start to do this, the synapses in the movement part of the right half of your brain accelerate their firing. If at this moment you had your head in a brain scanner which could measure your brain activity, it would detect the extra bloodflow needed to fuel the increased firing of the synapses.

If you had a mind to, you could practise this sequence of finger movements for 10–20 minutes a day over three weeks. Were you to do so, you would – not surprisingly – become faster and better at the task. At the beginning it would take you on average just under 2 seconds per sequence, while after three weeks you would be able to complete each finger run in roughly three-quarters of a second.

Anyone who has learned to type or play a musical instrument will recognize how you get better with practice. For decades psychologists have studied how we learn skills, but until recently they have been unable to see what, if anything, happens in the brain as we learn. Now, thanks to the latest brain scanners, which tell us what the brain is up to as we perform, we can see inside the brain as it learns.

In a nutshell, what happens is this: the part of your brain's hand-movement control system that springs to life when you do the 4-1-3-2-4 task on the first day gets bigger over the twenty-one days. In other words, as you get better at the finger dance, so the amount of brain tissue involved expands: the synaptic action spreads out.

Don't expect that practising this exercise will make you a top-class pickpocket, however: the training doesn't affect even quite similar finger routines. Take the finger sequence 4-2-3-1-4, for instance. (If you have practised the first sequence a few times, try this new one now. Notice the difference?) In the brain-scan study that produced these results, volunteers practised this sequence very briefly at the beginning, and then three weeks later, without practising it in between. The brain expansion for the trained finger exercise did not take place for the untrained finger aerobics.

Cells that fire together, wire together, and the more often cells fire together, the more likely it is that they will team up. As you practise finger exercises – or other skills such as typing, for that matter – each time you do the routine, the same sets of brain cells fire in the same sequence. According to the rules of Hebbian learning, over hundreds of such trials, these cells will become linked up through the changes in their synapses.

Learning, therefore, sculpts the brain, crocheting intricate new patterns in the trembling web of connections between neurones. But is this not just the artificial stuff of laboratories? Does it really relate to everyday life? Well, yes, it does. Let's turn to one of the most important things in life – music – to see brain sculpture in action.

As everyone knows, playing stringed instruments such as guitar, violin or cello requires a pretty dexterous left hand to finger the fret-board. So what happens to the brains of people who have played one of these instruments for much of their lives? What takes place in the brain areas that register touch and sensation for these virtuoso bodyparts? To find out, a group of scientists lightly touched each finger in turn on the left hands of a group of nine stringed-instrument players, while scrutinizing their brains to see where and how much they responded.

Compared to non-musicians, a much bigger area of the part of the brain that detects touch 'lit up' when the players' left fingers were stroked. This region was also much bigger than the equivalent part in the other half of the musicians' brains: that is, when their right hands were touched, the touch centres in the left half of the brain 'lit up' to a normal extent, and much less than the right-brain centres. This is exactly what was found in the artificial finger-tapping routine, but now, in the real world, here is evidence that years of practice at their in-struments had actually moulded new circuits in the brain clay of these musicians.

Here is the obvious question: did the musicians who practised most assiduously have the biggest brain areas devoted to their left hands? No, they did not. What determined how big the left-hand brain area had become was how old they were when they began to learn their instruments. This would be no surprise to any music teacher, who knows that the brains of adult students are much less mouldable than those of child pupils.

In fact, we now know that a part of the left half of the brain known as the 'planum temporale' is bigger in musicians than in non-musicians. This part of the brain is important in verbal memory, and musical training before the age of twelve is now known to lead to better verbal memory. In other words, musical training not only expands the body-area of the brain used by the musical instrument, but also stimulates more general physical changes in the brain, benefiting other faculties.

Does this mean then that experience and practice change only the brains of children? No, it does not. It may be that the differences in how much adults practise are too small to show up as differences in brain activity. What this research does show, though, is that the young brain can be particularly yielding to the moulding of life's experience.

Brain theft

An afterthought: where exactly did the extra neural clay come from to give the musicians their extra finger space in the brain? Answer: from the brain area normally devoted to the palm of the left hand. The palm sensory neurones seem to have changed allegiance in response to the daily practice demands of the hard-worked fingers of the left hand: instead of continuing loyal service to the palm, they threw their weight behind the fingers' taxing duties at the fretboard.

There is probably a cost for this type of neural theft. It is likely that the musicians would have had less sensitive palms, because they had fewer brain cells devoted to detecting touch there. Though this wasn't specifically investigated in the musician study, other research shows how such neural defections dilute the sensitivity of the body regions which lose their brain representatives.

So, if the palm's brain cells have been seduced by their finger-representing colleagues, then the palm itself becomes less good at doing its touch-detecting job. Not that most of us make great use of our palms when feeling our way through the average day, so it probably doesn't matter much; but there are times when this filching of brain tissue *can* cause big problems.

Tens of thousands of people throughout the world have to give up work because of a disorder known as 'repetitive strain injury' (RSI). At risk are workers who have to carry out closely similar movements with their hands and arms hundreds or even thousands of times per day. Data-entry workers and typists are just two examples of those who move the same sets of muscles in the same way again and again. People who fall victim to the disorder develop pain, stiffness and weakness, which can be so severe that they lose their jobs.

We saw earlier how about 20 minutes' practice each day for a few weeks of a finger-tapping exercise expanded those brain areas responsible for this set of movements. What then are the effects of doing the same routine for eight hours a day, five days a week, year in, year out? Clearly they will be greater than those involved in our finger exercise. Even the heaviest practice schedule will be harmless if the routine is frequently broken up with different actions and if rests are taken regularly. In cases where the same routine is repeated again and again without frequent enough breaks or a big enough variety of movements, however, then the risks appear.

One of the dangers is that constant firing of the same networks of cells builds up a formidable web of connections which becomes so dominant in the neural marketplace that it squeezes out other patterns of connections needed for different movements. Here, the principle 'cells that fire together, wire together' forms an unholy alliance with its sister principle 'when cells fire apart, wires depart'. Together they nurture a hungry Hebbian network through unremitting over-practice of the hand movements which the person uses at work.

What are the consequences? Well, according to the neural-theft principle, one should be a reduced ability to recognize objects with your hands through touch, and one study has indeed shown that people with RSI are affected in this way.

What has happened here is the converse to what happened to the person whose webbed fingers were surgically separated. There, the joined fingers always moved together as a team, and so by Hebbian learning the brain maps for the separate fingers blurred and merged. Once they started an independent life, they teased out separate brain zones for the different fingers, because the brain cells for the fingers no longer always fired together.

In the brains of workers suffering from RSI, on the other hand, the constant activity of networks of brain cells in the same areas and in the same sequences may have blurred the individuality of subgroups of these cells. The neurones became like good factory employees who work well together doing the same job for twenty years; then the factory closes and they find themselves unequipped and unskilled for work elsewhere.

Physical problems in the hands and arms also play a part in RSI, but it does seem likely that brain changes are also important. Recordings from the brain cells of animals show that repetitive activity does indeed cause a blurring in the individual brain areas that are normally precisely specialized for separate parts of the body.

Your job engraved in your brain

Does all this mean that your brain is shaped by the job you do? Yes, it does. Researchers studied the brains of people who had died, looking in particular at how many branches or dendrites each neurone in a certain area of the brain had. What they found was that the cells in the brain finger areas of typists, machine-operators and appliance repairmen were more richly branched when compared with brain cells responsible for other parts of the body, such as the trunk. These findings are preliminary, but they do make sense in terms of what we know about how experience affects the brain.

The same research group came up with even more striking results in a later study, though. They carried out a detailed post-mortem examination of the brains of a number of people of different ages. What they found was quite remarkable: the more education a person had had in his or her life, the greater the complexity and number of branches (dendrites) there were on the neurones in the language areas of the brain.

While they could not prove which came first – complex brain neurones or relatively high education – the intriguingly strong possibility is that education fosters the sprouting of dendrites in brain cells. In fact, we know that education protects against the ravages of Alzheimer's Disease in old age, and this supports the notion that education builds brains as well as minds. Education is a cornerstone of civilization, and it civilizes by sculpting people's brains, by growing connections in their brains. This is one crucial way in which culture has taken over from evolution as the main engineer of human destiny.

If your brain can be shaped by your job and education, so it can also be embroidered by other types of stimulation. Blind Braille readers, for instance, usually read with the forefinger of their right hand. They use the touch sensors in their skin to recognize the raised Braille shapes on the paper, feeding words into their brain through their fingers rather than their eyes. Given what happens to the brains of violinists and cellists after years of practice, you would expect that this constant stimulation of a tiny area of skin would enlarge the brain area responsible for sensing touch on the forefinger: and this is exactly what has been found. Researchers mapped how much of the brain was 'switched on' by touching the reading fingertip in experienced compared to less well-practised Braille readers. Sure enough, just as with the musicians, the Braille readers who had been using their fingertip to read for many years had a bigger area of their brain devoted to that finger than the less experienced readers had. Of course, this area was bigger than the equivalent area on the opposite side of the brain devoted to the non-reading forefinger of the other hand.

Not all Braille readers use a single finger to read. Some use two or three fingers, which run together across the raised surfaces of the print. Where three fingers are used, these digits get the same stimulation again and again at more or less the same time. In other words, in the brain's body map, cells for finger 1 fire with the cells for finger 2, and so on.

Now, cells that fire together, wire together. So, if this is true, then we should find that the body maps in the brain for three-finger Braille readers are quite different from those of one-finger Braille readers. Unlikely? Maybe – but it happens! Three-finger Braille readers are much worse than their one-finger colleagues at knowing which of their three reading fingers has been touched. Their brain body maps for the fingers were also quite different, because the maps had been moulded by experience, with the cells for the three fingers wiring together so that when one fired, they all fired. When the middle finger was touched, for instance, cells for the forefinger and ring finger would also fire. As a result, the brain could not easily tell which finger had been touched, because the separate maps for each had been 'smeared' together by Hebbian learning.

This is exactly what happened with the person born with the webbed hand that we looked at in the last chapter. While the fingers always moved together there was a single map for all of them, but when they were surgically separated, each finger began to develop its individual map. So, if the three-finger Braille readers wanted to reclaim some of the individual sensitivity of each of their reading fingers, all they would have to do would be to start using each on its own. After a while, the cells for one finger would not always fire when those for the other fingers did so. Once again, the principle 'when cells fire apart, wires depart' would come into play.

Braille readers who spend six hours a day proofreading Braille texts show an expansion of the brain maps that control movements in their reading fingers after a day's work. These brain areas are bigger then than they are after the same people have had two days off work. In other words, not only does your job shape your brain over years, but it also affects your brain on a day-to-day basis. No wonder it's so hard to get your brain into gear on a Monday morning!

A thought: a large area of the brain towards the back of the head is devoted to decoding the wondrous carnival of visual information that our eyes take in. But what happens to these millions of neurones in people who can't see? That brings us to our next question: what happens when you can't get into the mental gym?

What happens when the gym is closed?

If you lose your sight, then a huge part of your brain is cut off from sensory experience. However, blindness doesn't lead to this part of the brain just withering away. No, the vision brain areas of blind people can be triggered by other sensations, such as touch or hearing. This is the opposite of what happens to sighted people, whose visual brains, when they pay attention to touch for instance, *decrease* in activity.

People who lost their sight when they were young show a 'lighting up' of the visual areas of their brains when they have to pay attention to touch while reading Braille or while trying to recognize shapes with their hands. This research tells us that brain cells cut off from the sense organs they serve don't pine and wither away. Rather, they put their shoulders to the wheel of other mental activity.

Breaking a leg in your brain

Blindness is not the only problem that can starve a brain of sensory stimulation. Suppose you break an arm or ankle and end up in plaster for a few weeks. During this time of enforced inactivity, the part of your brain that normally moves these muscles is laid off. One study looked at people who had an ankle joint strapped up because of injury. The researchers plotted out the area of the brain controlling movement of one particular muscle – the tibial muscle of the bound-up leg. They found that the amount of brain tissue devoted to moving this muscle had shrunk due to inactivity. What's more, the longer the ankle had been in plaster, the more this brain area had shrunk!

This withering took place because the trembling web of connections in the movement centre of the brain was not refreshed by normal, daily movement. The brain is a marketplace, with continual, restless competition for connections. Brain nets stay strong through their synapses firing together again and again, keeping the Hebbian connections bound together with constant exercise. Once this stimulation stops, though, other active networks of brain cells may start picking off some of the bored brain cells from the unstimulated circuit. They are a bit like headhunters circling round an ailing company, picking off the best staff for other organizations.

But don't worry – if you break an ankle, you won't affect your brain permanently. The brain changes found in these people were quickly reversed once they were asked deliberately to tense up the tibial muscle. In other words, a little burst of activity in the web of connections quickly re-established the full network. So, even though the synapses between neurones in that muscle's brain network had become sluggish, the connections were still largely in place and needed only a few bursts of synaptic activity to revive them.

If you starve a network of input for much longer periods, however, then the shrinkage might be less easily reversed. When the mental gym is closed for a long time, the effects can go beyond just changes in the synapses. You can find, for instance, a pruning back of the dendrites – the branching onion roots of the brain cells. This has dramatic effects: in rats, for example, those living in stimulating environments have many more branches spreading out from their neurones than do animals living in less interesting quarters. This is also very likely to be true for human beings – more of this later.

So, when the mental gym closes down, the trembling web can lose a lot of connections and, if that happens, it may take much more than the simple flexing of a muscle to build up the connections again. If you have ever had a leg or arm in plaster for a long time, you will know this all too well: you need physiotherapy to build up the muscles again so that they can regain normal movement – and physiotherapy almost certainly works by stimulating the shrunken connections in the movement-control parts of the brain as well as by building up the muscle tissue.

The astronaut's brain

Astronauts floating in the weightlessness of space have to learn to use their eyes to tell them where their bodies are. After all, there is no gravity, none of Earth's disciplined verticality. So, as they float about the space shuttle, they have only their eyes to tell them where they are in relation to their spaceship – there is no other way to find out what is up and what is down. Weightlessness means having to think about every move you make: hence the spongy, shaky way astronauts walk from the spacecraft once back on Earth.

Researchers at NASA in Houston, Texas, have discovered that it takes between four and eight days for an astronaut's balance to return to normal after being in space. Though no direct measures of brain function have been taken, it seems highly likely that weightlessness cuts off some sensory inputs to the astronaut's brain, causing temporary changes in brain organization similar to the changes found in the brains of people with plastered legs.

This last suggestion is especially plausible given that even anaesthetizing the fingers of a hand can, by cutting off sensory input with the local anaesthetic, change the brain map for the hand. In one study, after plotting the brain maps for each finger of the hand some of the fingers were anaesthetized. It was discovered that the brain areas sensitive to the non-anaesthetized fingers expanded into the shrunken areas which shortly before had loyally served the now-silent fingers. What's more, these changes in the brain persisted even after sensation returned. The brain would, however, almost certainly have returned to normality once the fingers were used normally again.

Grow your brain from the couch

Take a few moments to do this exercise. Imagine that a heavy rock is resting on the ground in front of you. In your mind only – without actually moving – reach down and lift it up, taking care to bend at the knees to avoid hurting your back. Now, in your mind, slowly stand up. Steady yourself for a moment. When you are ready, raise the rock to your shoulders, then ease it above your head until your arms are straight. Now lift it slowly up and down, taking care to straighten your arms each time. Do this ten times, then put the rock carefully back on to the floor.

Some people can imagine such movements with great clarity, others less well. It takes some concentration to make your mind track the slow up and down of the movements over the ten lifts. Sometimes the rock lifts and falls far more quickly than it would in real life. But if you practise it mentally, you will find that at least some of the time the imagination creates an uncanny facsimile of the real thing. Some people even feel tired towards the end of the ten lifts, and slow down as they near completion because of the effort! Try the ten lifts again in your mind if you want to check this out.

The startling fact is that mental practice of this type can actually increase real-world strength. One study looked at the effects of mental versus real practice in tensing and relaxing one finger of the left hand. This mini muscle-building took place for five sessions per week over four weeks – a total of twenty training sessions. Half the participants actually did the exercises, while a second group just imagined doing them for the same number of training sessions.

At the end of four weeks, the finger strength of each person was compared with people in a control group who did not train at all. The physical-practice group's finger strength had increased by 30 per cent while the control group showed little change in strength. In other words, if you do the equivalent of finger press-ups, you can build strength in the fingers – no big deal. But what happened to the people who just pumped iron in the mental gym? Their finger strength improved by 22 per cent, almost as much as the physical-training effect! This is good news indeed for the sluggards among us, who would prefer to do our training on the couch than on the track or in the gym.

These results were not due to the two trained groups simply putting more effort into their grip. No other parts of the body showed these increases in strength, which were quite specific to the fingers whether the training was physical or mental. Nor did the mental training work by building up the muscles in the fingers. In other words, the improvements in strength were caused by changes in the brain – and these brain changes were in turn caused by the stimulation of the trembling web of interconnected neurones controlling finger movements. By firing together again and again, these brain circuits strengthened and expanded, just as happened in the brains of the violinists and the Braille readers.

But is there actually any direct evidence that pumping virtual iron – doing the kind of mental practice that you did when you mentally lifted the rock – *does* change the brain? Yes, there is. One study plotted changes in the brain regions that kicked into life as people learned a one-handed five-finger exercise on the piano. For five days, two hours per day, volunteers practised this exercise and, just as has been shown in other research, the area of brain activated got bigger.

To make sure that the brain changes were really caused by the specific learning of the note sequence, another group of people played one-handed piano for the same period without learning any particular exercise or sequence of notes. Their brain areas expanded far less than the specific-exercise group, while a control group who didn't practise at all showed no change in the brain areas controlling movement in that hand.

Most interesting of all, however, was how a fourth group fared. These were people who just pumped iron in the mental gym, practising – purely in their heads – the five-finger piano exercise for the same length of time each day for five days. What happened to their brains? They showed similar changes to those shown in the brains of the people who really did practise the exercise! In other words, pumping virtual iron not only improves strength and performance – it does so by physically changing the brain.

Earlier we saw how athlete Steve Backley kept in training through mental practice, in spite of a sprained ankle. In the light of what we now know about how pumping iron inside the head affects the brain, this makes perfect sense: Backley kept stimulating the networks of connected neurones where his skill was embroidered. By keeping these patterns of connections firing together via the mental gym, he preserved them and protected them from the competition of the brain's marketplace.

Just as in the ruthless multinational corporation, executives who are off sick for a while may come back to find someone else sitting at their desk, so it is for brain connections. Top-class athletes spend years building up these superb assemblies of brain connections; it is in them that their talent resides. However, unlike embroidery with real thread, where the pattern stays once sewn, the synaptic embroidery of Hebbian learning needs constant rehearsal – and this rehearsal can happen either in the real world of the athletics track or in the virtual world of the mind. Just as executives need to keep their profile and political muscle in an organization by visibility and action, so it is for the brain connections where the athlete's prowess resides.

Can we actually *see* what happens in the brain during mental practice? Fortunately, we can. Using a PET scanner – a brain scanner that shows which parts of the brain are active during different mental and physical tasks – people were studied as they imagined themselves moving. The movements were based on a simple task – manipulating a joystick – and the brains were watched to see which areas were switched on when people imagined moving it. The results were compared with what happened when the same people simply got ready to move the joystick, without actually moving it.

What was found was that very similar parts of the brain 'lit up' in these two different situations. In other words, mentally imagining a movement triggers much the same brain machinery as does preparing to make the same movement. It seems, therefore, that imagining a movement is not very different from actually making the same movement, as far as the brain is concerned. Just in the final stage – actually instructing the muscles what to do and when – does the brain call into action extra centres which are not involved during imagination.

So, the next time you are laid up with a cold and can't go jogging, you can console yourself with a mental run around the block. But it is important that while doing this you actually *feel* yourself running to get the beneficial effects. We know this because of a study that compared brain activity in people as they *watched* hand movements with their brain activity when they *imagined themselves* moving their own hands. Watching someone else moving a hand triggered just the visual parts of the brain at the back of the head. Imagining making the movements themselves, however, lit up the movement areas of the brain. So you won't get fitter if you lie in bed picturing yourself sprinting down the street, but you will probably get a little fitter if you feel yourself doing it. This is because fitness resides partly in the brain connections, and you don't exercise the brain connections of the movement areas when you watch yourself doing the exercise. No – you have to do the mental training with your own mental body!

The hurdler described earlier exhausted himself by running a second mental race too soon after the first. He couldn't finish the imaginary race, and in fact actually vomited as if he really had over-exerted himself. This anecdote from the track may seem a little farfetched, but in fact there is good scientific evidence to support the principle that mental practice mimics its physical counterpart in many ways.

One study, for instance, had people imagine they were running on a treadmill that was going at different speeds. Even though they were not physically moving, their heart rate and breathing increased in direct proportion to the speed of the mental treadmill. In the light of this and other similar findings, it is entirely plausible that an athlete could over-exert himself on the mental track. In other words, Steve Backley's story about the vomiting hurdler has the ring of truth about it, scientifically speaking.

Try this exercise. Imagine that you are about to write your name, address and telephone number on a piece of paper. Before you start, set a timer so that you can find out how long this mental exercise takes. Take care to imagine your hand movements precisely. Now start the timer and begin. Make a note of how long it took you. Now find a real piece of paper and do the exercise in reality. Time yourself, then compare the two times. Usually, people find a close relationship between the time it takes to complete the mental task and the actual one.

You will have done the last exercise with your preferred hand – in most cases the right hand. Now do the exercise again, but this time with your non-preferred hand – probably your left. Time yourself in the mental and the real conditions again. You will not be surprised to find that it took longer to write your name and address with the left hand. But if you did as the people taking part in another study did, then you may be surprised to find that *mentally* writing with your left hand (or right if you are left-handed) *also* took longer than with the other hand. In other words, mental simulation followed very similar rules to those applying in the real world.

The same happened when volunteers imagined writing things in large versus small letters. Just as writing in large letters took longer in reality, so the mental act of writing in large letters took longer than writing in small letters.The same was true for walking: imagining yourself walking 10 metres took longer than imagining yourself walking 5 metres. Furthermore, the time taken to walk the imagined 10 metres was very close to the time taken *actually* to walk 10 metres.

So, pumping virtual iron is uncannily similar to pumping real iron. It isn't at all surprising, then, that mental practice can sculpt the brain just as real practice can. Nor should you be surprised to hear that the majority of the world's top athletes use mental imagery – indeed, most say that it is a vital technique for building up their performance. Among world-famous athletes who report preparing for competitions by 'feeling' and 'seeing' themselves acting out their sports routines are US basketball player Michael Jordan, French skier Jean-Claude Killy, golfer Jack Nicklaus and figure-skater Nancy Kerrigan.

What's more, mental practice improves surgeons' operating skills, as well as bettering physicians' abilities to carry out internal examinations. And the world-renowned concert pianist Glenn Gould practised very little in the latter part of his career. Instead, he would read a score and then mentally practise it several times before going on to make a recording of it!

In short, mental practice can not only can make you fitter and better at what you do, but it also changes the brain. Let's look a little more closely at how this happens.

More brain than brawn

Your brain is not a muscle. As we have seen, it seems that just passively stimulating brain circuits may not be enough to sculpt the brain – for stimulation to change the brain, you must *pay attention* to the experience. So, first of all, we have to answer the question 'What is attention?'

Reading the first lines of this paragraph means paying attention to just this small area of space, while ignoring all the other information which is streaming into your eye. It also involves (maybe) inhibiting thoughts about what sandwich you will have for lunch, memories of last year's holiday, or fantasies about winning the Lottery. You can choose to focus all your attention on this next WORD or you can 'zoom back' and become aware of the geometry of the whole page, something which was probably outside your focus of attention when you were reading WORD.

We couldn't survive without this ability to select some things for attention. Some types of brain damage disable people hugely by removing their ability to select what is important from the deluge of information assailing their senses and bubbling up from memory. Our ability to select a small fraction of information for attention depends upon particular parts of the brain, especially the forward part of the brain – the frontal lobes. Being able to select is just one type of attention, though.

Have you ever set out to hear your local weather on a national forecast and yet noticed as the broadcast ends that you haven't the faintest idea of what it was? With their highly familiar mantra of cold fronts, spreading systems and blustery showers, such bulletins rarely contain new information which grabs your attention. Remaining alert for your region's moment in this stream requires your active attention throughout the forecast. The brain's selective attention system has a partner brain circuit whose job it is to help you keep your attention maintained over time. The right hemisphere of the brain has a particular job to do here. People who suffer strokes of the right half of the brain find it more difficult than normal to keep alert and sustain their attention over time. This 'sustained attention system' is a kind of 'monotony override' which lets us keep our minds on a task when there is nothing very much in the task itself to keep us alert and interested. You need this brain system to keep alert when you are driving on an empty road at night or trying to keep your mind on a boring lecture. People who suffer damage to the right hemisphere of their brains have more difficulty in paying attention to the environment. They also find it hard to pay attention to their own bodies, which means it is harder for them to exercise their damaged brain circuits and help them recover some connections.

When you lifted the rock in your mind, you had to keep your

attention on your own body, disciplining your mind to keep track of all the movements. This is what athletes have to do in their mental preparation. To do it you really need a good sustained attention system, and you can be sure that the brain's attention circuits are working overtime.

Another thing the brain's attention systems have to do during difficult tasks like this is to 'adjust the volume' in other parts of the brain. We know this by studying how attention affects the activity in the bodily sensation areas of the brain. The brain activity of volunteers was examined as they lay expecting to feel touch on one hand. Before they were put into the brain scanner, though, they were trained to expect stimulation to the hand. Then, with the volunteers fully expecting the same stimulation they had always got, the researchers looked to see what happened to the brain when they expected it but didn't get it. What happened, in fact, was that the brain activity *decreased* in regions of the brain that mapped the body parts where stimulation *was not* expected. In other words, attention 'turned down the volume' in those part of the brain.

Attending to one sense reduces activity in brain areas responsible for other senses. So, for instance, as you concentrate on reading this page, it is likely that the touch-sensitive parts of your brain are 'turned down' so that the visual parts of your brain can better do their work in decoding the funny little shapes that make up these words. This is why, for instance, if you are really concentrating on a book, you might not hear someone speaking to you. As you concentrate on what your eyes are showing you, your brain actually 'turns down the volume' of your hearing, so that it sometimes takes an irritated shout to arouse you to your forgotten duties!

What all this shows is that attention can sculpt brain activity by turning up or down the rate at which particular sets of synapses fire. And since we know that firing a set of synapses again and again makes the trembling web grow bigger and stronger, it follows that attention is an important ingredient for brain sculpture. Now this shouldn't be particularly surprising, given what we now know about how mental practice affects the brain – mental practice, after all, is partly about being able to attend to mental images.

In fact, it seems that brain sculpture needs attention in almost all cases. Let's assume, for example, that your attention is fully occupied reading this chapter. Supposing a machine was set up which rubbed your forearm over and over, thus stimulating the brain area where your forearm is mapped. Normally, stimulation should 'grow' these brain circuits in the ways shown in this chapter, but if you don't *attend* to this stimulation – because you are reading this – then the circuits *don't* grow as expected.

In other words, brain sculpture needs your active attention. Indeed, research with animals shows this quite clearly: brain areas that are passively stimulated aren't sculpted by experience. This is one of many discoveries made by a research team led by Professor Michael Merzenich of San Francisco, the world's leading researcher on brain plasticity. Brain sculpture generally only happens when attention is paid to that stimulation. What's more, the attention circuits of the brain are based largely in the frontal lobes and it is these that are crucial for the remoulding of the trembling web of connections during the learning of new skills, whether they relate to work, sport or home. Learning a golf swing for the first time, for instance, depends heavily on your frontal lobes. Once you have the swing perfected and automatic, however, the frontal lobes will be relatively redundant and will retire to leave other parts of the brain sending the ball sailing beautifully down the fairway.

The remoulding of connections which the frontal lobes help set up is part of the retooling which the brain needs to do in order to perform the new skill fluently. But the frontal lobes act like a fussy but expert nanny for the rest of the brain, deciding what information it is important for the brain to receive – and what should be suppressed. It is as if the frontal lobes are constantly changing channels or adjusting the volume on the television, thus regulating what scenes and information its brain-children can see and hear.

The frontal lobes can actually open and close gates for incoming sensory information at the very earliest stages of that information's entry into the brain. The frontal lobes can turn up the 'volume control' within hearing for instance, so that the particular aspects of the sound which are important are magnified almost as soon as they hit the brain.

This, of course, may also involve suppressing aspects of the sound that the frontal lobes have decided are not so important.

Next time you are having a conversation at a noisy party, you might pause to think about what the frontal lobes of your brain are doing to help you keep tuned in to the voice of the person to whom you are talking. If it is a woman with a relatively high-pitched voice, for instance, then it is likely that those parts of the hearing centre of your brain (the auditory cortex) that deal with that frequency of sound will actually get a boost in synaptic activation from the frontal lobes. This tuning up – possibly accompanied by a temporary dampening down of your ability to hear lower frequency voices – will actually improve your ability to hear what the woman you are talking to is saying among the babble of competing voices surrounding you.

It should not be surprising that people whose frontal lobes are damaged – say by a head injury or a stroke – tend to find it hard to keep in mind what they should be attending to. A bad nanny may be careless about what the children in her charge watch on television and may let them sit for most of the day through all sorts of unhelpful or even harmful junk. Rather than directing their attention to interesting or important things in toys, books, tapes or television, the bad nanny lets the children fall prey to whatever catches their attention: such children will have difficulty learning to control their own attention and to sustain it while reading, playing, listening or watching television.

Damage to the frontal lobes is a bit like employing a bad nanny for the rest of your brain. You try to concentrate on what the character in the film is saying, but instead the picture on the wall behind him grabs your attention. What happens? You miss a crucial part of the plot and lose track of the film. Half an hour later you are aimlessly and restlessly pacing about the house, making tea or flicking mindlessly through a magazine while your partner sits engrossed in the movie in the other room.

This is typical of what happens to people who suffer damage to the frontal lobes of the brain – particularly to the so-called 'dorsolateral' frontal lobes to the side of your head just above your eyes. It is thanks to these brain areas that you can read a book while music plays quietly in the background. This is because the frontal lobes 'turn down the volume' in the hearing areas of the brain to give peace to the visual and language parts to get on with the reading. A person with damage to the frontal lobes of the brain, however, can't 'turn down the volume' so easily. As a result, she can't concentrate on reading because – inside her head at least – the volume of the distracting music is turned way up compared to the person with intact frontal lobes. Some people who have never been in an accident or had a stroke seem to be born with a difficulty in paying attention and resisting distraction: sometimes they are called 'attention deficit disorder' sufferers. Some of them, however, haven't learned to pay attention properly because their brains haven't been taught to do so.

It shouldn't surprise you to find that people who suffer damage to the frontal lobes recover less well from their injuries than those whose damage affects other parts of the brain. The frontal lobes can target different areas of the brain, boosting synaptic activation here and suppressing it there. Given that repeated synaptic activity helps circuits remould and grow, then it follows that the repair and remoulding of damaged brain circuits is likely to rest partly on the frontal lobes' ability to nurture them with carefully targeted input.

Pumping iron in your sleep

Wouldn't it be wonderful if we could learn, effortlessly, as we slept? Well, we do – at least some things. First, a little about sleep, of which there are several different types. One of these is called REM sleep – 'rapid eye movement' sleep, for the obvious reason that during REM sleep you make numerous flickering eye movements behind your closed eyelids. During REM sleep, your brain is particularly active and you also tend to dream.

You will probably have noticed at some time a roommate's or partner's eyes flickering like this, while at the same time they may even mumble or speak – evidence of the brain's hyperactivity during REM sleep, which takes up roughly 20 per cent of your night, on average. There are, of course, numerous exotic explanations of what dreams mean – ranging from mystical revelation to mental garbage disposal – into which I am not going to delve here. But REM sleep and its dreams do appear to have one important role in brain sculpture.

The web of connected brain cells is moulded softly by the electro-chemical impulses cascading through it, triggered by sensations, thoughts, memories and actions. Stimulation can make nets grow, and this activity strengthens the learning and memories that are embroidered into the connections.

REM sleep may involve one particular type of stimulation of brain circuits that helps consolidate and strengthen the new learning and memory which the day's experience has half-crocheted into your brain. Evidence for this comes from research indicating that during REM sleep the weave of the crochet is tidied and tightened, leading to overnight – effortless – learning.

The researchers used a perceptual test at which they knew people improved if they slept on it! This visual test required people to detect small differences in a complex design. If tested after a night's sleep, the volunteers were found to be better at the task than they had been at the end of a session's exposure to the test the previous day. In other words, their brains were pumping iron as they slept, tightening and tidying the previous day's crochet-work of learning, and hence improving performance the next day.

The researchers then looked at what happened to this overnight learning if they interrupted REM sleep by rather unkindly waking up the volunteers whenever they started to show signs of REM sleep (between twenty and sixty times during the night!). Sure enough, when deprived of REM sleep, these people did not show the overnight-learning effect. This was not just because of tiredness – for when they were woken the same number of times during non-REM sleep the normal overnight learning was found the next morning.

Sports managers and trainers are very concerned that their sportsmen and sportswomen get proper sleep in the weeks and months leading up to competitions. During REM sleep, it seems likely that the skills of movement and perception they have honed during each day's practice may be consolidated. As in the case of mental practice, here is an example of scientific evidence in support of grassroots wisdom.

So, pumping iron in the mental gym changes the brain. Mind over matter – mind sculpture becomes brain sculpture. But what happens when the gym closes permanently? What happens in the brain when part of its input is irreversibly cut off? The ghosts that roam in the brain are the subject of the next chapter.

4

Ghosts and Phantoms

He wasn't sure exactly when it had happened, but some time in the last couple of months his third arm had appeared. It sat diagonally across his torso, growing out of the top-left corner of his chest. His doctors said they couldn't see it, so he would draw it for them. That was quite easy, because it didn't fit under his clothes. It felt cold sometimes – so cold that he thought it was dead and not really connected to him any more. Yet it was still part of him, this strange extra limb. The stroke he had suffered had left him paralysed on the left side of his body. He couldn't use his left arm and would often pick up its lifeless weight with his good right hand to show what the stroke had done to him. He knew it wasn't logical, but the simple fact was that he felt he had three arms. And it wasn't delirium. Here was an intelligent sixty-five-year-old man in Oxford, haunted by an impossible but hideously real ghost; but unlike the wraiths glimpsed on ancient stairways, this was a fleshy half-dead phantom sown into the very tissue of his body. Here was the ghost of nightmares — the ghost that clings to you, no matter how fast you run.

Sixty years earlier, in Germany, another man suffered a bodily haunting. He too had had a stroke. He complained to his doctor about the 'nest of hands' that was in his bed and asked if the doctor would please amputate them and dispose of them in a bag. Six days after the stroke, clear-headed and not confused, he had more complaints for his bemused doctor. His paralysed 'old' left hand had begun to shrink and a new hand emerged from the flesh. He now had two left hands. But he had no arms on the left – instead the two armless hands were grotesquely grafted on to his left knee. The patient – a cultured man – politely asked his physician what the likelihood was of such a thing happening. His perplexed doctor could only scratch his head and murmur unconvincing reassurances.

The things we take for granted. The feeling of our limbs ordered and assembled to make up the bodily 'me'. Close your eyes for a moment. Be aware of your two arms in their places, their curvature, the pressure of the surfaces where they rest. Notice what you seldom register during the day, of where they connect with your body at the shoulders, of the feelings in them, their weight, the heat in them, the whole complex of sensations that constitute the deceptively simple consciousness of your two arms.

To know where and how your arm is, however, is far from simple. Such knowledge rests on thousands of computations performed by millions of brain cells – the brain cells which respond to joint angles, others which register touch, pressure, temperature and a myriad of other sensations. Some of this we know only against the discipline of gravity. After a time in space, astronauts can lose a sense of where their limbs are and have to look at them in order to locate them. Nothing is self-evident, not even knowing where your arm is. Damage the brain cells that calculate this and the computations can go awry, and may spin ghosts out of the synaptic disorder. Phantoms and ghosts found trapped in the brain's trembling web are the subject of this chapter.

Battlefield ghosts

The Yom Kippur War of October 1973, like all wars, took its toll on the bodies of those who fought in it. Many lost limbs in the fierce desert battles. Later, while they were in a rehabilitation centre having artificial limbs fitted, a group of seventy-three of these casualties was interviewed about their experiences of losing a limb. Most of them were in their mid-twenties and some had been maimed just a month earlier; all had lost a leg or an arm, though some tragic cases had lost more than one.

What interested the interviewers was a phenomenon first given its name in a study of victims of another war almost exactly 100 years earlier. From his work in the gangrene-ridden hospital tents of the American Civil War, a Dr Mitchell coined the phrase 'phantom limb' to describe an eerie sensation which many of his young, mutilated patients described. This was the ghostly feeling that the severed limb was actually still in its proper place.

Unlike the two people described in the introduction to this chapter, these men's brains had suffered no damage. Yet in spite of this, the sense of still having a limb where none existed was formidably strong. Only the evidence of their eyes – and the cruel reality of their disability – let them see the illusion for what it was: a taunting spectre of their former wholeness. In the case described at the beginning of the chapter, the Oxford man who had suffered a stroke experienced a similarly strong sensation of a non-existent limb being attached to his body, only in his case not only was the limb an extra one, but it was also attached – bizarrely – to his chest.

In both these examples, we see the brain playing tricks to conjure impossible but vividly convincing experiences. The causes were different – brain damage in one, amputation of limbs in the other – but what they shared was a common haunting by a non-existent limb. Before trying to solve this puzzle, let us consider more of the experiences of these unfortunate victims of the Arab–Israeli conflict.

All seventy-three of the Israeli soldiers said that they had felt the ghosts of their amputated limbs lingering at their former location. As if this lurking phantom were not enough, many of the soldiers complained of pain in the absent limb. Some were even tormented by an unscratchable itch on it.

Professor Ramachandran of the University of California at San Diego has made a detailed study of these types of strange sensations. One of his patients had lost his right arm in an accident on a fishing boat when the boom fell on it. Like the Israeli soldiers, this man had a phantom limb, but it had 'telescoped' – that is, the hand felt as if it was directly attached to the stump with no forearm in between.

Intriguingly, though, this man was able to 'stretch out' the phantom arm until – in his mind at least – it assumed a normal length. In fact, he could even feel himself trying to reach out to grasp objects and on one occasion found himself fending off a threatened blow with his spectral arm! If he stumbled, he would stretch out the phantom arm to break his fall.

On one occasion, the man was asked to reach out to grip a coffee cup that lay within his reach. Suddenly, and without telling him, his doctor pulled the cup out of reach. His patient immediately shouted in pain, 'Ouch! Don't do that – it hurts!' He had 'felt' the cup being wrenched from his ghostly fingers and consequently experienced the pain that he would have felt had his arm actually been yanked.

Many of the Israeli soldiers told interviewers that they sometimes felt their phantom limb moving. Most only felt it move when they willed it to do so, but several complained that sometimes the limb moved of its own accord. Others even described how they felt cramps in their invisible limbs, and one was plagued by a permanently clenched phantom fist. The ghostly limbs would also sweat and – like the man with the extra arm described at the beginning of the chapter – the imaginary body parts could feel hot or cold. Even in dreams, their bodies were whole, not mutilated.

Just like the ghosts of haunted castles, these ghosts of arms and legs have a tendency to come and go. Almost all the Israeli soldiers, for instance, felt that they were more aware of the phantom limbs when they were quietly resting, and particularly just before going to sleep. Some of them felt their phantom limbs appear when they were having sex. Let's now try to understand how this kind of bizarre experience can come about.

Crossed wires and strange maps

Just as the world is transcribed on to paper maps in an orderly, if imperfect, fashion, so it is for body and brain. One of the imperfections of cartography is that places like Greenland get much less space on paper than they are entitled to by their actual square-mileage. In contrast, Europe is overrepresented, at least under some types of projection. Now while this may be unjust in terms of natural geography, the human geography of the situation dictates that it makes sense. After all, not much is going on in Greenland apart from the groaning of glaciers and the creaking of icefloes, in contrast to the manic buzz of the cities of overpopulated Europe.

The same is true of the brain's maps of the body. The European cities of face and hands get much more brain-cell map space than do the Greenland wastes of the lower back. But here is a puzzle: what happens when one of these crowded European body parts is torn from the body by an exploding mortar? Suddenly we are left with a large part of the brain map – the hand area, for instance – with nothing to represent. It is as if there has been a geological cataclysm, and Europe has slid into the Atlantic, leaving maps worldwide with large areas which correspond to nothing on the surface of the earth.

What happens to these brain cells? Do they just wither away and die? Is it a question of mapmakers replacing Europe with a blank space marked 'no longer exists'? Before answering this question, let's look at some other strange things that happen to people who lose a limb.

A seventeen-year-old boy had lost his left arm just above the elbow. His phantom arm too had 'telescoped': in other words, he felt as if his hand was stuck straight on to the stump with nothing in between.

When this lad was touched lightly on the face with a Q-tip, he felt the touch not just on his face, but also on his phantom arm. What's more, the fingers of the phantom hand were mapped out regularly on the side of his face. When his chin was touched, for instance, he felt a sensation on the little finger of his spectral left hand. Stroking his cheek made him feel as if his thumb was being stroked. A touch on the skin between nose and lip gave the sensation of touch on his index finger. When warm water was dripped on to the left side of his face, he felt warmth throughout his phantom hand, and as the water trickled down his face, he sometimes even felt the liquid running across his phantom hand. When his phantom hand itched, scratching his lower face could relieve it!

If people have had a paralysis in their arm before amputation, they tend not to be able to move the phantom limb voluntarily. It is as if the pre-amputation paralysis of the real arm leads on to the virtual paralysis of the phantom.

What is happening to produce such strange maps? Why should the phantom hand be grafted mutant-like on to the face? Well, in the brain's map of the body, though everything is precisely positioned, it is not drawn like a normal body. Rather, it is etched on the brain as if in a distorting, fragmenting mirror. In this mirror you see an enormous face, huge hands, impressive genitals but tiny feet, legs and torso. And nestling beside the hand on this distorting map is the face.

Now, after an arm has been torn from the body, the brain cells in the hand area of the brain are suddenly starved of sensory input. What do they do? After all, their only purpose in life is to register sensation to the body – so do they wither away when their body part disappears? The answer is no, they do not. Instead, these brain cells change allegiance to another part of the body that will feed them the sensation they crave. Where? The next-door neighbour on the brain map. Hence the sensation of the phantom hand grafted on to the young man's face. It seems that, just as training and experience remould brain connections, as we saw in the last chapter, so sensory starvation caused by amputation also leads to brain sculpture.

Another pair of neighbours on this map are feet and genitals. This explains why some people who have lost legs feel phantom sensations when they are having sex: the lost leg's brain cells have to wire up somewhere, and their neighbour on the body strip – the genitals – gives such an opportunity. Indeed, the intriguing suggestion has been made that if a man's penis were to be amputated, then rubbing his foot could reproduce some of the sensations which his penis used to give him.

The hand part of the map doesn't just have the face as neighbour: on the other side it has the map representing another part of the body, the trunk. Do the hand cells not switch over allegiance to this – albeit less glamorous – part of the body? Indeed they do. Maps of phantom hands have been found etched on to the trunk as well as the face.

Researchers looked at which parts of the brain's body strip 'lit up' when the trunk was touched. Exactly as would be predicted by the 'good neighbours' theory, rubbing the trunk activated the hand part of the body strip. The hand area of the brain had of course been starved of sensation, and as a result these cells shifted their allegiance to represent the trunk. This is a clear case of the brain re-sculpting itself in the light of changed experience.

The man we met at the beginning of the chapter with a third arm growing across his chest was experiencing a ghost spun out of the chaos of a torn web of synaptic connections. Though the brains of amputees have not been damaged in this way, their brains are clearly altered by the dramatic changes to the sensory input they receive. Their phantom limbs are also spirits created by, and then trapped in, the brain's machinery. True, the continued jangling of the severed nerves at the stump plays its part in nurturing the ghosts, as do changes in the pattern of connections between the nerve ends and the spinal cord; but to a considerable extent, these phantoms are the byproducts of brain sculpture.

What can be done about an itching, painful or cramped phantom? If these are ghosts trapped among brain cells, then dealing with them must surely involve changing the brain in some way. Scratching the cheek may work for a few, as the brain is tricked by the strange re-mapping into believing that the phantom limb has been scratched. However, we will return later to other ways of persuading the brain to free its phantoms.

Perhaps the most radical way of changing the brain is to destroy some of the brain tissue. Some people have been unlucky enough to lose first a limb and then, years later, to have a stroke which destroys brain tissue in the part of the brain where the body maps are located. Just such a group of people were studied, whose phantom limb had been 'amputated' by a stroke to the side of the brain which represented that side of the body.

Such mental amputations only work, though, when the stroke has cut-off sensation to the phantom's side of the body. One person, for instance, was finally rid of a phantom right leg after he suffered a stroke to the left side of the brain. As sensation gradually returned on the right side of his body, however, so the phantom leg grew again, like a newt growing a new tail. In other words, as the torn web of connections repaired itself, so it reconstructed the spectral limb.

While some phantoms may fade with time, then, others leech tenaciously to the nervous tissue, yielding only to the violence of a stroke. But the brain is not simply a collection of circuit boards, with connections soldered permanently in fixed patterns. While there is a considerable amount of such 'hard wiring' in the brain, and while there are limits to the brain's plasticity, the human cortex is also a shifting, responsive organ, constantly remoulded by experience. You would therefore expect phantom limbs and their echoing maps to change gradually with time and experience, and this does indeed happen. Phantom limbs may telescope with time, and the nature of their mapping on to the face may also change. Take one forty-three-year-old woman, for instance, whose right arm was amputated above the elbow. At first, her phantom felt normal, the same length as her other arm and joined normally to the rest of her body. True, it felt colder than her real arm, but it adopted postures and positions in line with what the rest of the body was doing. When she was walking, for instance, her phantom moved with much the same swinging rhythm that her real arm would have had before amputation.

Gradually, however, the phantom limb began to change shape. The hand and fingers gradually moved closer to the stump, and while it still felt colder than the other hand, she now felt pumping, tingling or throbbing sensations in her phantom. At times her illusory hand began to grasp and flex of its own accord, and phantom fingers sometimes moved in time with the fingers of the left hand.

Like the young man described earlier, this woman had a map of her phantom hand etched on to the side of her face – in her case the right side. When she was reassessed two years after the original amputation, however, the map on her face had changed. Now the map on the right side of her face was chaotic and disorganized, in contrast to the quite precise map that had been found shortly after her amputation. More surprisingly, she now had a similar, though equally chaotic, map of her phantom hand on the *left* side of her face. It seems that the brain's remoulding, which had taken place on the left side of the brain (corresponding to the right-sided amputation), had spread to the neighbouring cells on the right side of the brain.

Though most sensory nerve cells on the right arm wire up to the left side of the brain, there are also some connections that slip over to the right side. In other words, the right hemisphere also experiences a long-term change in stimulation caused by the amputation, albeit much less dramatic than the changes with which the left hemisphere has had to cope.

The strange changes in the form of the phantom limb experienced by this woman make sense in the context of what we know about brain sculpture. The real, moving, feeling arm is constantly bombarding the brain with a consistent and reliable barrage of stimulation. This repeated stimulation of brain circuits maintains in good order the synaptic connections in the relevant brain circuits, according to the principles of Hebbian learning.

But the phantom limb is just that – a phantom; its brain circuits receive no consistent stimulation from real fingers sensing and moving in the real world. In the absence of this discipline of experience, the phantom's circuits may spontaneously shift and remould themselves. They make and break connections in an undisciplined way, like a way-ward adolescent left to his own devices without adult supervision and control.

As a result, these shifting connections yield changing, but still uncannily real, experiences to the unfortunate amputee. In this light, the weird third arm of the man described at the beginning of this chapter is maybe a little less strange than it first seemed.

All in the brain?

While the 'good neighbours' explanation of these strange maps is an attractive one, it is almost certainly not the whole story. One reason for this is that phantom limbs are much less common and much weaker in one group of people whom you might expect to experience them. These are people whose spinal cord is cut in an accident. Depending on where the spine is damaged, such unfortunate people may lose all sensation and power in their legs (paraplegia) or in all four limbs (tetraplegia).

Given that their brains are starved of sensory input from the paralysed limbs in a similar way to the amputees' brains, then surely we should find strange maps and phantoms in these people also? However, while they do at times 'feel' the limbs – which as far as the brain is concerned are amputated in sensory terms – the experience is a pale shadow of the vivid sensation of people whose limbs are actually cut off.

One reason for this may be that the severed nerve fibres in the legs or arms of amputees keep firing sporadically, peppering the brain with a grapeshot of anarchic neural impulses. This barrage may be a necessary fuel to provoke the dramatic brain reorganization seen in amputees. In other words, phantom limbs and strange maps may arise out of a combination of the brain's remoulding and the forlorn jangling of cut nerves far from the brain.

This makes sense in the light of our knowledge of what influences the making and breaking of synaptic connections in the trembling neural webs. The restless and unceasing competition between the brain cells is the basis for brain sculpture. Anything which raises this general level of activity will similarly tend to make it more likely that the connections reorganize themselves.

In the case of spinal injury, the breaking of the spinal cord does not lead to chaotic sensory inputs to the brain of the type seen following amputation. As a result, though some brain reorganization may well take place, it will tend to be less dramatic than that found in amputees.

There is, however, one other important but related difference between spinal injury and amputation, and this concerns pain. While pain can occur in the legs cut off from the brain due to spinal injury, it is much more common to find phantom-limb pain after amputation. This may be because cutting sensory nerves may actually increase the level of activity in separate pain pathways to the brain.

Such pain-related input may play a part in stimulating the brain's reorganization. This possibility was raised in one research project carried out in Germany, when it was found that how much the brain had reorganized after amputation of a limb was closely related to how much phantom pain people experienced. The researchers went on to show that sometimes anaesthetizing the stump of a person suffering phantom pain got rid of the pain, and also dissolved the reorganization which had taken place in the brain's body area. This worked in only three out of six phantom-limb patients, however, and the anaesthetic had no effect on the non-painful phantom limbs of four other people. So, while pain pathways are not the whole story in understanding brain sculpture caused by amputation, they clearly play a big part.

Taming the ghosts

An itch you can't scratch can become a torture – and you can't scratch a ghost, unless you are lucky, like the man who could scratch his face to relieve the itch on his phantom arm. Pain in a non-existent limb is also a big problem, for if the limb exists only in the brain, then relieving the pain means doing something to the brain rather than to the body.

We will come back to the question of phantom pain later. Suffice it to say that anaesthetizing the severed stump abolishes neither the phantom nor the pain in at least half of all cases. So, what can be done to help gain some control over how the phantom feels, and of what it gets up to? How can we get at the brain's wiring to help the ghostly itches and aches that plague these people?

One man, for instance, had a vivid phantom arm, but it was virtually 'paralysed' – he could move it only with great effort. What's more, his hand often clenched painfully in a ghostly spasm: it could take up to half an hour to release it. Not only did the hand clench, but phantom nails dug painfully into his palm.

Now, as you will remember from the last time you cut your nails, nails are nerveless and so have no space on the brain's body map. How then can the brain create phantom nails? The answer to this lies with that old favourite – Hebbian learning.

Many thousands of times in your life you will have clenched your hands tightly, and on many of these occasions you will have pressed your nails into your palms. So these two sets of sensory experiences – the clenching of hands and the digging of nails into the palms – have been linked together in the brain through time. Cells that fire together, wire together. So in this man's brain the clenched phantom hand triggered its lifetime Hebbian partner – namely, the sensation of nails digging into the hand.

How can we get at the brain to change these strange, ghost-inducing sensations? One eminent researcher came up with an elegant answer to this question. He constructed a 'virtual-reality' device that was simply a box with a mirror in it and the man with the painfully digging phantom nails was asked to put his real arm into the box. When he did so, however, he saw a reversed image of his good arm in the mirror. In other words, suddenly he saw a visual illusion of a healthy limb in the place it used to be before it was amputated.

The man was then asked to move both his 'hands' – one real and one illusory – together. So, for instance, he clenched and unclenched his fists or moved them in circles as if conducting an orchestra. As he did this, he saw 'two' hands moving because of the mirror illusion – but, to his astonishment, this visual illusion now made him *feel* his phantom moving. Suddenly he found he was able to unclench his clamped fist and free himself of the pain of the ghostly nails digging into his phantom palm!

How could the brain be tricked into loosening its grip like this? Well, in the neural circuits that once controlled movements in the amputated arm, there was no longer any 'outlet' for their activity: after all, the arm had gone. They were a bit like scholars locked in an ivory tower, cut off from reality and able to carry on without facing the test of the real world. So, like scholars holding tenaciously to a theory that doesn't match the real world, they could lock the phantom hand into a painful grip without having the means in reality to change that grip.

When the man 'saw' his phantom limb 'moving' in the mirror, however, suddenly these ivory-tower scholars were exposed to a sort of reality, namely an apparently 'real' movement in the real world. Never mind that this was a trick and that the real movement was actually in the intact arm; the fact is that here was a powerful illusion of the phantom hand unclenching. So the visual images of this movement could, through their connections with the ivory-tower circuits, change the strange habits of the cut-off parts of the trembling web. In this way, they altered their patterns of connections and helped them 'get out of the rut' of the aching, clenched phantom hand.

Another man had lost his arm ten years earlier. His phantom limb was lifeless and paralysed, and he couldn't generate a flicker of movement in it. He was asked to put 'both' his hands into the mirror-box, then to move both of them in the same way that the previous man had. With his eyes closed, he said that his phantom was 'frozen', but when he opened his eyes and looked at the mirror-reflection of his 'moving' hand he suddenly felt movement in his paralysed phantom for the first time in ten years.

After practising with the mirror-box for 15 minutes per day for a few weeks, he found that his phantom arm had telescoped over the course of practice and that his phantom had changed. Now his illusory fingers and part of their ghostly palm dangled from the stump near the shoulder. This was a bonus for the patient, who for many years had had a painful phantom elbow; but now that he didn't have an elbow any more, there was no more pain!

The paralysed limb had been trapped in its ivory tower, cut off from any corrective feedback from body or eyes. What the eyes saw in the mirror – even though it was an illusion – was near enough to the real thing to get through at last to the ivory-tower connections. The experience remoulded these ossified connections by the activity it caused in the trembling web of synapses between the visual part of the brain and its body-sensation system. The movement glimpsed in the magical mirror was enough to sculpt the phantom's brain connections and free it from its prison.

Some people can also 'feel' touch in their phantom hands. In some cases, when the real hand was touched, and they watched this happening in the mirror, they 'felt' the pressure on their non-existent hand seen in the mirror. Connections may have emerged, or been unmasked, between the body-sensation areas of the two hemispheres of the brain, for it is hard to see how touch to one hand could be felt as touch to the other (albeit phantom) except across the fibres connecting the hemispheres.

In my own laboratory, we have seen something quite similar. We studied a man who, although his left arm had not been amputated, was nevertheless unable to feel that arm because of damage to the right side of his brain – except, that is, when he saw his hand being touched.

Perhaps there was some dormant touch sense left in the hand, which vision awakened? That could not have been the case, however, because when we put a plastic hand on the table – with his real hand hidden under the table, immediately below the plastic hand – and made it look as if it was being touched, he was better at feeling a real touch on his real hand.

The plastic hand – like the reflected hand in the magic mirror – looked somewhat like the real hand. When we touched it, the brain cells that 'saw' the touch activated their old partners, the brain cells that normally felt touch in that part of the body. This is another example of how the brain can be tricked when one part of the trembling web is tugged, causing changes in its distant but connected neighbours.

All this is brain sculpture in action – the remoulding of the brain's connections by experience. In the case of the magic mirror, though, the experience was carefully planned to change the brain. This is what rehabilitation is all about. In rehabilitation, neural circuits can be trained – in this case tricked – into changing their patterns of connections. Later in the book we will see more examples of this.

Big differences in what people feel in their phantom limbs probably depend partly on what each person does in response to the sensation. By studying these different responses, scientists may get some clue of how better to remould the brain to help it heal after damage – including the damage caused by age.

Some people, for instance, might learn to ignore these strange maps on their face and elsewhere. You need attention to remould connections in the brain, and it may be that what you attend to (and conversely what you ignore) determines how much you are haunted by these ghosts. One way of learning to ignore the feelings on your face caused by touching the stump, for example, might be to use your eyes to convince yourself that only one part of your body is being touched – namely, the stump. By focusing attention on just the stump, you might be able to make the crossed wires causing the phantom wither from lack of attention. Indeed, some doctors have reported success in using hypnotic-type methods, which depend on just such a use of attention, to help change the phantom. There is no good scientific evidence yet that this method can banish phantoms from the trembling web, but theoretically it is quite possible.

Another way in which you might change the brain's wiring is by stimulating the stump area, say by rubbing it. It has been suggested that such stimulation may help protect the arm and hand area from the overbearing influence of its face neighbour. Hence some people may inadvertently mould their brains by the things they do after amputation.

All these ideas for therapy are still speculative and scientifically unproven. Quite how the brain changes after amputation is not yet properly understood. It may be that the brain sculpture consists mainly of changes in the strength of connections in the trembling web – for instance, existing connections that have hitherto been inhibited might be 'unmasked'.

Before amputation, these connections might have been 'bullied' by stronger connections in the competitive stockmarket of the trembling web. But new physical connections might well grow too. There might be a sprouting of dendrite twigs as well as of axon branches in response to the changed experience. Both these things almost certainly happen, but while the synaptic juggling takes seconds and minutes, new growth probably takes weeks, months or even years.

Phantoms in the ear and the taste of clouds

Deafness is a kind of amputation – the severing of sound. What happens to the parts of the brain which register sound when they are starved of input? It would be surprising if the auditory cortex – the hearing part of the brain – behaved in a very different way from the body areas of the brain.

We should expect to find brain sculpture in the brain's hearing areas, and so we do. In a Japanese study of people who were deaf in one ear, researchers found that the brain had indeed been remoulded and changed by this unbalanced sensory diet.

What's more, phantoms can fill the sound vacuum, just as they do the body vacuum after amputation. Tinnitus – a humming or ringing in the ears – may reflect the brain's undisciplined response to starvation of sound. One seventy-year-old woman, for instance, began to be tortured by tinnitus after she had a tumour removed from her brain by a neurosurgeon. The operation made her completely deaf in one ear, and the result was a humming tinnitus in that ear, which came and went.

What was astonishing about this woman was that these phantom sounds could be brought on by stroking a particular spot on her left wrist. Also, she could switch her tinnitus on if she turned her eyes towards the left. This mirrors the remapping of phantom hands on to real faces, showing that the brain's response to its loss of experience is to remould its connections, sometimes with quite strange parts of the brain.

In this woman's case, however, the brain sculpture spread far beyond the hearing parts of the brain, and strange connections between the body areas, eye-movement regions and hearing parts of the brain were sculpted out of the chaos in the trembling web which the surgery caused.

Such crosstalk between the senses can also happen naturally, even without any injury to brain, body or senses. Some rare individuals are born with 'synaesthesia' – the ability to perceive something in one sense through another. For instance, some people 'see' certain musical notes and chords as having their own colours; others 'see' colours when they hear certain words. One person said that when he heard the word 'Moscow' he saw the colour 'darkish grey, with spinach green and pale blue' vividly in his mind's eye.

Tasting clouds or touching the scent of roses is not just the whim of an idle mind. These individuals really do see what they hear and feel what they smell. We know this by studying their brain activity when they are having such strange sensations. As they listened to words, they saw various different colours, depending on what the words were, and their brain activity differed greatly from that of people who didn't see colour when they heard words. In fact, their brains 'lit up' in precisely the parts of the visual brain where colour is registered.

It may be that the brains of these people have somehow kept connections between different sensory areas that are normally 'pruned' away in childhood as the brain grows. There are, however, many other possible reasons. What these cases show is that the woman who heard phantoms in her ear when her wrist was touched may not be as bizarre as she appeared at first glance.

Synaesthesia shows us that the strange experiences of the haunted people in this chapter are not due to some random and mysterious craziness that can be easily dismissed. An extra arm sprouting from your chest can feel as real as the arm holding this book. A phantom arm can clench and itch as much as a real arm can. What all this tells us is how dynamic the brain is, and how much it responds to, and is moulded by, experience.

We have considered how the brain reacts to dramatic changes in its sensory diet. Now let's consider the other side of the coin: how the brain reacts when it loses some of its own substance. Do brain areas keep behaving in a neighbourly way when some of their own neighbours die? That is the question for the next chapter.

5

The Torn Web

She never saw the car, nor did its driver see her. No screech of brakes – just the thud which a car travelling at just 27 miles per hour makes when it hits a human body. One moment there was a mind bubbling with the memories, thoughts and emotions of a young woman entering her intellectual and personal prime, the next there was unconsciousness.

The accident happened in Cambridge on a December evening in 1992, as twenty-year-old Jessica Mnatzaganian was crossing the road, returning from a concert in King's College Chapel. Talented musically as well as academically, she was a member of Cambridge University Chamber Choir and a straight-first student of Natural Sciences at Cambridge University.

Jessica had no awareness of the ragged wailing of the ambulance siren as it sped through the mist to Addenbrooke's Hospital. In that split second's impact, this sharp and vivacious student had entered the oblivion of coma. By the time she reached hospital, Jessica was neither opening her eyes nor moving her limbs, even in response to pain. Mercifully, she remembers nothing of the next two months, during which time she was paralysed in three out of four limbs, and her bodily functions, including breathing and feeding, were conducted via a network of tubes and machines.

Jessica's mother Madeleine spent the next three months by her side. Throughout she talked to her daughter and when, twelve days after the accident, Jessica first opened her eyes, she showed her photographs to try to stimulate her memory. She also played music to Jessica, including a recording of a piece for piano, cello and voice in which Jessica had sung. 'When she heard the music Jessica sobbed yet never opened her eyes,' Mrs Mnatzaganian told me. 'I could see a change in her breathing in response to the music – this was at a time when it was thought that she would never recover.'

Then, sixteen days into the coma, the son of a Muslim family tending to another patient in the unit came over to Jessica and said to her, 'My mother prays for you every night. Would you pray for her?' To the astonishment of those around her, Jessica replied, 'Yes,' the first word she had spoken since before the accident. Her next words were, 'My mouth's sore . . .' followed by '1, 2, 3, 4 . . . Oh my God, where's my logic gone?'

But Jessica remembered nothing from minute to minute and from day to day, even after she began to speak. The one limb she could move – her 'manic left hand', as her mother described it – flailed about, abnormally strong and wild, repeatedly pulling at the tubes and lines which were keeping her alive. She didn't know where she was – at times she thought she must be in Leicestershire, at others in the South of France.

'She would look up at me and say "Where's my real mother?"' Mrs Mnatzaganian told me. 'She was disorientated and felt that she was sixteen years old. But then she realized that she had had experiences which weren't appropriate to that age. So she worked out that she must have been time-travelling. The scientist in her kept trying to work out why she felt so strange.'

In spite of this disorientation, almost as soon as Jessica was able to speak she began to ask for science books to be brought in. 'Of course, she couldn't read them,' her mother told me, 'but she was utterly determined, even through her confusion, to get back to her studies. One day, she was in a particular kind of hell, wailing "Where's my logic gone?" and she just wouldn't go to sleep. So I played a tape which her tutor brought in of a class teaching session on taking blood pressure. The moment she heard it, she fell back utterly relaxed! Another day, a friend brought in a book on brain histology. Slumped paralysed in her wheelchair, her head half-shaved from an operation to remove a large blood clot from the brain, and lolling to one side, Jessica said, "You wait, I'm going to be clever again."

'It must have seemed like a conspiracy of fools!' Mrs Mnatzaganian smiled. 'We all had this faith that she would get back to college – we took it from her, of course – it all came from Jessica. Her friends and tutors all came in regularly, bringing books, talking to her, playing music ... We knew the statistics were appalling, but we didn't want to know them – we wanted to hear nothing that would threaten our faith that she could make it back ...'

Even as Jessica was beginning to walk again, she was still remembering nothing from day to day – she was still in a state of 'post-traumatic amnesia' two months after the accident, suggesting that her brain injury was a severe one indeed. The breakthrough came when Richard – her boyfriend, who had witnessed the accident – was to play cello in Elgar's Cello Concerto at a concert in Cambridge. 'I decided I'd like to get her there,' Jessica's mother said.

Jessica listened to a recording of the concerto on the day of the concert. 'I remember thinking, "I'll get my crying done now so that I can go to the concert," Jessica told me, 'and I sobbed my heart out. When I stopped, I began to worry that I wouldn't remember enough about music to appreciate the concert. But when I got there, I never moved – I concentrated on every note.' This concert on 7 February 1993 was the turning-point for Jessica, with the return of new memory – although she has lost for ever the recollection of most of the term before the accident, as well as – mercifully – the months in coma and confused amnesia. Whether the concert was a spur to recovery or whether the timing was a coincidence isn't known. But she started singing with Clare College Chapel Choir in early 1994, and then returned full time to her studies in October 1994, passing her second-year exams in Natural Sciences in June 1995. Talking to her now, you would never guess that she had had such an injury – she is as vivacious and sparkling a student as you could meet.

But hers was an unusually good recovery for such a severe injury and she never showed any of the changes in personality which devastate the lives of so many people with similarly severe injuries. Whether intensive stimulation of those in coma improves chances of recovery is not yet scientifically established, and Jessica may have recovered even if she had not had so much stimulation from relatives and friends.

'Without you, I'd have gone under,' Jessica told her mother simply, as if in answer to these scientist thoughts in my head. 'I stood between her and the world,' Mrs Mnatzaganian answered quietly. And it's certainly hard to rule out the remarkable sense of the positive which sparks between the two women as a contributor to Jessica's outstanding rehabilitation.

'It's one thing to travel hopefully, but one mustn't travel blindly,' Mrs Mnatzaganian added, like her daughter apparently reading my thoughts. 'Of course for many people there comes a time when you must accept that they're not going to make the kind of recovery that Jessica has. When someone is in coma, you must come to terms with it . . . but not too soon.'

(This account was first published in The Times, *London, 25 July 1995.)*

The healing sculptor

Jessica was one of the lucky ones. Many others whose trembling neural webs are torn do not make such a remarkable recovery. In addition to her determination and her family's support, she was also blessed with high intelligence. On average, people of high IQ make better recoveries than those with lower intelligence if their brains are damaged in an accident. One reason for this may result from the education that tends to go hand in hand with higher intelligence.

We saw earlier that more educated people's brains had more complex and richly interconnected neural webs than those of less educated individuals. Of course, it is possible that, rather than education producing these rich connections, the same genetic factor could cause both the intelligence and the complex brain structure. This cannot, however, be the whole story – education and experience can change brain structure.

Why should a more densely connected network of brain cells recover from damage better than less richly interwoven webs? One answer to the question may lie in Hebbian learning. The more brain cells that have become wired together through firing together, the more likely it is that the skills and memories woven into these wired connections can be recovered.

When the brain is damaged – say by a blow to the head or a stroke – you might, for example, lose the ability to make the complicated hand and foot movements you need to drive a car. This skill, remember, is stored as patterns of connections in the brain, built up through Hebbian learning during years of driving practice. You cannot drive the car any more after the damage because many of the connections between brain cells have been cut. The overall result of this is that you lose the 'memory' of how to drive the car.

Let's now suppose that, as part of the rehabilitation, you try to learn to drive again. You are taken to a deserted airfield where you can't do much harm, you sit in the car and put the key in the ignition. Your instructor then coaches you in making the right sequence of movements with gearshift, handbrake and clutch. What happens in the damaged network during this training?

First, some of the cells in the web where the memories of driving were stored are 'switched on' when the movements are made. Not only that, but they are switched on in a pattern that is quite like the original pattern of connections involved in driving. When this happens, the other cells in the web that are still connected with the switched-on cells are turned on too; this is because of the old connections sculpted by Hebbian learning during years of driving. The result is that most of the relevant cells are switched on by your going through the routine of driving. Of course, when cells fire together, they wire together. So even the cells that have been cut off from each other by the brain damage may connect up again through Hebbian learning. With practice, these connections should become stronger, so that eventually you may well be able to drive again. Your surviving brain cells have been stitched together by being switched on as a team through starting the driving routine.

This is exactly what happens in wartime, when platoons re-form even though they have lost some of their men. The corporal may be wounded, thus breaking the link between sergeant and privates, but new connections are made – say by promoting one of the privates to acting corporal – and so the platoon can begin to function again, even though it has lost some of its individual units.

Similarly, you can learn to drive again despite the fact that some of the brain cells that used to help you drive have died. Like the army platoon, the ability to do what you used to do lurks in the damaged *pattern* of connections *between* cells. Armies depend on strong roles – ranks – to make sure that the loss of any one individual isn't fatal to their ability to keep fighting. Privates can step into the role of other privates who have died. Likewise, your knowledge and abilities can be rescued by the right kind of brain sculpture, even if some of the cells die. Of course, if you lose a lot of brain cells, then the trembling web may be so torn that no patterns can be resurrected, even by the most careful brain sculpture. So it is too for army platoons. If they lose too many men, then after a certain point they can't really function as an effective fighting unit.

Things aren't always quite so easy, though. Sometimes other healthy circuits in the brain can have sinister effects on a damaged network that is struggling to regain its old abilities. This is one of several reasons why many people are not so lucky as Jessica in their recovery from brain damage.

Intelligent and well-connected brains such as Jessica's may have a better chance of healing reconnection than less well-endowed brains, however. The richness of the embroidery of the trembling web is one very strong candidate to explain the link between intelligence and recovery from brain damage.

Jessica suffered what is known as a closed head injury. When the head hits against a hard object, the soft brain tissue is shaken, stretched and twisted inside the skull. This bruises and tears the long, soft, white wiring – the axons of the brain cells – which packs the inside of the skull, connecting up the thin layer of grey matter that is the cortex. Though the neurones in the cortex are often also damaged in a head injury – for instance, by friction against the bony inside of the skull – it is the connective wiring of the brain that is particularly at risk and when the connections between cells are damaged or destroyed, cells that normally get input through these fibres suffer. This is because they are starved of the stimulation which keeps them strong and healthy. Yet some recent research has discovered a remarkable ability for the trembling web to repair itself when the connecting fibres are torn.

The researchers studied the neural webs of rats and found that, in certain parts of the trembling web, provided that at least 10–15 per cent of the connecting fibres survive, then over the course of 2–3 weeks reasonably normal abilities can return. Indeed in some parts of the brain reasonably normal abilities can be maintained even if up to 95 per cent of cells have been destroyed by disease. Only when this minimum threadwork of the surviving web is lost does the system collapse completely and become unable to recover by reconnecting itself.

One such example is Parkinson's Disease, which is linked to a loss of the brain chemical messenger dopamine in a part of the brain called the 'substantia nigra'. People who suffer from Parkinson's Disease have problems moving and walking, yet these difficulties really only become apparent once more than four-fifths of the dopamine cells in the substantia nigra have died.

Circuits can reconnect when the wiring between cells is damaged. In Parkinson's Disease, however, the actual cells themselves are lost. It seems that the remaining cells respond to this carnage by increasing their firing in order to keep up reasonable levels of dopamine. This is another way in which the trembling web can re-invent itself when it is torn.

In Jessica's case, the bruised and torn axons plunged her into a coma and, even when she had come to, the damage made her confused and muddled. Gradually, however, with her own effort and the stimulation of those around her, her torn webs reconnected and reorganized – at least to some extent. The end-product was the remarkable recovery that saw her back studying at Cambridge University.

Good neighbours?

The clogging up of arteries that causes heart attacks – myocardial infarction – has its equivalent in the brain: cerebral infarction. An artery in the brain becomes so furred that it blocks off the blood flow, causing the brain cells that depend on blood from that artery to die of starvation. According to where the blockage occurs, part of the brain will be damaged. A similar fate can befall brain cells when an artery bursts and bleeds into the brain.

A complicated chain of events cascades through the brain after a stroke. Gradually these chemical and physiological mix-ups sort themselves out, and in the ensuing hours and days the victim gradually regains some of the abilities that were lost. Quite what these abilities are depends on exactly where the brain has been damaged. One side of the body might become weak or even paralysed if the movement areas are affected. Or the vision on one half of each eye might be lost, if the wiring between the eyes and visual part of the brain is cut. Some unfortunate people suddenly find they can no longer understand what people are saying. Others completely lose their sense of direction so that they are constantly getting lost.

Immediately after suffering a stroke, the American actor Kirk Douglas was able to walk from his car into the hospital. His first inkling that something was amiss had been a strange sensation in his face, beginning in his head and spreading round to the corner of his mouth. He started to talk, but what came out was just babble. At first he wasn't sure if the words were nonsense or not, but gradually the realization dawned that something awful had happened.

Douglas steadily recovered his speech, though three months after the stroke he could still speak only about as well as his four-year-old granddaughter. One day, however, he felt so pleased with his progress that he said to her, 'Kelsey, say the word "transcontinental".' She couldn't and he could, so at least he was moving ahead of a four-year-old!

A year and a half after the stroke, Kirk Douglas was still having to struggle with English as if it were a foreign language, speaking slowly and sometimes infuriatingly unable to find the right word. In his book *Climbing the Mountain: My Search for Meaning*, he talks about the subsequent remarkable recovery of his ability to express himself. The dramatic changes he experienced in the months following his stroke could only have happened through some pretty impressive brain sculpture.

This recovery could not just be explained as some settling-down of the brain chemistry. In order to understand these improvements over the months and years after a stroke, it is necessary to consider how experience and effort slowly sew connections in the torn web, re-embroidering the patterns in which human language resides.

Amputation of an arm leaves millions of brain cells starved of input. Similarly, the death of brain cells cuts off their neighbours from the cosy stimulation and companionship they are used to. So how do these bereaved neighbours react to their loss?

We can see what happens to them by studying the brain's activity using PET scanners. Scientists peered into the brains of six people who had endured the same kind of devastating problems with speech and language as Kirk Douglas. Like him, these people got better over time, but what happened in their brains to explain this healing? All six men had had large strokes on the left side of their brains, where most of the main language centres are situated. A particular part of the left brain called Wernicke's area had been largely destroyed in all six. This part of the brain is thought to be crucial for adequate language. But if it is so crucial, how come these people learned to talk and understand again?

To answer this question, the men had to undertake various spoken-word exercises while the researchers carefully looked at what their brains were doing as they spoke. What they saw was that extra brain regions outside Wernicke's area 'lit up' – suggesting that these good neighbours had stepped in to help out with the tricky business of speaking.

Both the front parts of the left brain, which had not been affected by the stroke, as well as parts of the right brain, sprang into life as they spoke. In other words, the web of connections into which the intricate skills of language had been embroidered had changed, grown and reconnected to let these men speak again. Almost certainly, similar changes happened in Kirk Douglas's brain as he struggled to reclaim the gift of words.

Douglas, like his six fellow stroke victims, had been given intensive speech therapy and it is very likely that this helped to resculpt the connections in their damaged brains. Not everyone is so lucky, though.

While rehabilitation helps many brains to reorganize, there are limits to what it can achieve.

These limits depend partly on enough of the threads and cells remaining joined together in the torn web. The precise figure could be as low as 10 per cent, but that may only be true for some parts of the brain, like the substantia nigra – the culprit in Parkinson's Disease. Certainly in Kirk Douglas's case, and in the six men he never met, enough connected cells survived in a widely spread brain circuit to let brain sculpture carry out its healing reconnection.

Another powerful demonstration of the brain's 'good-neighbour policy' comes from a study of people in whose brains tumours had been found growing in the movement-control areas. In the six people studied – four men and two women – the tumours had destroyed the brain cells in the part of the movement area controlling one hand. Despite this, these six people could all move the five fingers of their affected hands.

The researchers were intrigued to find out which parts of the brain were now controlling these movements. When they asked the people to move their fingers while their brains' activity was monitored using a PET scanner, what they saw was that parts of the movement area that normally gave instructions to quite different parts of the body now became active.

In some of these people, though, areas of the brain totally outside the movement area 'lit up' and seemed to control the finger movements. Just like the men who had lost the power of language, other parts of the brain stepped in like good neighbours to help out.

This study shows how parts of the brain near afflicted areas can help with the daily chores previously carried out by their neighbours. Here is brain sculpture in action – the extensive restitching and repair of the brain's network of connections.

This research also shows that the webs are spun quite widely, and that parts of the brain that were thought to be specialized for only one thing can turn their hands to neighbourly chores that no one realized they could do. Like people, the brain's regions can sometimes rise to the challenge of an emergency.

It could be that these helpful neighbours do the chores in a slightly different way, though. In other words, the restitching may not be a perfect, invisible mending of the original web. Sometimes, indeed, people can regain lost mental and physical abilities after brain damage because totally different brain systems come into play in order to do what is necessary in a completely different way.

This type of brain sculpture is called 'functional reorganization'. It involves the help of quite distant neighbours in the brain and often this sort of reorganization leaves the torn web unrepaired. In reality, though, there probably isn't a clear dividing line between restitching of torn embroidery and functional reorganization. For most people whose brains are damaged, it is probably a question of both things happening.

Repair of the web itself depends on the survival of a rump of connected cells in the circuit – 10–15 per cent is a rough estimate for some circuits. But how can such a small huddle of neurones do the job of five or ten times as many cells?

Well, scientists have looked through an electron miscroscope at these hardy surviving cells in the brains of people suffering from Parkinson's Disease. What they saw was that these survivors had sprouted longer threads to keep in touch with each other. They also made more connections with other survivors. Like survivors of the *Titanic*, they reached out and held on to each other in the icy water, clinging to life by joining hands.

In other words, the surviving cells in the caudate nucleus adopted a 'wartime spirit' and responded to the carnage around them by reaching out to each other, stretching across the corpses of dead neighbours to do so. As in all warfare, however, once a fighting group falls below a certain critical strength, then the rout begins. In Parkinson's Disease, movement becomes badly affected when the dopamine-producing cells fall to between one-sixth and one-tenth of their former strength.

A similar principle seems to hold in other types of brain damage. Take stroke, for instance – that cruel and sudden killing of brain cells. One way of finding out what the brain is capable of after a stroke is to put a large magnet against the skull and stimulate the neurones by a brief magnetic pulse. If this is done just above the movement-control part of the brain, and if some of the neurones are still working, then the pulse should cause a twitch in the muscles on the opposite side of the body. In this way, it is possible to measure how much this part of the brain is still capable of, even though the person may not yet be moving the paralysed limbs.

One study looked at around 100 stroke victims. The researchers stimulated the motor-control area in the damaged half of the brain and measured whether the relevant muscle groups in the affected arm and hand twitched obediently. Some people's hands gave a quite normal twitch, while others, though responding, did so in a slowed way.

In a third group, however, their arms were limp and unresponsive to the magnetic tickling of their brain cells. Not surprisingly, a year later these people had not recovered nearly as well as those who had shown a normal response to the magnetic stimulation. They could only move their arms about half as well and were far clumsier in their hand movements. Walking was also difficult for them, because they had quite poor control of the leg on the affected side of the body.

What was most surprising was the state of the middle group – those whose muscles had reacted sluggishly to the brain stimulation. Twelve months after the stroke, they were doing just as well as the normal response group. It is likely that their brains had recovered in part by reorganization and reconnection of surviving brain cells.

So, brain sculpture and reconnection of this type need some cells and connections to work on: if too many are lost, then the system may collapse. So, a very large stroke that destroys most of the motor cortex on one side of the brain may leave a person permanently paralysed on one side of the body.

But what if a stroke of the same total size were to be divided up into a series of mini-strokes split over a few weeks or months? In both cases, the same total amount of brain tissue would be destroyed, the only difference being that in the second case the total damage would be divided up over four or five occasions.

Which scenario would produce the best outcome? The answer is the second, where cell death comes by several cuts. Why? Because in between each of these cuts, cells can reconnect and reorganize, so that when the second wave of destruction arrives it is assailing a better connected and hence better defended brain circuit. On the other hand, where the damage comes on one single devastating occasion, then not enough cells may survive to form a viable network for reconnection.

All is not lost, however, even in this last gloomy scenario. Later in the chapter you will see how ingeniously the brain can conscript quite separate systems in order to get back to some kind of functioning. But first there is another puzzling phenomenon to see in the brain's looking-glass world.

Help and hindrance in the magical mirror

We saw earlier how the brain reorganizes itself when an arm is amputated. So, for instance, the out-of-work brain areas offer their help to neighbours who are responsible for the face or trunk. Normally, it is the half of the brain opposite the lost limb that changes, but sometimes the changes spill over to the other half of the brain. One result is that the brain connections in the mirror-image location on the opposite side of the brain are sculpted too.

Not that the two halves of the brain are complete mirror replicas of each other. Each half has quite distinct duties – the left for certain aspects of language, the right for mapping the space around us and so on. As we will see later, the two brain hemispheres are to some extent engaged in a constant struggle with each other. They can be like two overcompetitive sportsmen, each constantly trying to get the better of his rival.

If, for instance, the movement part of one side of the brain is stimulated by magnetic impulses, then activity in the equivalent, mirror area of the other hemisphere is suppressed – dampened down. Activity in one half of the brain leads to inhibition of the other, via a bundle of connecting fibres known as the 'corpus callosum'. Not surprisingly, in those rare people who have a damaged corpus callosum, we find less suppression of one side of the brain following activity in the other.

Damage to one half of the brain should therefore give its competitor free rein to flex its mental muscles. Indeed, scans of people with damage to one side of the brain often show a higher than normal level of activity in the opposite, undamaged hemisphere.

The triumphant hemisphere doesn't always just bully and suppress its vanquished opponent, though. Sometimes it actually takes over some of the work that the damaged half of the brain used to do. We saw earlier how people whose left-brain language centres had been damaged seemed to use their undamaged right hemisphere more when they learned to speak again.

Another example of this was shown in an elegant study by some researchers in St Louis, Missouri. From their research into the workings of normal brains, they knew that a particular small region of the left frontal lobe became active when volunteers carried out a particular verbal task. What they had to do was to complete words from three-letter word fragments; for instance, given the letters 'tru. . .', they would produce the word 'trunk'.

One of the patients happened to have suffered a lesion in precisely the area of the brain that was known to underpin this mental activity. Yet, several months after suffering this damage, the man was able to do the task reasonably normally. He could not be doing it with the usual brain area, because the cells in that area were dead.

Suspecting that the brain's magical mirror may have had something to do with it, the scientists circled the precise mirror-image part of this man's brain – that is, in the equivalent region of the right frontal lobe.

If the mirror-image areas of the brain can indeed help out in taking over the functions of their partners in the other hemisphere, then studying this patient's brain as he did the word-completion task should reveal activity in the circled region of the right frontal lobe – and this is exactly what the St Louis researchers found. Precisely the mirror image of the point in the brain activated in non-brain-damaged people was triggered into life by the task in this patient.

A similar interplay between the two sides of the brain seems to happen in the areas controlling movement. Normally, in undamaged brains, magnetically stimulating the hand-movement areas in one hemisphere will cause twitches and movements only in the other side of the body. After strokes or other damage to these brain areas, however, magnetically stimulating the undamaged motor cortex in some cases causes the muscles on *both* sides of the body to move. In other words, the neural net of connections has been sculpted, so that now activity in the brain cells in the one hemisphere causes muscle responses on the *same* side of the body.

This brain rewiring may not always be entirely beneficial, though. One study in Cambridge found that people who had suffered strokes tended to show better recovery of hand and arm movements over a twelve-month period if they *didn't* show same-side responses to brain stimulation.

Other scientists, however, have concluded that these mirror-image reorganizations *can* be helpful. Almost certainly, it depends on exactly how the brain sculpture takes place. Perhaps in some cases the takeover bid from the undamaged hemisphere might squash out the repair potential for the torn circuits in the damaged hemisphere.

An example of such cross-brain rescue operations comes from a thirty-one-year-old Italian man who had had a stroke when he was only twelve. Paralysed on the left side of his body at first, he had steadily regained the ability to move his left arm and leg. When, as an adult, his brain activity was studied while he moved each of his hands in turn, the extent of brotherly love between formerly competing hemispheres became apparent. Whichever side of the body he moved, it was always the left-hemisphere sensory and motor circuits that lit up. It seems that the left brain's movement circuits had charitably taken on responsibility for the orphaned left arm as well as keeping up their own right-arm duties.

Certainly, research on rats shows that when one half of the brain is damaged, the other half tends to expand in size. The more it enlarges, the better the rats are able to run, showing that the brain growth is not an irrelevant quirk, but rather is a form of brain sculpture underlying recovery.

An even more dramatic form of brain sculpture is to be observed in human beings. That is the amazing rewiring that takes place when one entire half of the brain is sliced out of the skull.

Living with half a brain

Little Alex had a normal birth, but six days after he was born his alarmed mother noticed that at times his right arm and leg would jerk. Eventually doctors diagnosed a rare condition called Sturge-Weber syndrome – a congenital disorder of the brain. The jerking in Alex's limbs was caused by epileptic-type seizures in the left hemisphere of his brain.

A brain scan at the time showed that the left half of the brain was quite abnormal and Alex went on to suffer terrible seizures over the next eight years, each bout lasting two, three or even more days, with ten to twenty seizures each day. He was placed on high doses of strong anti-convulsant drugs.

As a baby, Alex didn't babble or gurgle very much and was said to be a 'silent infant'. When he was seven months old, the right side of his body wasn't moving normally, and his vision was absent on the right side. Alex remained essentially speechless throughout the first eight years of his life, tending to rely on pointing and gesture to make himself understood.

Brain scans taken when he was seven showed all too clearly the reason for these right-sided problems in his vision and body, as well as his lack of speech. The left hemisphere of his brain was withered and hardened, and as a result there was relatively little activity on that side of the brain. But, as you would expect of brain sculpture, his right hemisphere was bigger than usual.

When Alex was eight years old, neurosurgeons cut out his entire useless left hemisphere. When they eased the half-brain out of his skull, they found that it was a strange dusky-blue colour, and firmly calcified, quite unlike the usual blancmange softness of the human brain. Because this diseased tissue had been removed, Alex no longer had epileptic seizures, and the heavy drugs that he had been on for years were stopped nine months after the surgery.

A month after coming off the drugs, Alex, who for his entire life until that point could say only one word – 'Mumma' – began to speak. At first he managed only single words, but after just a few months he was able to make up and speak long stories. Here is an extract from one of them recorded by the scientists and doctors in London who studied Alex's recovery:

> Once upon the time there was a very naughty bus. While his driver was trying to mend him, he decided to run away. He ran along the road beside a train. They made funny faces at each other and raced each other. But the bus had to go on alone, because the train went into a tunnel. He hurried into the city where he met a policeman who blew his whistle and shouted, 'Stop, stop.'

Alex's ability to understand speech had always been much better than his ability to speak it. Even so, just four months before half his brain was removed, his understanding of words was only at the level of a four-year-old. Like his speech, this steadily improved, so that by the time he was fourteen years old his word comprehension was at the level of an eight-year-old and he was able, for instance, to understand words such as 'isolation' and 'tubular'.

Before the operation, Alex also had problems in moving his right arm. He was just about able to hold a cup and catch a ball with both hands, but his right arm was otherwise very limited in its movements. Immediately after the surgery this got worse, but over the next few months such movement as he had had in his right arm returned. Indeed, he could now use his right hand to grasp objects between thumb and fingers.

Magnetic stimulation was then used to activate Alex's 'good' movement centre on the right side of his brain. Usually, stimulating the right motor cortex will give twitches only on the left side of the body and vice versa, but in Alex's case magnetic stimulation of his surviving right-movement centre produced movement in both his hands, showing that his brain had reorganized for movement, just as it had for language.

It is very likely that some of this brain sculpture had taken place before his left brain had been removed, and it may be that the diseased half of the brain was inhibiting and interfering with the functioning of its right partner. Nevertheless, what is utterly remarkable in Alex's case is the complete absence of speech before the operation, compared with the good level of speech he was capable of after neurosurgery. This could only be explained by a most dramatic kind of brain sculpture.

Of course, Alex's is an exceptional case and there are a lot of children who lose half a brain and do not show such incredible changes. Studies of many such children do show, however, that some sort of brain reorganization occurs in most cases. Before the age of five or six in particular, the right half of the brain seems to be able to take on speech and language about as well as the left half does. Children who lose half their brain before this age are much less likely to have problems in speaking and understanding than are older children or adolescents.

Even older children, though, tend to have better speech and understanding than adults who suffer large strokes affecting the left hemisphere. This is in spite of the fact that the children have lost the entire left half of the brain, while the adults have only lost part of the left hemisphere.

Adults' brains too can rewire, however, even when the language centres have been affected by brain damage. So, while very young brains are more amenable to brain sculpture, the trembling web of connections in the damaged brain can to some extent grow and reconnect at any age, albeit with more or less ease.

Emergency relief

There are some nets that simply get torn too much, and repair is not possible. Though damaged networks of brain cells can survive with as few as 10–20 per cent of their neurones, if brain damage destroys this minimum reservoir of cells, then repair embroidery of the tattered net is out of the question. Many people are therefore left with a permanent disability after their brains have been damaged. Some are unable to move the arm and leg on one side of the body; others may be blind on one side; and some may lose the ability to recognize faces – even of their closest loved ones. Memory can go, as can concentration, while a few people can lose the ability to use common objects such as knives, pencils or even doorhandles. And, of course, there are some who lose the ability to speak, understand speech, or both.

The reason that people can lose just one very specific mental ability is that the human brain is 'modular', at least to some extent. True, in some circumstances, neighbouring parts of the brain appear to be able to 'help out' when neurones in different modules die; but, in many cases, the loss of an entire 'module' often means the permanent loss of the job done by that brain area.

Fortunately, however, there is usually more than one way to skin a cat. To take one example, different aspects of our ability to see are 'contracted out' to separate brain areas. It is, for instance, possible to 'see' an object's movement without being able to see the object itself. This is because the movement-detection machinery of the brain is located in a separate brain area from the apparatus that allows us the normal conscious visual experience of objects in front of us. If the latter is destroyed in a car accident, then you may still be able to use the remaining undamaged visual areas of the brain to give you some kind of information about the visual world.

To give another example, if a stroke has affected movement in the right leg, the victim may never regain full, normal movement in that leg. He may, however, be able to walk fairly effectively by tilting his body slightly to the left, hence taking the weight off the right leg. This sluggish, slightly disobedient limb can then be swung forward from the hip, compensating for the poor control of movements lower down in the leg. With practice, this sufferer's walking can come to look not that different from the way other people walk, and it may take the eye of a professional to pick up the difference.

In other words, people can behave in ways that look pretty similar to the way they acted before their brains were damaged, but they are in fact using quite different brain systems to control that behaviour. In fact, some of the brain sculpture we have explored in this chapter may be explained by this compensatory reorganization rather than by repair through embroidery of the torn net in the damaged brain circuits themselves.

In reality, this distinction between embroidery and compensation may be difficult to make and it is likely that, after all but the most trivial types of brain damage, both types of brain sculpture take place.

In the next chapter, we will look at a strange condition called 'unilateral neglect'. This can appear after strokes to the right half of the brain, and leads to people 'neglecting' – not noticing – other individuals, things or events towards the left side. Scientists in Scotland and Canada studied a group of people who had suffered from unilateral neglect but had recovered. In other words, in everyday life they no longer seemed to 'miss' things on the left side. The researchers did not, however, simply leave it at that. Instead, they asked these individuals to sit in a darkened room and point to lights as they came on in front of them. True enough, the recovered stroke patients reached out and touched all the lights just as well as people who had not suffered strokes. A video camera on the ceiling, however, revealed the secret of their recovery. It showed that, whereas people who had not had a stroke reached out in a relatively straight line towards the lights, the patients were different. Rather than moving directly to the light, their hands took an excursion towards the right before suddenly veering leftwards in the correct direction. Why was this?

What is happening is that the brain circuits that normally control attention to the left have not actually truly recovered. When the arm movement begins, it is skewed off to the right, showing that these people's attention is still tilted to the right. The mid-course correction is a kind of 'Oops, we seem to be going wrong – let's look at the map' response by the brain.

This makes sense in terms of what we know about the brain's attention systems. If, as you are reading this book, a large moth were to flutter into the leftmost periphery of your vision, your attention would automatically be attracted to it for a moment. The parietal lobe of the right half of your brain would have done much of the work in directing your attention to the beast. Such automatic or reflexive attention to the space around you is one of the jobs that this brain area sitting towards the back of your head has to do.

Now take a second to look up at the left high corner of the room you are sitting in. This voluntary movement of your eyes was controlled by a separate brain system in the frontal lobe, far from the parietal lobe. People with unilateral neglect can often notice things to the left if they are asked to look, but they tend not to attend automatically to things on the left. This is because unilateral neglect is usually caused by damage to the brain areas surrounding the parietal lobe. So, while they find automatically attending to the left (for instance, flicking their eyes towards the giant moth) difficult, in many cases they can use their undamaged frontal lobe to attend voluntarily to the left, just as you did when you looked up at the corner of your room.

The sudden mid-reach swerve may show the 'kicking in' of the voluntary attention system to help out the errant automatic attention system. This is an example of a sort of 'emergency relief' by a healthy brain system to a damaged network that has not managed to embroider itself well again.

To illustrate further how many different brain systems work together for much of what we do, take a moment to do this task, developed by Professor Alan Baddeley. Simply close your eyes and mentally count how many windows there are in your house.

Did you do it? If so, you will have used several different mental processes, including at least two types of memory. The first of these is a visual or spatial memory that allowed you to tour mentally about the house, counting the windows. The second is a verbal tally of the number of windows as you counted them. The left half of your brain is specialized for this second type of verbal memory, while the right half specializes in the first – namely, visual or spatial material such as shape or location.

If someone suffers damage to the left-brain memory centres, they may have difficulty in learning or holding in mind verbal information. But like the people with unilateral neglect just described, the individual with verbal memory problems can use non-verbal memory systems in the other side of the brain to compensate. For instance, a shopping list of 'bread, milk, butter' can be remembered both as a list of words and as a series of visual images. In practice, we all use both memory systems much of the time in everyday life. In this way, we get 'two bites of the cherry' to help us remember things. If one of these memory systems suffers because of brain damage, then we can learn to compensate for it by relying more on the other. In fact, we could all improve our memory abilities if we took time to use our non-verbal memory systems more when learning.

'You wait, I'm going to be clever again'

Jessica *did* become clever again, though perhaps not as clever as she was before the accident. Nevertheless, her incredible recovery shows the remarkable ability of the torn web to stitch itself back into at least a semblance of its former intricate embroidery.

Jessica's recovery probably came partly from undamaged areas of her brain helping other parts of the brain, partly from changes in the synapses in the surviving brain cells and also to some extent from the sprouting of new connections in her brain.

Whatever the reason for Jessica's exceptional recovery – and unfortunately it is rather unusual to have such a good outcome after such severe damage – it does highlight the brain's ability to sculpt and reshape itself. But here's the challenge: can we find ways to nurture and accelerate this sculpture? Are there ways of pumping iron in the mental gym that help the brain reconnect after it is damaged? That is the question for the next chapter.

6

Fixing the Torn Web

From across a room, you see a handsome, grey-haired man – animated, an enthusiast clearly – his face expressive and intelligent, and from that distance you hear his voice rising and falling in the subtle cadences of a fine teacher who loves his subject. Move a little closer and you might wonder what language he is speaking. Sit down beside him and you hear a single sound mellifluously constructed into whole sentences and paragraphs intelligible only to Sir John Hale.

The great Renaissance historian John Hale finished writing his last book, The Civilisation of Europe in the Renaissance *in June 1992, one month before he suffered a stroke in the left half of his brain which deprived him of the power to communicate by speech or written word. He is a man whose delight in using language is phosphorescent, but now his still-formidable intellect is severed from its means of expression, like a computer disconnected from its printer.*

To Sheila Hale, it is as if her husband is imprisoned behind a screen: everything about him is there – personality, intelligence, humour, patience – but locked up by the want of language. At one point after his stroke, her wordless husband was given a weighty academic book on neuropsychology, and asked to turn to the section relevant to his problems. Without hesitation, he skimmed through it and opened it at the chapter on dysphasia – disorders of language.

As Sheila Hale and I talked together, John Hale listened quietly, occasionally interjecting wordless comments, some of which could be pinned down by offering him interpretations to which he nodded or shook his head, appearing to understand everything we said. At other times we would give up and Sheila would say, 'I'm sorry John, we just don't understand.' He would grimace, then shrug and smile, patiently, from his prison.

John Hale can make complex judgements about the distinctions between words like 'discordant' and 'jarring', or 'frugal' and 'thrifty', by multiple-choice questions with words or pictures, demonstrating his understanding by pointing to the correct answer. Yet he cannot say the word 'cat'. He has access to the precise meanings he wants to express in language, but the moment he tries to express this high-level thought in written or spoken words, everything breaks down. John can copy written words beautifully, but cannot imitate spoken words; he can comprehend complex sentences but cannot say which part of the sentence is the subject and which the object.

In his last, exceptional, book, John Hale narrates a story by Rabelais. During a voyage, the protagonist, Pantagruel, jumps to his feet, cupping hand to ear, hearing 'first voices . . . then whole words'. A ship's captain tells him that they are the sounds of a great battle which had been frozen by winter and are now beginning to thaw. They see some of the voices fall on deck, and after they had 'warmed them a little between our hands, they melted like snow, and we actually heard them'.

(This is part of an article first published in The Times, *London, 8 March 1994.)*

Trying to find ways of melting the words frozen within John Hale's brain – rehabilitation – is the subject of this chapter.

Invisible mending?

If the brain can be sculpted by experience, why do Sir John Hale's words stay trapped in his skull? Why can't we just stimulate the parts of the brain controlling language and force the trembling web of connected neurones to make more synaptic connections? After all, violinists can do so by practising, so why can't John Hale?

The puzzle deepens in the light of the remarkable recovery of people who have had half of their brains removed. If the brains of these amputees can reorganize to 'fill up' the vacant neural space in the brain, why can't John Hale's brain reorganize itself?

What's more, if our brains can sprout new connections to compensate for changes in the brain as we get older, what's stopping John Hale's brain doing the same? Later we will see that we can improve mental skills in children by giving them the right education and stimulation, and we will discover how emotions and emotional thought can be changed by therapy. So the question won't go away: 'If the brain is so malleable, why are Sir John Hale's words frozen in his skull?'

This question is as important practically as it is theoretically. Taking Britain as an example, roughly half of all money spent in this country's National Health Service is devoted to disorders and diseases of the brain. Stroke, head injury following traffic accidents, Alzheimer's Disease, schizophrenia, depression, multiple sclerosis, brain tumours and alcoholism are just the most common examples.

In this chapter, the question to be answered is whether we can help repair these torn nets by stimulation and exercise – in other words, through rehabilitation. Connections within the brain wax and wane in response to different experiences. So can we apply this principle to all people whose brains are damaged? The answer to this is 'Yes – but within limits.' Here are some of the factors limiting this flexibility.

'Hey! That's my job!' Different parts of the brain have become specialized for different mental functions – i.e. the brain is partly *modular.*

'United we stand, divided we fall!' If too much of a particular

module is damaged, then rescue may be impossible: a *critical mass* is lacking.

'Oh get out of the way! I'll do it!' Parts of the brain which are not damaged can squash out activity in other partly damaged areas. *Inhibition* can suppress potential, just like a dominant child can inhibit the confidence and talents of a less confident sibling.

Restitching the net. Brain circuits may decay without proper stimulation and input – but if we give it the right kind of input, we may be able to 'rescue' it by providing the stimulation needed to repair the torn areas of the damaged brain centres.

Tuning the mind's ear. The wine connoisseur's brain has learned, through Hebbian learning, to make different responses to subtle variations in flavour that most of our brains would register as identical. Our brains are 'tuned' for different skills and these can go out of tune as we grow up or after brain damage. By giving the right training we can sometimes 'retune' them.

'Pay attention!' You can improve your golf by practising swings in your head while sitting on the Tube. The parts of the brain controlling attention do this by sending signals to the circuits which control the movements. These same attention systems may help damaged brain circuits recover by stimulating them into action.

Let's now look in detail at these six constraints on brain sculpture.

'Hey! That's my job!'

The brain is a specialized machine with different parts doing different jobs. Let's take speech, for instance. Arriving at your ears is the string of pips and squeaks that we call spoken language. In response to these, the eardrum vibrates, sending minute electrical impulses through the auditory nerves that lead to the brain. Eventually these impulses reach those parts of the brain whose job it is to decode the signals into words.

Imagine a Morse-code operator in a 1940s warship, huddled over his radio, earphones clamped to his head, translating the dots and dashes he hears into a series of letters which he scribbles on his pad. To this particular individual, the words he writes are meaningless because they are in code. The radio-operator passes on the message to the second lieutenant who has the codebook and decodes the message: 'Enemy submarine ten miles north.'

To some extent the brain works like the crew of this warship, with different parts of the brain doing distinct jobs in the task of decoding speech into meaningful ideas. Just as in wartime the radio-operator may be killed or disabled by an explosion, so the part of the brain which decodes the Morse signals into codewords can be selectively damaged after stroke, disease or injury.

One stroke victim to whom this happened described his family's speech as sounding like 'an undifferentiated continuous humming noise without any rhythm': this is known as 'word deafness'. This unfortunate man was like the ship's second lieutenant, listening desperately to the Morse code coming through the dead radio-operator's earphones, but hearing only meaningless beeps and blips.

The second lieutenant and radio-operator in Sir John Hale's brain both survived his stroke: he can read and understand speech. Furthermore, the captain of this metaphorical ship is alive and well, for Sir John can think and reason normally. But what he *cannot* do is translate this thought into speech. This is because in the human brain the circuits responsible for the production of language are quite different from those which receive it. In other words, the stroke's explosion in Sir John's brain knocked out the output side of his communication system, leaving the incoming side intact.

Let us return to the question of why, if the human brain is so malleable, Sir John has not learned to speak again? The reason is the very modularity of the brain which we have just described. By adulthood, certain parts of the brain have become very specialized indeed for particular mental functions. If most of the neurones in one of these modules die, then it can be extremely difficult for other neighbouring neural circuits to take on this highly specialized job. In Sir John's case, the parts of the brain responsible for translating ideas into words have been damaged badly.

Speech is a highly specialized mental function which is not readily taken over by neighbouring parts of the brain. In fact, in most cases only the left hemisphere – in particular the front half of the left hemisphere – can talk. However, the right hemisphere can deal with *some* aspects of language and this makes it somewhat easier to find recovery in reading abilities which have been lost after brain damage.

While listening to speech means translating pips and squeaks into ideas and images, reading words involves triggering these ideas by staring at lines and squiggles on the page. As with so many other mental activities, the parts of the brain that allow us to read are different from those which help us understand spoken language. At the very heart of all these spoken and written word systems is a vast storage network whose sophistication and complexity puts all the supercomputers in the world to shame. This is the brain's semantic system – the huge storage system of concepts, meanings and all the images and associations linked to them.

Access to this storehouse of knowledge can come through spoken or written words. Where reading is concerned, however, there are two alternative doors into the storehouse – and this is good news if you have to learn to read again after a stroke. But *why* are there *two* reading routes into the semantic store? Quite simply because some of the semantic information is stored in the undamaged right hemisphere of the brain.

Strange things can happen because of this arrangement. Let's suppose someone with a damaged left half of the brain tries to read the word 'stone'. To do this, first the lines and squiggles picked up by the eyes must pass back to the visual areas of the brain at the back of the head. These make sense of them as purely visual objects, with no meanings linked to them. After they have done this, they pass the words forward to the language-decoding area in the left hemisphere.

The person understands the word perfectly – the lieutenant who decodes incoming messages is alive and well – but when he tries to utter it problems arise. Let's assume that the stroke has cut off the brain's language-reception centre (which is called Wernicke's area) from the language-despatch centre (known as Broca's area). So the word which has been perfectly well comprehended cannot be transmitted – as is the case with Sir John Hale.

Sometimes, though, people who have had strokes like this do something very peculiar. When they try to read the word 'stone', they may actually mutter a word such as 'rock'. A moment later, asked to read the word 'bush', the word 'tree' may be spoken. What on earth is going on here?

What is happening is that the information about the word 'stone', because it is blocked from going *directly* forward to the speech-output centre, passes back across to the undamaged right hemisphere of the brain, into the semantic system there. It then hops back across to the left hemisphere upstream of the blockage, and into the undamaged speech-output system. The only problem is that the right-hemisphere semantic system is pretty lax in the way it works. Instead of precisely giving out the concept of *stone* to the written word 'stone', like a sloppy librarian it throws on the desk some approximation of this – i.e. 'rock'. And so it is the word 'rock' that is passed on to Broca's area and then spoken. Similarly, 'bush' triggers 'tree' in this rather careless system.

As we saw in the last chapter, the brain can compensate for damage – and in this case it does so by finding different pathways using undamaged brain circuits. I have concentrated on language here, but there are many such examples for every other type of mental activity. As we learned earlier, the general rule is that if a highly specialized brain circuit is completely destroyed and there are no alternative pathways, then the mental function may be lost. But what happens if the circuit is only partially damaged or if it is not quite so specialized as in the case of speech? Let us now look at these possibilities in turn.

'United we stand, divided we fall!'

If too much of a particular module is damaged, then rescue may be impossible: a *critical mass* is lacking. We also saw how torn webs can reconnect themselves simply by the surviving connected brain cells being activated: when they become active, then through Hebbian learning the other partly disconnected cells can become reconnected.

It is also the case – as we saw in the last chapter – that a minimum critical number of cells must remain in a torn web for it to have a chance of repair. Skills which are stitched into its embroidery can thus be recovered, despite the fact that some of the brain cells previously controlling these skills were killed by the stroke. This is because, as we have seen, skills lie in the *pattern* of connections *between* cells.

Such a pattern can therefore survive even if some of the cells die. On the other hand, if more than a critical number of cells in a circuit are lost, then the pattern of connections cannot survive and that particular brain circuit will permanently lose its ability to do what it used to do.

Things are sometimes not quite so clear cut, however: other healthy circuits in the brain can have sinister effects on a damaged network which is struggling to regain its old abilities. That brings us on to the third limitation on brain malleability – inhibition.

'Oh get out of the way ! I'll do it!'

In the same way that a dominant child can inhibit the confidence and talents of a less confident brother or sister, so parts of the brain that are not damaged can squeeze out activity in neighbouring partly damaged areas.

You could see this happen in your own brain if I were to give you a burst of harmless magnetic stimulation to one side of your head, over the part of the brain which controls movement on the other side of your body. When this was done in people with quite normal brains, for a fraction of a second the movement area in the opposite half of the brain was suppressed and made less active by the magnet-induced activity in the other.

In particular, the two halves of the brain are in constant competition with each other – so much so, in fact, that in certain rare cases a second stroke affecting the opposite side of the brain can sometimes *improve* disability caused by the first stroke. What happens here is that the second stroke reduces the bullying of the previously healthy hemisphere, allowing the damaged hemisphere to show off some of its latent abilities, which until then have been squashed down by the healthy half of the brain.

Competition between the two halves of the brain really shows up where paying attention is concerned. For instance, if a stroke damages the right hemisphere of the brain, in very severe cases the person's attention may be dramatically shifted over to their right-hand side of space – i.e. to what takes place on their right side; in fact, he or she may be quite unable to give any attention at all to things on the left. This is known as 'neglect' of one side of space – which you read about briefly in the last chapter.

One reason for this loss of attention to things on the left is that the undamaged left hemisphere of the brain has suddenly become freed of all competition and so completely overwhelms the right hemisphere, inhibiting even what ability the right hemisphere *does* have to wrestle attention over to the left side of space.

Having this problem is a little like watching a film with half the screen blanked out. But, more than this, to you the film seems complete and you are simply not aware of the fact that half the screen – usually the left half – is blanked out. One of my patients – let's call her Pat – who suffered from unilateral neglect drew a flower that she thought was perfect and complete. Yet all the petals were crushed over to the right side, with none on the left.

Unilateral neglect nevertheless gives us a fascinating glimpse into the nature of human consciousness, for it isn't a problem of *seeing*, but rather a disorder of *awareness* of what is seen. The thing about neglect is that, even though all the information is arriving from the eyes at the visual part of the brain, the information is not reaching consciousness, and this is why people with unilateral neglect tend not to realize that half their world is missing.

Can anything be done to help the damaged brain overcome this problem? Yes, it can. Let's take the example of the dominant brother whose overbearing talent prevents his sister from showing her abilities. The parents of these two children may try to curb their son's behaviour, but they could also try to boost their daughter's confidence and self-expression. Similarly, in the case of neglect, an alternative to dampening activity in the undamaged hemisphere would be trying to boost activity in the weakened, damaged half of the brain.

One way of doing this is to 'switch on' networks which are known to be connected with the damaged system. One key ally of the attention system is the neural web which prepares the ground for movements – the so-called 'pre-motor' system. When we plan to reach out to grasp or touch something, it makes sense that our attention should be shifted to that object, so that we don't miss it or knock it over. As human beings have evolved through the millennia, the pre-motor system has become intimately linked with the attention system. That makes it a good candidate for helping out a limping, malfunctioning attention network.

Unilateral neglect after right-sided brain damage often leaves people with a partially paralysed left arm and leg. Often, however – and this was true in Pat's case – they *can* make small movements with the left hand, arm or leg if they concentrate enough. When Pat did move her left hand – exactly as you would predict – her awareness of the left side of space improved so that, for instance, she could read more on the page and miss out fewer words.

The story is a little more complicated than this, however. When Pat simply crossed her hand to the other side under the table, placing it on her right knee, moving it there didn't improve her neglect. Nor did moving her right hand when it was crossed over to the left side. How come? Well, just as we saw earlier in this chapter that different parts of our brain do different jobs in the task of understanding speech, so there are separate attention systems for dealing with different areas of space.

When you have read this, put down the book for a few seconds. Close your eyes and pay attention to the feelings in your left foot. Now move your attention to your right thumb. Then again to your left shoulder.

In doing this exercise, you were exploring one particular area of space – your body. The part of the brain that controls attention to body space is quite separate from that which attends to the space outside your body. Hence, following some types of damage, a person can have difficulty in paying attention just to the left side of their body but not to the left side of external space. For instance, they may not comb their hair on the left side, or they might leave the cuff of their left sleeve unbuttoned.

Now glance around the area surrounding your body. What objects could you reach out to pick up if you wanted to? Is there a cup or a glass at your side, or a spectacle case? This area of space surrounding your body is known as 'reaching space'. As with body space, certain types of brain damage can lead to a person having problems in paying attention to the left side of this zone of space. For instance, Pat sometimes missed the food on the left side of her plate, wondering for instance why her partner had not given her any vegetables this dinner time.

Finally, look around the room where you are sitting. Glance at the corners and, if the curtains are open, look out of the window. You are now in the realm of 'far space' and, as with the other two types of space, this is controlled by a somewhat different brain circuit. As you might expect, therefore, you can find some people whose brain damage causes them to have problems only within far space. For instance, one group of scientists in Oxford described a man who missed almost everything to the left on the table in front of him, but who was a key player on the pub darts team!

Although the circuits controlling attention to these three spatial areas are independent, they also collaborate closely, which explains Pat's puzzling results where only left-hand movements made on the left side of her body improved her attention to the left.

What is happening here? The answer is quite simple. When the left hand moves on the left side of the body, two brain circuits are switched on together – the right-hemisphere circuit for body space (the left arm is moving) and the right-hemisphere circuit for reaching space (it is moving to the left of the body).

Taking our hypothetical little sister who is in the shadow of her big brother, this is equivalent to winning the school sports and coming top of her class on the same day. Either one of these on its own might not be enough to boost her confidence vis-à-vis her brother, but the two together give a combined boost which shakes off his inhibiting influence on her self-esteem.

More or less the same thing happens with the right-hemisphere circuits for body and reaching space. When the left hand moves on the right side of the body, only one right-brain circuit is activated (the one controlling attention to the body), and when the right hand moves on the left side of the body, again only one circuit in the right hemisphere is switched on (the one controlling attention to reaching space).

Given a domineering left hemisphere, one switched-on circuit in the right hemisphere is simply not enough to shake off its influence: you need two, which is why only moving the left hand on the left side of reaching space has an effect. But what happens if both left and right hand are moved together? The benefits are lost. When Pat was reading, she read more on the left side when her left hand was moving, but when both hands moved together, she went back to square one.

This is because switching on the left-hemisphere attention circuits to make the right hand move at the same time boosted the inhibition of the left hemisphere over the left. It was as if on the day that little sister had her two triumphs, her older brother was made school captain!

So here is an example of how damaged parts of the brain can shake off inhibition from non-damaged parts if the correct sister circuits are activated together. We have put this principle of brain malleability to practical use in treating Pat's unilateral neglect, using a 'neglect alert device', a timer clipped on to Pat's belt, which buzzes at random. When it buzzes, Pat switches it off with a movement of her left hand or arm. In this way, the inhibited circuits in her damaged right hemisphere are continually activated and so ward off the bullying inhibition of her non-damaged left hemisphere. Pat's ability to look after herself at home was improved by this training: she bumped into things on the left less often, and was more inclined to notice people and things on her left.

Cajoling the bullied right brain into making movements isn't the only way it can rise above the bullying of its left-hemisphere brother. The right half of the brain has a particular set of jobs to do, just as the left has. One of these is to keep the brain alert and attentive, as we saw earlier. This 'alertness' system, though quite separate, is closely linked to the system that pays attention to the left side.

We can use this fact to help out the damaged right hemisphere which is having trouble paying attention to the left side in Pat. How? Well, one way is briefly to 'switch on' the alertness system and see what happens to Pat's ability to pay attention to the left side. We did this with a number of people suffering from unilateral neglect. They were asked to look at a computer screen while we measured how much they tended to 'neglect' the left side of the screen. Then, sometimes, we played a loud sound less than a second before the screen flashed its picture. When they were 'alerted' by the sound, they were far better at noticing the left side than when they weren't; in fact, for that brief second, on average their neglect was abolished by the brief surge of alertness that the sound caused.

This was because the space-attention system was helped out by its neighbour, the 'alerting' or 'wake-up' circuit which is also based in the damaged right half of the brain. Working together in this way, they managed to lift themselves away from the dominance of the left hemisphere and show the world what the right brain was capable of in spite of its damage.

Now, curing neglect for a second or two is obviously not much good practically in the real world, but this experiment gives us a sneak preview of the damaged brain's potential. Armed with this preview, my colleagues and I set out to help people with neglect overcome their handicapping disability. First we showed them that we could change their brain temporarily by sudden alerting sounds. If someone were to sneak up to you just now and burst a balloon just behind your head, you would probably leap to your feet with a racing heart, staring eyes and dilated pupils. Your brain state – its entire chemistry – would be changed by the sudden noise. If this prose had been making you a little sleepy, then that drowsiness would have been banished.

We didn't burst balloons behind our patients' heads, but we did show them how sudden sounds could change their brain in quite a dramatic way. We then said to them: 'Well, if I can change your brain so simply, then why can't you learn to do that yourself?' After all, most of us can ward off sleep or keep ourselves alert in monotonous situations like driving down a long straight road at night. So why can't people with brain damage that makes it hard for them to stay alert do the same?

That's just what we did. We gradually trained these people to 'switch on' their brain's alerting system by linking the loud sounds to a pithy command that they came up with, like 'Wake up' or 'Pay attention'. We trained them to check periodically how alert they were, and if they found that they were not very alert, then they had to rouse themselves to alertness using this phrase, often sitting up straight at the same time.

After just ten hours of this training, the patients were not only much more alert, but their neglect had reduced dramatically, just as it had for the brief second after the loud sounds; this time, however, the effects lasted twenty-four hours and more, not just for a second or two. One of our patients had made a pizza before this treatment, but the cheese on top was spread only on the right side of the pizza, leaving the left side as mainly dough. After the training he made another pizza. This time the cheese was equally spread all over!

So, by understanding how different brain systems help and hinder each other's functioning, we can 'trick' the brain into doing things of which at first sight it doesn't seem capable. It's not just with unilateral neglect that you can do this, though: the principle applies to almost all the different things that the brain does.

Restitching the net

What you do and what you think can change the patterns of con-nections with the neural networks of your brain. But can we put this principle into practice with brains which are functioning abnormally? The answer is yes. Take, for instance, the many unfortunate people who suffer a stroke with a consequent paralysis of the one side of their bodies. The paralysis may be complete or partial, and arms are more commonly and severely affected than legs. This happens because the brain circuits controlling movements are damaged. A substantial number of such people are left with a more or less useless left arm and end up getting around in life by just using the other arm.

These movement problems are treated with various types of therapy, including physiotherapy and occupational therapy. By encouraging people to move their paralysed limbs, we hope to give just the right stimulation to the brain's torn webs to help the networks reconnect, using the principle of Hebbian learning as described earlier in the example of the man learning to drive again after his brain had been damaged.

But how can we get paralysed limbs to move in order to provide the stimulation which the damaged neural webs so badly need? One way is to give the patients as much support as possible so that the flickering residue of function in the affected limbs can emerge, thus kindling reconnection in the circuit.

Researchers in Germany have done just that, using a parachute harness and a treadmill! They took people who could not walk by themselves and gave them just enough support with a pulley system and harness to enable them to walk on a slowly moving treadmill. By the end of training, of the seven people who couldn't walk before the training, three were walking independently, while another three could walk with just the supervision of a therapist.

It is important to give the *right* kind of stimulation to the torn webs. Cells that wire together, fire together: this means that sometimes the *wrong* brain cells may wire up together. Some types of spasticity – painful and handicapping contractions of muscles in paralysed limbs – may arise because the brain cells controlling contractions of the muscles are connecting up wrongly. As we saw earlier, people who become deaf are sometimes plagued by tinnitus, which may be caused by the brain cells which are starved of sound rewiring in unhelpful ways.

In rehabilitation, therefore, you should *target* the stimulation so that it helps the nets to reconnect in the right way, without making faulty connections. How? Well, one way is to give precisely the same input again and again. Parents know all about this when they are talking with their babies: you will often see a mother saying, over and over again, 'Ma-ma', to a chuckling infant, until the triumph of an approximate imitation by the child.

Similarly, a golf coach will get you to practise a swing over and over again. You won't be asked in the first few lessons to try a drive first, then a putt, then a chip and so on. No, you will practise a particular sequence of movements over and over again to help your brain form and then strengthen a particular pattern of connections in your trembling neural webs.

Now, as we discovered earlier, this can sometimes go too far, as anyone who has suffered from repetitive strain injury will testify. If a particular pattern in the web is practised by millions of trials per month over years, then that pattern may grow so much that it squeezes out other patterns in the network, leaving you unable easily to make other movements.

This is not a likely problem after brain damage, however. Therapy often consists of teaching a whole range of different movements: this is understandable if people are trying to learn the complex activities of daily life such as dressing, cooking, writing and walking. But there is a problem about teaching all these different things in the relatively small number of hours of rehabilitation that most people receive. The problem is this: the torn web of connections may never get enough of the *same* pattern of stimulation over and over again for it to rc-lcarn thc old pattcrn of conncctions undcrpinning that particular skill.

These ideas were put to practical test. Researchers compared standard therapy (with its mixture of different movements intermingled in each session) with a highly repetitive style of training. Taking twenty-seven people who had semi-paralysed arms and hands after a stroke, they simply had these people use their affected hand to squeeze together two metal bars separated by springs, in and out, over and over again for thousands of trials. This was just like weight-training in a gym, only it was the hand that was being exercised.

Compared to normal therapy, this type of training resulted in a much better recovery of hand function. This is not too surprising: Hebbian learning requires brain cells to be active at the same time for connections to be formed. If these connections are to become strong and reliable, however, then the same cells have to be active at the same time over and over again – hundreds or even thousands of times.

So, after brain damage, pumping iron in the mental gym needs an even greater discipline of repeating the same actions over and over again in order to nurture gently the unfolding trees of synaptic connections in the torn circuits. In very few places in the world, however, is this principle put into practice during rehabilitation.

Another way of targeting torn nets was developed by the same research team. Even if an arm is paralysed, the attempt to move it can produce tiny movements in the muscles of the arm, detectable only by electronic sensors. The German group amplified these tiny responses using a special machine, which immediately stimulated these same muscles electrically, making them move. In other words, tiny levels of activity in the muscle were translated into significant movements.

As the patient's hand movements improved, so the research team raised the threshold of the machine. In other words, slightly higher levels of muscle activity were needed to trigger the extra stimulation from the machine. In the twenty people with strokes who were treated using this method, marked improvements in their ability to move the paralysed hand were found.

Even months or years after a stroke, many people no longer use the paralysed arm. In roughly a quarter of those who end up with such a chronic loss of arm use, there is actually *some* movement in the hand if the person is tested by a doctor or therapist. But these individuals don't make much use of this small residual movement, relying instead on the other arm and hand for all their activities.

One group of researchers made a startling discovery, however. If for a couple of weeks these people are discouraged from using their good hand and arm, *and* they are encouraged by therapists to use their paralysed hand for a few hours each day, then lo and behold their ability to move the previously paralysed hand and arm improves.

Why is this surprising? It is surprising because most of these people had had their stroke more than a year before and were long past the stage where natural recovery is normally thought to take place. Yet here we have a very simple method – keep the good hand in your pocket for most of the time for a couple of weeks, and try to use the paralysed hand as much as possible. This results in *long-term* improvements in the paralysed arm.

The explanation for this is quite simple. For a while the paralysed arm really cannot be moved because the brain network controlling its movement is badly damaged. So for a while the patient relies on his good arm. The result? The damaged circuits controlling the movements of the paralysed arm are starved of the kind of stimulation which will help them reconnect.

In short, then, the principle 'use it or lose it' applies to these brain circuits. But only by discouraging people from using their non-paralysed hands could these shrunken networks starved of stimulation have the freedom to be activated and hence grow.

The results with human beings are supported by observations of monkeys who had lost a small area of their brain which controlled particular hand movements. It was discovered that neurones around this damaged area seemed to wither, which meant that the monkey's movement abilities were impaired even more, over and above what would have been expected from the damage itself.

This happened because the surrounding neurones – which were themselves quite healthy and unaffected by the damage – were starved of input because of the damage and so their neural webs shrunk through lack of input. These researchers showed, however, that this extra loss of function could be prevented by rehabilitation which gave the monkeys practice in moving their affected hands in particular ways. These movements stimulated the circuits which would otherwise wither because of lack of input from the damaged area. This is quite like what was done with the people who had suffered strokes: encouraging them to use the limb causes reconnection of the neural webs shrunken from disuse.

There can be problems in the brain other than those caused by injury or disease, though. As we will see later, as a child's brain grows and learns, it can develop quirks. Some of these are genetically programmed and others may arise from circumstances in the womb or at birth. Others, however, may happen because of the way the child learns and the experience the child does or does not have.

For instance, children who have hearing impairment at a critical time in language development may have problems in the way they take in spoken language. These problems can, in turn, cause difficulties in reading later in life. This is because their brain networks don't get the same kind of stimulation as those of other children and so are sculpted in a different way. Is it possible to resculpt these networks to improve things? At least in the case of one type of common problem – specific language impairment – it seems that we can.

Tuning the mind's ear

We all know people who are less good with words than others. They can't spell very well, and long words perplex them. While for some people this is just a reflection of their general abilities, for a substantial number the difficulty is quite specific to their language abilities and does not reflect their more general skills. This so-called 'specific language impairment' (SLI) severely handicaps such children through-out their lives.

Among the problems they experience is in distinguishing 'phonemes' such as /p/ and /b/. According to researchers in the USA, this is because in part these children's brains have learned to process spoken language in a different way from other children. In particular, they are unable to distinguish very rapid changes in sound taking place over just tens of thousandths of a second. Yet it is precisely such rapid changes which allow us to distinguish phonemes such as /p/ and/b/.

In these children the neural webs controlling language compre-hension have for some reason learned to break up language into larger rather than smaller chunks – i.e. syllables rather than phonemes. Distinguishing between syllables such as 'plate' and 'gate' only requires a time resolution measured in hundreds rather than tens of milliseconds. SLI children can cope with this, and therefore can get along with the less subtle aspects of comprehending spoken language.

For an intelligent brain, however, this is clearly not enough. So much of what we learn depends on our ability to make subtle distinctions between phonemes. According to these researchers, the difficulty is part of a more general problem in the time resolution of hearing in these children. They have shown, for instance, that single clicks become 'lost' to the children if they are presented close to another sound. This is in marked contrast to other children, who are able to detect the clicks even when they are very close to the sound. Normal children, therefore, have a much finer microscope on the heard world than do SLI children. They can dissect a stream of sounds into much finer elements than can SLI children, and therefore can build up a much more accurate body of language.

While this is not the whole story regarding the language problems of such children, it is nevertheless a significant part, and the question arises: what can be done about it? Can the neural webs in the mind's ear be retrained to increase their time resolution and improve discrimination of spoken language? Yes, they can!

Researchers used specially designed computerized games to train SLI children to distinguish and detect sounds presented at smaller and smaller time intervals. They also gave them games involving discriminating phonemes with which they had difficulty, such as /p/ and /b/. The critical difference between these two phonemes occurs within a tiny time interval at the beginning of each, while the rest of the phoneme is the same in each. Yet it is precisely within this time interval that SLI children cannot make discriminations because the critical sound is obliterated by the much longer end of each phoneme. In addition to training the SLI children to make finer and finer discriminations in time, therefore, the computer was also programmed artificially to exaggerate the differences between phonemes at that critical beginning. The result was that the children showed very big gains in their language abilities, almost certainly because the patterns in the neural web had been altered through the experience of this training.

'Pay attention!'

Pumping iron in the mental gym changes the brain. This is so even when you just pump iron inside your head – namely, with mental practice. You saw earlier how paying attention to different parts of your body, or to different senses, actually changes the activity in those areas of the brain where the sensations are registered. In fact, all the stimulation in the world will not sculpt the trembling webs of your brain unless you pay attention to that stimulation!

Repairing the torn web after brain damage should, therefore, depend heavily on how well these attention circuits in the frontal lobes of the brain are working – and indeed it does. People whose frontal lobes are damaged recover less well from injury to other parts of the brain than people whose frontal lobes are unaffected. In support of this idea, my research group showed that how well people can pay attention just after a right-brain stroke predicts how well they can use their left hands two years later!

There are also some hints that, even if an individual cannot move his or her paralysed arm, just *imagining* the movements may cause the kinds of improvements that my research showed that real movements could have. In other words, in the future some rehabilitation may be carried out in gyms inside people's heads!

Can experience help fix the torn net?

Yes it can, but there are limits, as Sir John Hale's enduring problems demonstrate. A net can be repaired by experience only if there are enough neurones left to connect, and if there is a bare minimum of connections left between these survivors. The concept of 'triage' is used in dealing with casualties in emergencies or battlefields, in order to concentrate limited medical resources on those who would benefit most. One group of casualties will survive without medical help, and a second group will probably not survive no matter what is done with them. For a third group, however, medical attention is critical for their survival and it is on them that emergency medical teams concentrate.

A similar principle may apply to damaged brain circuits. If only some of the network is damaged, Hebbian learning will ensure that the circuit repairs itself without much need of specialist help: just the act of learning to walk or talk again will provide the necessary stimulation to reconnect the network.

At the other end of the spectrum, sometimes so many neurones and connections are obliterated that there is little possibility of recovering the lost function, except by some other part of the brain taking on the job. But for many mental functions this is not possible, and so recovery for these patients means compensating for their lost function by learning to do things in a different way.

In the third group, however, there are the most exciting possibilities for sculpting the damaged network back into its correct shape. We have seen in this chapter how such sculpting has to be done with care. One problem, for instance, is that you might shape up and encourage networks which *inhibit* the damaged system.

Another possible problem is encouragement of bad habits within networks. For example, just bombarding SLI children with words in the hope that they might learn to take them in better might just strengthen their habit of breaking spoken language into over-large chunks and prevent them from learning to make the fine discriminations which will help them tell /p/ and /b/ apart.

The challenge for science is to find out for every individual how best to help the brain maximize its potential. In the future, this may happen by combining the kinds of treatments we have looked at here with drugs that make the brain more malleable and open to the sculpture that these rehabilitation methods offer. This is because the brain's connections are remoulded – the synapses altered – more readily when particular chemical messengers are available. These include the neurotransmitters noradrenaline and acetylcholine. When deprived of these, the trembling web is more readily 'stuck' in a particular pattern. If given a dose of them, however, the trembling web more easily yields to the urging of experience, remoulding itself through Hebbian learning.

This principle has been put into practice – again following stroke – in people relearning to use their limbs with the help of physiotherapy – that well-established form of brain sculpture. Drugs that increased the availability of noradrenaline boosted the effects of the physiotherapy and accelerated physical recovery. These drugs may work a bit like oil on rusted machinery: you can't move the machinery without the oil, but no more can the oil itself make it loosen. What you need is the combination of effort applied to the machinery and oil to get it working again.

Sometimes, though, no matter how much oil and effort you apply, part of the machinery is missing and it simply won't work. In such cases you have to replace the missing bits. This happens in the human brain too, with transplants of brain cells into areas where they have died – for instance in Parkinson's Disease. A trial of brain-tissue transplants for Huntingdon's Disease is for instance due to start soon in Europe.

It seems likely that simply putting these brain cells into the brain may not be quite enough, however. These healthy cells may well need stimulation and input to help embroider them into the brain's trembling web, so that they can really do their job. Research on rats shows that indeed they do need 'physiotherapy' to help the new tissue 'bind' into place and become a useful contributor to the damaged brain's recovery.

So the brain sculpture of the future for people with brain damage will almost certainly involve some combination of carefully planned stimulation (making sure not to stimulate brain areas that will inhibit the damaged ones), drug therapies to 'oil' the synapses and make them more willing to be sculpted, and – probably in many fewer cases – actual transplantation of brain cells into the torn net.

In the next chapter, let's turn to the kind of repair which eventually all of us will have to face – sculpture for the ageing brain.

7
Use It or Lose It

The man sitting opposite me on the London train looks as if he is in his seventies. Tufts of white hair spiral out from beneath the tweed cap that he has pulled tight and straight on his head. His anorak is buttoned up to the collar and his brown polyester trousers are neatly creased: army habits engraved in his brain even fifty years later. The grey-white hairs of his thin moustache can barely be seen against the pallor of his skin. Plastic, half-frame glasses droop below pouchy eyes. He sits with his head slightly bowed, fingers interlocked. Though his eyes are open, he does not glance about him. Hard to know what is going on behind his eyes. Occasionally his jaw moves as if he is chewing something.

He is with two women – one his wife, it seems. Both have bunched, permed hair and sit together, neat, prim and alert. One of them smiles at me as I sit down, tries to engage me in some conversation. For the length of the journey the two women chat, judge, plan and debate, in between dipping into the newspaper for more material to discuss. I let my hearing blur the better to watch the vivacious mime show of nods, conspiratorial smiles, darting glances and pursed lips. Above all, they are noticing, sifting and grading the world and their fellow human beings, with a bright-eyed intentness.

I glance back at their companion. He hasn't moved. His eyes are dreamy and unfocused. 'Sometimes I sits and thinks, sometimes I just sits': studies in older people have shown lower levels of activity in the frontal lobes than in younger people when they are asked to sit and do nothing in particular. But, as you will see in this chapter, there is huge variation in how people age. If I were to guess about the man in front of me, I would estimate a much lower level of activity in the front 40 per cent of his brain than is the case for his two companions.

Perhaps he is roaming his memory banks, pleasantly detached from the daily grind. If he is, it is a kind of passive meandering, a random buffeting from recollection to recollection, not an active, focused, targeted search of memory. No, if I am to guess, here is a brain sluggishly free-wheeling, under-used.

Who knows what this man did before he retired? He probably made it until he was sixty or sixty-five before being laid off. The thing about jobs is that they make you use your brain; even the streetsweeper has to solve problems of parked cars, schedules and targets. However, the demands on initiative are being sucked out of more and more jobs, and with increasingly sophisticated computers, even professionals may end up using their brains less and less.

At a recent conference of the International Airline Pilots Association, one speaker described the sort of passenger aircraft that might exist in 2005. He said the crew would consist of one pilot and a dog. The pilot's role would be to feed and look after the dog. The dog's role would be to bite the pilot if he tried to touch anything. Bank managers have to gauge risk when considering loan applications, yet even this human judgement is becoming increasingly automated. Managers key the data about the person looking for a loan, and about the business. The computer then calculates the risk and comes out with a recommendation. Computer 'expert systems' have been shown to be much better than the vast majority of doctors at diagnosis in certain specialities. The only reason they are not used is because doctors don't like to think that a machine can have better clinical judgement than they have.

So the man on the London train might have given up trying to self-start his brain even before he retired. On the other hand, his wife and her friend may never have had a job, but that hasn't stopped them from raking the carriage with searching, curious eyes. They are so manifestly actively using *their brains. The question I pose in this chapter is whether by using the trembling web of synapses in this active way, they are less likely to lose mental abilities as they age.*

First, the bad news

As any professional sportsman or woman will tell you, the older you get, the slower your reactions become. Learning new techniques is also harder. If you have any doubts about that, try learning to ski in a class full of young children: by the second day, they will be skimming contemptuously past you as you lie face down in the snow after your umpteenth fall.

Age also dulls memory – but not all types of memory equally. Older people can, for instance, learn new facts pretty well, in fact, compared to younger people. So, for example, if you decide to go back to university in your fifties or sixties, you won't be too disadvantaged when it comes to cramming in the facts, compared to your younger classmates. What you will find hard, however, is remembering *where* or *when* you learned any particular fact.

This so-called memory for the *source* of knowledge may not seem particularly important. Surely what counts is that you remember the fact, not who or what the source of the fact was? In reality, however, it is very important to know where we heard that rumour, in which book we read that fact, or when it was that we paid that bill which a credit agency claims is still outstanding. Knowing where or when you learned something helps you go back and check, and perhaps pick up some new information as you do so. If you can remember where you read something, then that memory may help trigger off other facts which you learned on the same page. And remembering where you told that joke will help you avoid the embarrassment of telling the same joke to the same people again. Most of us can think of some elderly relative who tells us the same anecdotes from their youth over and over again: 'Yes, Uncle Jim, you *have* told us the story about Aunt Mary's false teeth and the octopus . . .'

Of course, elderly people have little problem in remembering events from years ago. This is because the memory apparatus that lays down new memories is to some extent separate from the parts of the brain where these memories are stored; and the new memory circuits – located partly in an area of the brain known as the 'hippocampus' – may be more vulnerable to the effects of age than the fact-stores in an area known as the 'lateral temporal cortex'.

It will probably come as no surprise to many older readers to find that recognizing faces is harder for older people than for younger ones. In particular, with age comes the tendency to say 'Oh hello!' to complete strangers because you mistakenly 'recognize' them as people you have met before. Such embarrassing slips have their origin in the same quirks of the older brain which make it hard to remember the 'source' of facts.

This is because many faces are quite similar, so a particular face might easily trigger the pattern of synaptic connections in your brain's trembling web corresponding to a similar but nevertheless quite different individual. What your brain does to make such mistakes less likely is to pull out the 'context' for the face, to help sort out to whom the face belongs. By 'context' I just mean the circumstances – time, place, people who were also present – in which you encountered that face before.

For example, you meet someone at a party whose face is vaguely familiar. Your brain races to search for a name, where you know him from and what you should do – give a jolly smile, nod respectfully or flee. Suddenly your brain comes up with the heart-sinking answer: he is the bore from last year's Christmas party who pinned you to the wall with a monologue about tariff structures on the Belgian rail-freight network. The context of the memory thus remembered, you have your answer – flee! The older you are, however, the less likely you are to have such a merciful release and the more readily will you suffer the attentions of the half-remembered party bore.

Age also brings with it a difficulty in ignoring distraction. Whereas teenagers seem able to concentrate against blaring background rock music, older people tend to become harassed and irritable if their teenage children are talking quietly beside them as they try to read.

This is a problem of 'inhibition', where the activity of one set of brain cells suppresses the firing of another set.

Though inhibition can cause problems in a damaged brain trying to repair itself, in fact we could not function properly in the world without it. How else do we listen to the airport flight announcement against the babble of voices in the crowded departure lounge? We have to inhibit the billions of bits of irrelevant information assailing our senses in order to concentrate on the fragments of information which are crucial for us at a particular point in time.

This difficulty in suppressing the irrelevant causes particular problems with driving in older people. Whereas older people are more vigilant, careful and generally less error prone, they tend to make *more* mistakes at busy road junctions. At such complicated traffic intersections, everyone – young and old – is faced with a barrage of lights, signals and speeding streams of traffic. Some of this information is critically important for deciding when and what we do next, while much of it is irrelevant. For instance, the roaring trucks on the motorway overhead may be noisy and intimidating, but they pass right over this complicated junction and are quite irrelevant to the task of managing to turn here. A young driver will be much better able to 'screen out' this irrelevant distraction than an older driver, and so will be better able to focus attention on the lights and traffic which *are* important for surviving this particular turn. It shouldn't be surprising, therefore, that older drivers tend to have more accidents in complicated situations like this than do younger drivers.

While older people may be better than their juniors in some types of problem-solving where they have experience and expertise, they are worse at solving novel or abstract problems at which they have no previous experience. This type of 'raw' problem-solving ability is sometimes called 'fluid intelligence'. It rests much less on past experience with a particular problem, depending instead on the ability to wrestle with a completely abstract or unfamiliar kind of puzzle. 'Crystallized intelligence', on the other hand, rests substantially on a lifetime's knowledge and learning – such as general knowledge, vocabulary and experience in solving particular kinds of problems.

Mathematicians, advanced computer programmers and theoretical physicists are working, by the very nature of their job, at the outer limits of knowledge in their field. Hence they cannot draw nearly as much on past knowledge as can, for instance, lawyers, historians or other scholars in the humanities. The former tend to make their names much earlier in life – often in their twenties or early thirties – whereas the latter tend to reach their peak somewhat later in academic life, because their work is more heavily based in accumulated knowledge and experience. For similar reasons, most top managers in major corporations tend to be grey-heads: running a big company needs as much stored knowledge and experience as it does raw, fluid intelligence.

So, if age brings with it a decline in some of our faculties, what is happening to the trembling webs of connections in our brain to explain this?

Age and the trembling web

There is some good news and some bad news as far as the brain is concerned, too. The good news is that the number of brain cells – at least in one important part known as the temporal lobes – stays much the same between your fifties and your eighties. The bad news is that your brain begins to shrink in your fifties. The average brain weight of a twenty-year-old man is approximately 1.4kg, while the average brain weight of someone in his fifties is approximately 1.34kg. By the time men are in their eighties, their brains have shrunk to an average of 1.2kg! Albert Einstein's brain, for instance, weighed just 1.23kg when he died at the age of seventy-six.

These are average figures, however, for some brains show scarcely any shrinkage over these thirty years and approximately only half of people studied in their late sixties showed any shrinkage in their brains at all. As we will see later, we find this increasing spread in the effects of ageing for mental functions too.

It seems that age particularly hits the connecting fibres of the brain – the so-called 'white matter' – more than it does the central parts of the neurones themselves. This is confirmed by a study showing that neurones in the temporal cortex of the brain shrink back over these three decades, their dendritic trees gradually withering.

This bad news is compounded by the fact that the all-important frontal lobes of the brain may suffer more from the ravages of ageing than do other areas. As noted at the start of this chapter, when asked simply to lie back and do nothing, older people tend to show less activity in the frontal lobes of their brains than younger people. It is when we are thinking and planning that our frontal lobes are particularly active, and they are also important for controlling movement and responses, through their connection to other parts of the brain that also control movement, known as the 'basal ganglia'. It seems that ageing particularly hits the speed and efficiency of responses and movement, in contrast to the 'input' functions of the brain that are located more towards the back of the brain.

Next time you feel irritated by the old person fumbling for coins as the queue grows behind him, calm yourself with this thought. Actually he may be mentally much more agile than he appears and his slow, fumbling movements are probably not a fair gauge of his mental competence.

So, our brains are shrinking as we get older. A depressing thought, but at least we may not be losing brain cells – rather, the cells are shrinking. Here is an optimistic thought, however: experience can shape the connections between brain cells. So, can it also affect the shrinkage in connections between cells which age brings on? In other words, is 'use it or lose it' a viable possibility? Before tackling this question, let's look at how the brain adjusts to time's onslaught.

The old dog's tricks

The brain doesn't simply sit back and take it when it is damaged and its reactions to the ravages of age are no exception to this rule. Though the brain doesn't seem to lose brain cells in the temporal cortex with age, it may lose them in some other areas. When it does, it seems that the surviving brain cells respond by sending out more and longer connections to other survivors. This is what happens in Parkinson's Disease, for instance, as we saw earlier.

One group of researchers studied brain cells taken from people in their fifties and seventies as well as from a group of people suffering dementia. They found that the average length of dendrites – the branches and twigs sprouting from the brain cell's trees – was *greater* in seventy-year-olds than it was in fifty-year-olds. This was interpreted as the trembling web's response to loss of neurones: another case of good neighbours helping out when brain cells die.

The brain's systems also reorganize to cope with brain shrinkage, just as they do to cope with damage caused by stroke or injury. Older people seem to do certain mental tasks differently from the young. For instance, the brain activity of old and young people was studied as they learned a series of faces, and later as they tried to recognize which faces they had seen before and which were new. While they were learning the faces, younger people's brains became active in a number of places, including the left frontal lobe. Older volunteers in this study did not activate the same brain areas during learning, however, and did not for instance show a 'lighting up' of activity in the left frontal lobe. This suggests that some of the memory problems of older people happen because their brains do not put the same 'effort' into laying down memory traces for later recognition.

But up comes the old chestnut again: older people differed from each other in brain function to a greater extent than younger people did. With age, it appears, comes the separation of sheep and goats, cognitively speaking. It's time we took a look at this spreading out of abilities as people get older.

Getting older means getting more different

The contrast between the man and the two women on the London train illustrates something that is really quite obvious – some people get old faster than others. Going to a school or college reunion can be a sobering experience, a time of *sotto voce* gasps: 'God, he's aged!' Other old boys and old girls look disconcertingly unchanged from decades before.

It shouldn't be surprising to find that the brain – like other organs of the body – ages at different rates in different people. What this means when you test older people's mental functions is that, while *average scores* on mental tests go down, the *spread* of scores goes up. In other words, some old people stay just as mentally fit as whippersnappers half their age. Indeed, older people who do not show brain changes are much sharper than many of their juniors.

The question is why some people age more than others. A lot of it may be genetically determined, while lifestyle – smoking, diet, alcohol, stress, etc. – plays a part too. There is, however, another lifestyle factor that has been shown to affect mental fitness, and that is physical exercise.

Certainly, keeping physically active seems to extend life: one Finnish study showed that men and women in their seventies and eighties who took regular exercise were less likely to die over the next five years than those who did not. And the brain seems to benefit from physical fitness too. Older people who keep fit have faster reaction times than those who do not. It seems that this increased speed of reaction is not simply that toned muscles are responding more quickly; rather, the quicker reaction times are caused by speedier brain functioning. When this brain power is measured with EEG brain waves, physical fitness seems to produce faster and stronger brain responses. Physical exercise may influence brain function by stimulating the secretion of 'neurotrophins' – substances which encourage sprouting between brain cells.

So, physical activity seems to benefit the brain and may offer some protection against the assault of age on mental function. But does the same apply to mental activity? This brings us to the matter of 'use it or lose it': in other words, can the brain's trembling, ageing web be preserved and nurtured via mental activity? First, let's look at mental activity in early life, long before age begins to take its toll.

Education – an insurance policy for the brain?

Primary-school education was not made compulsory in Italy until many years later than in most other European countries. Because of the widespread poverty that prevailed in many parts of Italy then, relatively few people could afford to pay for education themselves. As a result, a substantial number of Italians in their sixties, seventies and eighties have had little or no schooling in their lives.

One group of researchers was interested to find out whether the amount of education people had in early life had any effect on the state of their brains in old age. The results were very surprising: rates of Alzheimer's Disease – the most common type of senile dementia – were *fourteen times* greater among illiterate people with no education than among those who had more than five years' education. Just over 7 per cent of illiterate people had Alzheimer's Disease, while just under 3 per cent of those with less than five years of education suffered this dementia. Among those who had more than five years' schooling, the rate of Alzheimer's Disease was just half of 1 per cent.

When educational deprivation is so widespread, you can be sure that there are plenty of intelligent people whose brains were starved of the stimulation that schooling provides. It can't be the case that these Italians who had low levels of education just happened to have genetically compromised brains, making them vulnerable in later life to Alzheimer's Disease. On the contrary, it seems very clear that brain sculpture produced by education in early life had long-term effects on the brain, and that these effects were sufficiently dramatic to increase substantially the likelihood of Alzheimer's Disease in old age.

Researchers have found the same result in many different countries. However, quite how education affects the brain's trembling web is not yet clear. One possibility is that the actual disease process in the brain tissue is stopped or delayed. Another is that education nurtures a better-connected network of neurones. When this web is afflicted by the disease, so the argument goes, it keeps functioning better and longer than less well-connected webs because – with the help of our old friend Hebbian learning – patterns of memories, skills and knowledge are stitched more densely into the connections, and hence are less easily lost.

Another possibility is that education fosters lifelong habits of mental activity. The more education you have, the more likely you are to stimulate your brain with reading throughout a lifetime, and probably you will tend to debate, discuss and think more about the world around you. It is also possible that this ongoing mental activity in old age offers protection to the old brain against the decay of Alzheimer's Disease.

We saw earlier how there is indeed evidence that education may nurture a better-connected trembling web. In fact, as we discovered, researchers have actually measured the richness of connections among brain cells in people with different levels of education. While they could not prove which came first – complex brain neurones or relatively high education – the Italian research strongly supports the notion that education has effects in the brain which either delay the onset of disease or protect the brain against the disease when it does come on.

Before considering whether we really must 'use it or lose it', however, let's look at what the older brain *can* do as well as the young brain.

. . . and now for the good news

Even if you are thirtysomething, you might have felt the hot breath of mentally sharper twenty-year-olds on your neck, particularly if you work in a job such as computer programming, commodity trading or pure mathematics. These types of work demand the kind of razor-sharp mental agility which mirrors the physical super-fitness required of top sportsmen and women. You don't, after all, find many forty-something international soccer players, and we happily accept it when sports pundits describe some thirty-two-year-old athlete with chiselled muscles and translucent skin as 'over the hill' and 'past his best'. But sometimes it's harder to swallow the fact that we are mentally less agile than our juniors.

Are older people less mentally competent in all respects? Take judges, for instance, who are not renowned for their youth. Why are they not replaced by lightning-sharp market traders with the scent of middle-aged blood in their nostrils? Or politicians? Even Bill Clinton and Tony Blair are no spring chickens.

The answer, of course, is *experience*. The accumulated knowledge of decades may be essential to navigate the bewildering complexities of human behaviour as manifested in case law or politics. Publishers and editors, wine-tasters and art historians, are just some examples of jobs where the cool wisdom of experience beats the hot blood of youthful mental speed. In fact, research confirms that older people are often better than younger people at making judgements about complex chains of events. This is particularly the case in ambiguous situations involving human behaviour. Older people tended to view these events in terms of interaction between external circumstances on the one hand, and the personal qualities of individuals on the other. Younger people are less likely to see events in such a sophisticated and mature way.

Not only can older employees draw on experience to do the job, but they are also less likely to be involved in accidents at work; are less likely to take time off sick; and are generally more satisfied with their jobs. So, in spite of their lower average mental sharpness, older workers can end up doing at least as good a job as their younger colleagues, depending of course on the particular job.

The British television general-knowledge programme *Mastermind* used to test highly accomplished competitors in their knowledge about their specific area of interest, as well as in their general knowledge. One research study compared old and young *Mastermind* contestants and found that, even in the general-knowledge questions on which the older people had no specific practice or learning, they were just as fast and accurate at pulling out obscure facts about the world as were younger contestants. In other words, at least as far as this part of the mental practice is concerned, their brains appeared to have escaped the ravages of ageing.

Another mental arena where age beats youth is absentmindedness and carelessness. People in their seventies are less likely to forget to do things they set out to do than are younger people. So, for instance, they are less likely to forget an appointment or to make a phone call. They also take more care when they are working on tasks and make fewer mistakes than younger people. So, therefore, if you have to ask a stranger to keep an eye on your bags in an airport while you go off to buy a newspaper, then ask an older rather than a younger person. They will be less likely to let their attention drift and let your bag be stolen.

Older people are therefore *better* than younger ones in some types of mental activity. How can this be squared with a story of inexorable brain shrinkage as we get older? First, roughly one-third of older brains scarcely shrink. Second, some older people will have used certain mental faculties more than younger people and such experience may strengthen the connections in the trembling web.

In other words, one reason why older people are mentally better than younger people in some respects may be because their mental faculties have been stimulated more often over a larger number of years. Here, therefore, is the possibility that not only is 'use it or lose it' true, but that 'use it and improve it' may also be true. So let's now look at how pumping iron in the elderly brain might slow or even reverse the biological effects of ageing.

Pumping mental iron in the over-fifties gym

If you are over fifty, then your brain probably differs somewhat from that of the average twenty-year-old, but perhaps not too much. Certainly your brain is capable of learning, rational thought and the odd withering put-down which makes up for all those quips about your receding hairline or widening hips; and the neural webs of the older brain can tremble and change in response to experience and learning in much the same way that young brains do.

So, brain sculpture for the over-fifties is feasible, desirable and to be expected. In other words, age is no barrier to pumping mental iron to keep the trembling webs strong and connected. In fact, it may be even more important as you get older to pump mental iron – to keep mentally active and to give your brain challenges. After all, the connections between brain cells do begin to shrink and may need extra help to keep connected.

Better-educated people probably have better-connected brains. Some of the less diligent over-fifties among you, therefore, might be tempted to rest on the laurels of your excellent Masters degree and stop taxing your brain with difficult puzzles like how to programme the video or reorganize the marketing department. But this would probably be a mistake. True, the more education you had in your formative years, the better bolstered is your brain against the ravages of age, disease and injury, but it seems very likely that you will maximize this advantage by continued exercise of your brain.

How do we know this? Well, one way is to give old and young people tests at which older people tend to perform poorly. This generally involves making them respond at speed in complicated tasks – like some computer games, for instance. Such tasks favour the young over the old. What happens, however, when you give old and young *practice* on these tasks? If the oldies' poor performance is all down to unravelling brain embroidery and watered-down neurotransmitters, then no amount of practice is going to narrow the gap between young and old. If, on the other hand, poor performance with age arises because older people are simply not used to fast responding in complicated situations (you don't see many seventy-year-olds playing the virtual-reality machines in amusement arcades), then practice *should* narrow the age gap in performance.

And indeed this is what happens. Older people, given half a chance to practise, narrow the lead which their younger competitors have, showing that they have the potential to perform better if their brains are given a chance to catch up. The scientists who showed this reasoned that as you get older, generally speaking, fewer demands are made on your brain – you are, for instance, less likely to have to study for exams or learn new skills. In other words, your brain is less 'in training' as you get older.

Older people's poorer scores on tests may therefore be in part due to this 'disuse'. The more practice you give both young and old, however, the less of a factor this 'disuse' becomes. In other words, older people should benefit disproportionately from practice. This is exactly what has been found, though practice never completely eliminated the differences between young and old. In other words, some but not all of the mental slowing was caused by 'losing it through not using it'.

It seems very likely, therefore, that the increased spread in mental abilities which comes with age is in part caused by differences in how much individuals use their mental functions as they get older. In fact, 'using it' may not only help maintain connections in the neural web, but may also help neurones repair themselves against the damage caused by ageing.

Professional musicians know this intuitively. If you earn a living by making music, then in your fifties, sixties and even seventies you must compete with much younger talents on precisely these measures of dexterity of hand and brain which age particularly affects. How do musicians manage this? One study looked at how older amateur and professional pianists fared over several years. As you would expect, the amateur pianists lost some of their skill over this period, but this was not the case for the professionals. In fact, they kept up a level of skill that was only very slightly lower than that of their younger professional colleagues. And what determined whether the older professional pianists kept up with the younger ones? Practice! Quite simply, the more they deliberately practised as they got older, the more likely they were to keep up the same level of skill as younger pianists. In other words, by musically 'using it', they could almost definitely avoid 'losing it'.

Further evidence in support of this principle comes from researchers who were interested in measuring the mental capacities of a group of older people who were still mentally active in order to test the notion that such mental activity forestalls some of the effects of ageing. Still-active Californian university professors were compared with less mentally active people of the same age to see how well they did on mental tests; they were also compared with a group of younger people. Over a range of tests, the mentally active people in their sixties and early seventies outstripped their contemporaries, and were just about as good as the younger people.

This leads on to an obvious question: how does your brain respond when you take your pension and retire from a demanding, mentally stimulating job? One study has found that while people in boring, routine jobs can *benefit* mentally from being released from the grind of daily work, people in highly complex and mentally demanding jobs may be more likely to *decline* cognitively.

This is not very good news for the Californian professors contemplating retirement, but it is of course entirely what you would expect of a brain composed of a trembling tissue of neural connections which is sculpted by stimulation and experience. Of course, it is far from inevitable that retirement means that you starve your brain of the stimulation it needs to preserve its connections.

One of the great privileges of education is that you *learn to learn*. A good education – particularly at university level – turns your brain into a sort of self-programming computer. As such, your brain can provide itself with stimulation through new learning, thought and imagination. We have already seen a concrete example of this earlier in the book, where purely mental imagery and practice made new brain connections grow. With retirement, then, you can – no, *must*, if you want to keep the dendritic trees blooming in your brain – substitute new types of mental activity for the old. This might involve anything from reading your way through the Russian masters to collecting pre-war Asian model locomotives. The important thing is that your brain places demands on itself.

Sometimes it is not so easy to generate all the stimulation yourself. We all need people and organizations around us to keep us stimulated, and to make us do things at times when we might not feel like doing them. Pure, 100 per cent self-starters are rare indeed.

So it is likely that our brains will undergo a certain amount of 'disuse' after we retire. One factor that protects against such effects is long marriage to an intelligent spouse! But is there anything else we can do – say some kind of mental aerobics – which will ward off some of the disconnection that comes with disuse?

Well, it seems that therapeutic mental workouts can indeed help maintain mental agility, just in the way that regular exercise can keep up physical health and fitness. For instance, research has shown that older people can be trained to use their memories more effectively, with the benefits of this training lasting several years after its completion. Logical reasoning abilities can also be trained and improved with the right kind of mental workout.

Of what exactly do such mental aerobics consist? Let's take the example of memory. To remember something, you have first to take it in, or 'encode' it. Then it has to be 'stored' until it is needed, when it must be 'retrieved'. A distinction needs to be made between verbal and visual memory. For instance, if you have to learn the way from the conference centre to your hotel in a strange town, you can do it in two ways. One of these is *verbal* (turn left at the department store, second right at the fire station, then left at the pharmacy); the other is *visuospatial*, in the form of a mental picture or map. To make the most of your memory, you have to learn to use these different systems – encoding, storage, retrieval, as well as verbal and visual – to their full capacity.

Most people rely more on verbal than on visuo-spatial memory. This means that as memory starts to fail with age, we have only a single memory system on which we tend to rely – in other words, all our memory eggs are in one basket. If, however, we can develop the habit of using visual imagery to help us learn, then we have two back-up systems, rather than one.

Memories are like the strands of wool knitted together in a pullover: the more completely they are connected with each other, the less chance they have of unravelling. Hence, if what you want to remember is connected with mental pictures, then there is less chance that it will unravel and be lost.

Memory is also improved by *linking* what you are trying to learn to things you know already. For instance, if you *actively* listen and read, by relating what you are hearing or seeing to what you know already, then you will better remember the information. A simple study method known as PQRST – standing for preview, question, read, state and test – gives a practical method for improving recall of anything you read, using the principles of linking and relating to what you know already, as you can see in the following example.

Preview
Before reading an article or chapter, briefly scan it, perhaps

reading the first line of each paragraph, as well as the first and last paragraphs. Form a rough idea of what it is about and what it is likely to tell you.

Question

What do you already know about this topic? What have you read about it already? Most importantly, what questions do you have about the topic that you would like answered by the article?

Read

Read the article actively, with the questions you have raised foremost in your mind.

State

When you have finished the article, review its contents, again relating it to what you know about the subject already, and in particular asking yourself whether or not it answered the questions you had about it.

Test

Test yourself for your memory of what you have just read.

The brain has another type of memory system, known as 'implicit memory' which allows us to learn some types of information without consciously paying attention to them. One study has shown that people with poor memory can learn by using this implicit memory system, which is often unaffected by age, illness or brain damage. Crucial to the system's efficient use, however, is that you should not make mistakes while learning. For example, when learning to use a complicated electronic notebook, the people with damaged memory systems were much better at remembering how to use it properly if they were never allowed to make any mistakes during learning. Because it is not a conscious system, implicit memory does not cope well with mistakes and does not shake them off easily. This means that if, say, you are trying to learn a list of French vocabulary, wrong guesses during learning lead to the implicit memory system holding on to these wrong responses and so they interfere with learning of the list.

The practical consequence of this for improving memory is that when we are trying to learn something – from using the new video recorder to building up our Italian vocabulary – we should use the principle of 'errorless learning'. In other words, we should study in a way that minimizes guessing and maximizes trials where there is a strong chance of our getting the right answer. For instance, you might just learn two words of Italian first, and keep testing yourself on just these two words before trying to learn any more. By very gradually building up the list you are learning, and constantly testing yourself only on words you are confident you know pretty well, you will learn much better than if you try to learn a list of twenty words in one go, making wrong guesses in the process.

It seems then that mental aerobics can preserve mental agility and memory as we get older – to some extent at least. But age isn't just about memory and mental challenge. Old age brings with it big changes to health, finances, relationships and opportunity. How people respond to these changes is critically important in determining how age affects them. We will see later how these emotional factors have very strong effects on brain function – how *belief* in your mental abilities protects and fosters these abilities.

The man on the train

Returning to the elderly man on the London train with whom I began this chapter, you might speculate about the source of his apparent listless, dull-eyed demeanour. Was it depression? Certainly, like many other emotions, depression changes the brain profoundly, reducing, for instance, the amount of activity in the frontal lobes. But he didn't *look* depressed.

Perhaps age had done to his brain what it had done to his wispy white hair. Senescence may have culled and withered the cells of the trembling web so that it could no longer sustain the probing, watching curiosity which the brains of his two women companions displayed.

Or perhaps his trembling web had withered from disuse – from the lack of demand of work, from the slow drift of his life in the company of these two pert and active women. Maybe he had given up control over much of the decision-making in a life constricted by retirement.

Perhaps, indeed, the vibrant initiative of these women sapped what belief he had in himself to control and influence his life.

This is all speculation, of course. The point is to illustrate how life sculpts your brain, how *you* sculpt your brain and how the trembling web must be all the more nurtured and stimulated as age tries to prune back its connections.

However, there is an even more important stage in life when the trembling web must be nurtured and stimulated: childhood. Let us now turn to a particularly precious kind of sculpture – the shaping of a child's growing brain.

8
Fingerprints on the Brain

Sam's tongue and brain wrestle for the sound. Something to link to the peculiar, curved little mark on the page. Kuh? Why 'kuh' for C? Why not 'blah'? And where is he to look, anyway? All these rows of anonymous squiggles, and he has to force his eyes not just to one of these rows, but to an arbitrary little point on the row. Start on the left? Where's left? Why left? Now move right to the next letter? Why right? What's a letter, anyway?

'Ah . . .' 'Good boy!' he hears his father say, feeling the squeeze of encouragement from the arm round his waist. In his brain, another arbitrary correspondence between a squiggle on the paper and a sound in his ear is made. Somewhere behind his eyes a trembling web of synapses bind together a fraction stronger. Next time he sees that 'a', an electric whisper along the filigree connections will evoke a shadow of the half-linked sound and it will come out more easily. Sam won't have to knit his five-year-old brow so tightly tomorrow night, as he tries to bind together these tiny, disconnected and random features of the world which the adults so badly want him to do.

'Tuh . . . !' he announces triumphantly, duly accepting victor's laurels

from an admiring father. But then his face falls as he is asked to run them all together. All what together? 'Kuh . . . ah . . . tuh . . .': what does that spell, Sam? Spell? Yes, run them together, Sam. OK, here goes: 'T . . . ac!' Tac? 'What's a tac, Daddy?' No, no, not a 'tac', Sam. Say the first letter first, then the second . . .. But what's first? The one at the beginning, Sam! 'Kuh': left is always the beginning.

Not in Arabic, Daddy. Now don't get precocious on me, Sam – it's your brain we're sculpting tonight, not mine. OK, OK, Dad, keep your hair on: 'Kuh. . . . ah . . .' Good, now run them together, Sam – like this: 'kuh . . . ah' . . . kuh.ah . . . kuh–ah . . . 'Kah!' Great, Sam – excellent – 'ca'! Now the last letter . . . what's the last letter? 'Tuh.' Good, now run 'ca' and 'tuh' together 'Ca . . .tuh'.

'Kahtuh!' Kahtuh? Kahtu? Kaht? CAT! Cat!' Brilliant, Sam, brilliant – that's right, it's 'cat'.

Sam is beginning to learn the secret code of written language, changing his brain as he does so. Next week he will look at the scratches on the paper which we understand as 'cat' and the sound will come effortlessly, fluently borne on an electrochemical wave across the newly embroidered neural tissue.

So his intelligence will be slowly built on the scaffolding of literacy, each day bringing a tranche of new words with their retinue of concepts and categories and understanding about the self and the world. Just as his father helped him bind together the unrelated sounds to their secret code of arbitrary squiggles, so words will for Sam begin to bind together the disconnected aspects of the world.

Here is the brain being engineered to do what Sam's genes never planned it to do. Here we see humanity leapfrogging its genetic patrimony to sculpt a brain using the tools of human culture. What a privilege, and what a responsibility, to be able to leave fingerprints on our children's brains.

Mind's triumph over matter

What an awesome responsibility it is, physically shaping a child's brain like this. The words we speak, the actions we take, sculpting the brain as surely as any surgeon could. Here is an immortality of sorts – traces of ourselves physically bound into the brains of the children who will survive us.

Our civilization rests on the written word. Human culture, human knowledge, would be nothing without it. Yet the ability to read and write is an artifice of human ingenuity, contrived in the absence of genes to guide our use of the mysterious squiggles with which Sam grapples. Here we have the central engine of human civilization and culture – perhaps the major determinants of our fate – spun from pure mind. Like an adolescent outgrowing the shelter and constraints of family, mind rides out in its white convertible of culture and language to make its own way in the world. Meanwhile its family of inherited biology can only look on with a wringing of hands, fearfully hoping that the headstrong offspring they no longer control will choose a sensible path in the world.

Just as Sam, one day, will grow up and away from his parents, so it is for the human mind. Of course there are genetic foundations to all this. Our genes bequeath us the ability to make out the shapes of squiggles on the page; they give us the ability to make the intricate movements needed for writing; and they also give us the ability to speak and understand language, albeit that these abilities need the nurture of experience for the genes to express themselves.

Written language, however, is different. There is no gene for this. For millennia during which human attributes were shaped by evolutionary selection, the ability to read and write was not being selected. Spoken language, yes: the early hominoids who could best communicate with each other would probably survive better and thus favour the transmission of these genes. But not reading and writing, those flagships of human civilization; no, these are the work of the human mind.

So humans like Sam's father have learned to pass on this essential skill of literacy to their offspring. And it *is* essential. Research in the United States shows that illiterate adults account for 75 per cent of the unemployed, and that 85 per cent of juveniles appearing in court are illiterate. Forget the evolutionary selection of abilities and attributes that helped early humans survive in the wilds of Africa: these aren't what's needed to survive in the wilds of Detroit, Jakarta or Mexico City. No, literacy and the education it brings are the keys to survival now. The literacy that the human mind painstakingly sculpts into its own neural tissue – mind's triumph over matter.

Thanks to modern brain-scanning methods, we can see just these effects of childhood mind sculpture – on the brains of twelve elderly women in a small town in southern Portugal. In this part of Portugal in the 1930s, poverty was such that not all the children in a family could be educated and so a cultural tradition developed whereby the eldest daughter would often stay and work at home, remaining illiterate and uneducated while the younger sisters and brothers whom she had to look after had at least a few years of education.

This cultural tradition meant that it couldn't be the case that these illiterate elder sisters were in some way born with less intelligence or ability. In fact, the eldest child in a family usually has a higher achievement educationally than other children, so their illiteracy was purely a product of the culture they grew up in, not of the biology they inherited.

Of the twelve women studied, six had been kept at home and were illiterate, while the other six had gone to school for just four years and could read and write, albeit at a modest level after so little schooling. The two groups of women didn't differ in mental ability in tests such as general knowledge, naming of objects and most types of memory, and they were more or less the same age, in their sixties and seventies. All that differentiated them was whether or not they had been taught to read and write.

It was already known that illiterate people are poorer on certain tasks than literates. In particular, they find it hard to repeat nonsense words like 'calmetic' or 'trimey'. Similarly, they can't easily play word games where you have to repeat a word while missing out its first letter – for example, hearing 'table' and responding 'able'. Researchers think this is because learning to read involves your brain learning to 'chop up' words into their component sound-parts, or phonemes. This is what Sam's father was doing when he taught Sam to say 'kuh . . . ah . . . tuh' for 'cat'. This way of reading is called 'phonological' and learning by this method means that you can repeat words that you have never heard before – nonsense words or words in a foreign language, say – by applying this 'chopping-up' strategy.

There are other 'reading routes' in the brain, though, as we saw in Chapter 6. One of these is called the 'lexical-semantic' route, which consists of the written word triggering directly the meaning and images associated with that word, without its being decoded into its sound chunks.

Most of us use both types of route when we read, but there are some people who use only one. This may be because a part of the brain responsible for the other route is damaged, or it may be because they never learned one of the ways of reading. The Portuguese women who hadn't learned to read never had a chance of learning the phonological route, so tended to rely on the lexical-semantic route. This is why they could not easily repeat words that had no meaning – their brains hadn't learned the code that Sam was struggling to master. They could, however, easily repeat words that they knew, because these words burrowed straight into the meaning stores of the brain, without having to be first decoded by their sounds.

Sam's brain was being physically moulded by his father's coaching, I argued. But can we be sure that teaching physically sculpts the brain in this way? Thanks to these twelve doughty Portuguese women, we can now be sure. They were flown from their mountain village to Stockholm in Sweden, where their brains were studied as they wrestled with the task of repeating spoken words.

If our brains really are physically sculpted by learning to read, then they should work differently when doing mental tasks that we think have been built up by learning to read. One such task is 'phonological decoding', namely repeating unfamiliar words that you hear spoken to you. It *shouldn't* show up differences on familiar words, because mostly we can read them without bothering to break up words into their sounds.

So, while lying in a PET scanner that measures brain activity, the twelve women repeated word after word, some of them real and familiar to them, some of them unreal and made up. The six illiterate women were just as good as their literate companions at repeating the familiar words, but they weren't much good at repeating the unfamiliar words: while the women who could read were able accurately to repeat 84 per cent, those who had never been to school managed to repeat only 33 per cent of them.

While they were repeating the real words, the brains of both groups of women showed much the same pattern of activity. When they listened to and repeated the nonsense words, though, the six illiterate women's brains behaved in a quite different way. Compared to the literate women, they failed to show activity in several regions of the brain, particularly in the left hemisphere. Instead, their brains showed activation in the right frontal part of the brain.

Here we have concrete proof that what we learn as children physically sculpts our brains and makes them work in quite different ways. This result is all the more striking because the literate women whose brains were so different had only four years of education. You can imagine what the differences might be after fifteen or twenty years of learning.

It is unlikely that it is just learning to read that changes the brain. Education trains many more skills than this – skills of thinking, remembering, planning, problem-solving and many others. All this nurtures the trembling web, building the brain and the intelligence and abilities it controls.

Pruning the shrubs of our children's brains

Next time you get a chance, watch a child like Sam learning to read, trying to do arithmetic, or struggling to master any of the thousands of complex mental tasks which children must learn in order to forge a decent life in this demanding world. Inside Sam's skull, there is a brain more densely connected and using up more energy than his father's. Each neurone in Sam's brain has up to 50 per cent more connections with other brain cells than those in his father's brain have. So next time you wonder about the bright-eyed energy of children, just visualize the power stations in their heads, throbbing at 50 per cent higher energy than those of the exhausted adults around them. Little wonder the sudden collapse into dreamless sleep after a day's play. Not until the twenties does brain activity reach adult levels and the brain become fully 'wired up'.

We know this in part from PET studies of brain activity in people of different ages. PET brain scanners detect how much electrochemical firing is going on among the synapses in the brain. Even when children are not taxing their brains with new learning, their brains are more active than those of adults. This is because of the greater number of synapses between the neurones in children's brains.

Take a seven-year-old, for instance. At this age, the brain is almost identical in size and weight to an adult's. Yet in the frontal lobes there are 40 per cent more synapses per brain cell. But just as a rose bush has to be pruned in order to grow well formed and healthy, so in the child's brain the synapses are gradually trimmed back until they reach stable adult levels. This happens at different times in different parts of the brain, but the peak of connectivity typically happens between the ages of four and seven.

What causes this pruning back of connections? Remember Sam's knitted brow? Do you recall his father's careful coaching, helping him master these strange links between completely unconnected features in eye and ear? One of the main things which determines which synapses stay and which go is learning. Those synapses which don't become connected to other neurones, through learning and experience, simply wither away in the great competitive free-for-all which is brain activity.

As the study of the Portuguese women showed, the fingerprints of adult sculptors on children's brains can be detected decades later when these children are themselves grown up. In another PET-scanning study, this time with literate English speakers, part of the brain was found – called the 'left ventral occipital cortex' – which became active only when adults saw English words, or pronounceable made-up words like 'glomp'. This part of the brain did not respond to strings of letters or shapes that looked like letters.

This 'reading area' of the brain is quite reliably found in many different adults, and you might be tempted to assume that nature had – through genes – programmed it to carry out this mental activity. Of course this is quite impossible, because we have been reading for only a few thousand years, while our genetic make-up was established by natural selection long before the strange cultural activity of reading began.

In other words, the part of the brain needed for reading has been programmed – sculpted by experience and learning. As we PET-scan Sam's brain thirty years from now, we will see the fingerprints of his efforts and his father's coaching, as they huddled together under the bed light so long ago.

The recent rise in genetic explanations of behaviour has made us forget quite how important learning and experience are in moulding the connections in that trembling, responsive brain web. For this web is so enormous and complex that our genes are simply not extensive enough to specify and control all the possible trillions of sets of connections that can occur.

It is a bit like Marxist versus free-market economics. Centralized planning of complex economies is simply not feasible, if you want to see a reasonably efficient supply of goods and services. The system is too complicated and too unpredictable for a central-planning office to be able to command all that goes on. Well, the brain is much more complex than any economy, and so this fact applies even more to the genes that control the human brain.

Like liberal free-market economists who want to see free enterprise tempered by some state regulation, our genes set limits on what our brains can and cannot do, while leaving the trillions of connections in the trembling web to fend for themselves in the carnival of life's experience. In some cases genes take over essential services – eating, sleeping, breathing, reproduction – leaving little room for the mind to mess about and risk killing itself off. This is just like governments, who regard certain bodies – the police and armed forces, for instance – as core services to be dictated by the central state.

So, rather than try to specify all our behaviours, our genes have bequeathed our brains with a sensitivity to the fingerprints of experience. In other words, it is the gift of natural selection, and the secret of our enormous success as a species, that we can programme and reprogramme the very apparatus that controls our behaviour. Given this awesome responsibility, how should we nurture our children's brains?

What's best for children's brains?

By the age of three, the average child of a professional family in the United States will have heard approximately 30 million words addressed to him or her. This contrasts with approximately 20 million words heard by children of working-class families, and 10 million by children whose families are on welfare. This is one reason why children of professional families have much bigger vocabularies than working-class children, who in turn know many more words than children whose parents are on welfare.

So, as we speak to our sons and daughters, nephews and nieces, or friends' children, we leave our fingerprints on their brains, nurturing great daisychains of synapses. Of course, if we strengthen some synapses, we simultaneously weaken others. Thus we play a small part in the great pruning of synapses which takes place throughout childhood and adolescence.

This then raises a tricky question: does it matter what form of care we give our babies and children? Yes, it does. It seems that young children in some nurseries tend to have a very different experience from children who are looked after by childminders, relatives or the parents themselves.

In a study carried out in London in the 1980s, three-year-old children in four different types of childcare were assessed. These were private day-care nurseries, childminders, care by relatives and parental care. The researchers studied moment by moment the nature of the interactions between the adults and children, as well as among the children themselves. Every 10 seconds, observers would record what each child was doing at that moment, and whether and how any adults were responding to the child. There were dramatic differences between the four types of care. The parents of children looked after at home talked more than three times as often to a particular child as did the staff in the nurseries. Childminders spoke to each child 50 per cent more often than nursery staff did. Parents, relatives – and to a certain extent child-minders – were significantly more responsive to the children's speech and facial expressions than were nursery staff. Nursery staff also showed affection to the children only half as often as did childminders.

But do these differences in exposure to language have anything but transient effects on the children? Yes, they do. The language develop-ment of eighteen-month-old children in the four types of day-care was studied. Even by this age there were differences in the vocabularies of the children. Of the children looked after by a parent, 41 per cent had a vocabulary of more than sixty words, compared with 23 per cent of children in the nurseries and 22 per cent of those with childminders.

The use of two-word combinations is a very important stage in the development of language. Phrases such as 'John hungry', 'go shop' etc., are the beginnings of grammar. Approximately 40 per cent of children looked after by parents, relatives and childminders used at least one such two-word combination during the observation, in contrast to 26 per cent of children in the nursery group.

In other words, just as you would expect from the 'fingerprints' view of language development, the brain's store of words is built up by learn-ing and experience. But hold on: perhaps the nursery children came from lower social-class backgrounds?

In fact, quite the reverse was true. The average income of the parents of the nursery children was the highest of all four groups, and only 6 per cent of the nursery group had two parents of low occupa-tional status, in comparison to 51 per cent of the home-based group and 67 per cent of the relative group. What's more, 78 per cent of the nurs-ery-group mothers had higher-education qualifications, in comparison to only 20 per cent of the relative group and 35 per cent of the home group.

In other words, these effects of day-care *reversed* the effects of social class on language development. It's hard to avoid the conclusion, therefore, that the low vocabularies of children from families on welfare mentioned earlier are caused by the lack of verbal fingerprints and not by some innate genetic process.

The good news is you can leave fingerprints on children's brains throughout childhood and beyond, and it is very likely that the nursery children would catch up later in childhood, once their brains began to get normal levels of language stimulation. Also, the private nurseries of 1980s London have probably improved. The point is, of course, that whether you are eight or eighty, your brain craves the caresses of stimulation and learning.

As you will remember from Chapter 7, however, education builds up a robust brain which protects you from the ravages of ageing later in life. The earlier this education starts, and the better it is, the more strongly connected will be millions of brain cells; and these connections are made through Hebbian learning, when cells that fire together, wire together.

When Sam finally realized that the 'c', 'a', and 't' marks on the paper corresponded to the 'cat' sound and meaning in his memory, then a long string of synapses also 'clicked' into place: suddenly brain cells at the back of his head in the left side of his occipital cortex became significantly more strongly connected with distant brain cells in his temporal lobe, on the left half of his brain, in the area approximately above his ear.

So Sam's father sculpted his son's brain by patient coaching and encouraging feedback. Because, of course, what is important in helping a brain grow is not the crude quantity of stimulation: you can speak at a child all you like, or you can talk around the child to other adults, and he or she will probably not benefit from this untargeted language stimulation.

What *is* important, on the other hand, is how much adults *tailor* what they say to what the child says and does. This makes perfect sense in terms of our knowledge about what makes the trembling web grow. If a child who is learning to speak points at a passing dog and says 'Woof', then the responsive adult will say something like 'That's right, Sophie, it's a dog! Clever girl!' The unresponsive adult, on the other hand, will either ignore the child or respond with some quite irrelevant comment such as 'Come on, hurry up, we don't want to be late for Granny.' When the responsive adult meshes with the child's valiant attempts at applying words to the world, the fragile synaptic web between object seen (hairy living thing with four legs) and verbal label recalled (woof) is strengthened. When the adult does not reinforce this tentative link with confirmation and praise, then the child is left uncertain as to whether 'woof' is the right label for the slavering beast towering over her at the moment. And so the synapses between two parts of the brain may not link up so strongly, if at all.

Tuning in to a child's brain

It has been estimated that mothers give well-tailored feedback about language to their infants approximately 2000 times in a twenty-four-hour period – that is, roughly twice per minute. Over several years of childhood, this corresponds to millions of carefully crafted coaching trials that mould the brain's connections and help develop language.

In fact, this learning begins in the womb: a new-born baby prefers its mother's voice to other voices as soon as it is born. This is because the baby has been hearing its mother's voice for several months before birth. New-born babies also prefer music that they have heard in the womb. So even before birth, learning begins and the brain's wiring is fostered by experience. Of course, mothers cannot tailor their speech to what the baby is doing the way they can once the child is born and such targeted feedback is much more potent in helping the brain's connections to develop.

Some parents don't provide this feedback because they never experienced such attention themselves when they were children. Others may be too busy, worried or depressed about making ends meet, or concerned about a troubled relationship. Many different factors can make it difficult for parents to respond to their children and provide these millions of instances of brain-shaping coaching.

Does it, in the end, matter how parents respond to their children? Do the children not learn anyway, with brains genetically programmed to develop language? Well, yes, language will develop in most children with normal brains, unless they are subjected to the most terrible deprivation. But *how well* language will develop, and hence how well more general mental abilities will develop, *does* seem to depend on how parents – and particularly mothers – conduct the millions of brain-shaping coaching sessions involved in rearing a child.

Evidence for this comes from a study of a group of children aged five, who were followed up from birth. Researchers who had watched the mothers interact with their children noticed that some mothers were much less 'sensitive' to what their children were saying and doing when they responded to them. This was true even when their children were babies. For instance, a baby might be lying on its back kicking its legs. A sensitive mother who was tuned in to what her baby was doing would say something like, 'You're trying to kick your legs there!' A mother who was not as sensitive, on the other hand, might say something quite irrelevant like, 'You're a beautiful boy.' Warm and pleasant though this last comment may have been, it didn't at all help the infant make sense of the world. To the baby, the sensations in his legs and the urges to move them are all a rather mixed-up and fuzzy blur. The sensitive mother helps direct the infant's attention – maybe even just by looking at them as she speaks – to the parts of the body which are the source of the mysterious but exciting sensations he's having. In so during, she is helping synapses form in the brain, helping knit a strong and well-connected web of neural connections. What's more, she is helping him to link a word to these strange, moving objects that produce such funny feelings. By eighteen months of age, the researchers already found differences in mental development between infants whose mothers communicated well and sensitively with them and those with mothers who did not.

One consequence of not having their trembling brain webs well nurtured by sensitive coaching over millions of mother–child interactions was that these children's brains did not develop so well, and so they were mentally less able at school at the age of five. Of course, such disadvantage at the beginning of education tends to lead to further disadvantage, as these children will not learn so well. The likelihood is that many of them will fall increasingly behind at school – and hence in life.

Can these harmful effects be reversed? No one really knows yet whether they can be completely undone. There may be a 'critical period' for the best development of early mental abilities in infants. However, we do know for sure that children can bounce back from the most dreadful early deprivation – far worse than the well-meaning if insensitive brain-coaching of mothers – so it seems very likely that children's brains will respond to the right kind of stimulation and coaching, even though they have not had it earlier in life. We can see it in this particular group of five-year-olds: the amount of stimulation they were getting at home at five years of age affected their cognitive abilities and, for boys, the quality of their schooling also shaped their cognitive abilities.

We do need a note of caution here, though. Genetic factors may make some babies and children more easy or attractive to interact with, and the same genetic factors may also favour their mental development. If this were the case, then the apparent relationship between mother's sensitivity on one hand and children's mental development on the other would be a spurious one.

The only real way to check this out is to show that mental abilities can improve if children are adopted into a different family, or if some other changes are made. Later we will see how this indeed can happen, along with evidence that the right kind of education can improve mental abilities. That will take us on to the hoary old problem of intelligence and whether it is a product of nature or nurture. But first let's look at other reasons why certain children may miss out on some of the millions of brain-sculpting interactions which grow the brain.

Are you receiving me?

Sometimes there are practical reasons why the children of the most tuned-in of parents may miss out on a few hundred thousand brain-shaping interactions. Having a twin sister or brother can be one such reason. Parents are not super-human, and having two infants of exactly the same age places limits on how much individual attention can be given to each. It is not surprising, then, to find that twins have slightly delayed language compared to non-twins, though there is no evidence of any lasting effects later in childhood or in life.

It has to be said, however, that only children have higher academic achievement than children who have brothers and sisters, and the oldest child of a family also tends to have a higher achievement than his or her younger siblings. Whether this is because only children and first-borns experience more brain-sculpting interactions with their parents, or whether it is because of more complicated social and emotional reasons, is not clear. It may well be a combination of both. But sometimes other things happen to a child that can dilute the effects of attention from the most diligent and sensitive parents.

If a child cannot hear properly, then the brain will obviously fail to pick up all the subtle changes in sound waves that make up speech. And if experience does make the brain grow, then children who are born deaf should show differences in their brains because they have been cut off from sound and because they have learned language using a different sense modality – vision.

This is exactly what has been discovered. In people who were born deaf, the part of the brain that normally specializes in decoding speech sounds – the auditory cortex of the temporal lobe – was found to be doing a different job. This brain area was now tuned to detect visual stimuli on the periphery of vision.

Why should this happen? Children in the United States who are born deaf learn a sign language called 'American Sign Language', or ASL. When using ASL, you learn to focus your eyes on the eyes and face of the person with whom you are communicating. This means that you must rely on your peripheral vision to detect what signs the other person is making with his or her hands.

To be sure that these brain changes were caused by the brain sculpture of learning ASL, the researchers also studied people who could hear normally, but who had been born to deaf parents. As children, these people also had to learn language through ASL. If experience really does change the brain, then they should also show the types of brain organization that the deaf people showed. This is exactly what was found: normally hearing people born of deaf parents showed very similar results to the people who were born deaf.

We saw earlier in this chapter how in the first few years of life children have many more connections between brain cells than they do as adults. Growing up involves culling some of these connections, which happens in part through learning and experience. Some of the connections that exist in early years but disappear later are located between the visual and hearing parts of the brain.

If experience and learning strengthens these synapses, however, then they will survive the pruning of the ruthless competition for survival between the over-abundant connections. Learning ASL involves just such a process, rescuing these visual–hearing synapses, and so these children's brains are shaped differently from the brains of hearing children by what they learn, as surely as if it were surgery.

There is a less dramatic reason why children may not get the same quality of input to their brains during the millions of synapse-building interactions with parents and teachers. Some severe ear infections, if they happen repeatedly, can result in a condition known as 'glue ear', or 'otitis media', which can cause temporary problems in hearing. Unfortunately, this problem is most likely to occur at precisely the time when children's brains are being shaped by the spoken language they hear and the feedback it brings them.

In the pre-school years, when this problem is most common, children are building up their knowledge of grammar and syntax. Syntax means the relationships between words in phrases and sentences, and it is in these relationships that all but the most simple of ideas are conveyed. What's more, these connections between words depend heavily on brief, easily missed words like 'on', 'of', 'in', 'with' . . .

Syntax also depends on very slight changes to the ends of words, which are nevertheless critically important in understanding the sense of a sentence. 'Walk' may not be easily distinguishable from 'walked' or 'walks' to a child whose hearing is blurred by glue ear. In fact, truly deaf children have very great difficulty in learning syntax because they are not exposed to the subtleties of grammar contained in these tiny changes at the ends of words. Though our brains seem genetically programmed to develop language, how well we develop it – and in particular how well we develop syntax – depends a lot on the brain-sculpting experience of childhood.

To understand spoken language, you must also be able to hold words in mind for a few seconds so that you can decode what they mean. This is the type of memory needed to look up a new telephone number in the directory and hold it in your mind for the few seconds it takes to dial it. This type of memory seems particularly important for children learning to read. Think of Sam at the beginning of this chapter. He had to store up the sounds 'kuh', 'ah' and 'tuh' in this immediate memory store long enough for him to work out their combination into the word 'cat'. It won't be long before Sam will have to master much longer words, such as 'hospital' or 'terminator'. Learning to read these words will place even bigger demands on this immediate-memory storage system.

If the raw material in the form of speech sounds which comes into this store is degraded because of hearing loss, then it is possible that the child's use of this important memory store will not develop properly. For instance, because things tend to be a bit blurred, the child may not develop the habit of breaking up words into their constituent chunks – phonemes – perhaps because many of them do not sound particularly different from each other to the child. In other words, exactly the same problems that the illiterate Portuguese women experienced may emerge.

Researchers have studied the abilities of children suffering otitis media to break up words into phonemes and hold them in memory. Compared to five-year-olds who had not suffered otitis media, these children performed slightly less well at these tests. It seems, however, that otitis media may have its strongest effects on brain development in children who are already vulnerable, for instance because of being premature. Their brains may have fewer resources to compensate for the lack of stimulation caused by the loss of hearing.

They were also a little behind on vocabulary and reasoning tests, as you would expect if their brains had been deprived through hearing loss of some of the subtleties of spoken language. It may be, however, that these children were initially sent to hearing clinics because their language was not apparently developing properly. If that is the case, then again the difference between the otitis media group and others may have been due to some other reasons – family, genetic or educational – quite unrelated to the hearing loss.

As with the maternal-sensitivity evidence which we considered earlier, one critical test of the link between hearing loss and language development is to see whether correction of the hearing loss results in a marked improvement in language. So far this has not happened, so for the time being the question remains unresolved.

There are many other ways in which the brain can be starved of the stimulation it needs, and one of these is the nature of the social conditions in which the brain develops. Let's take a look at this now.

A great hunger in the brain

The synapses in Sam's brain needed his father's patient coaching in order to form and strengthen as he was learning to read. All the nets of connections in children's brains need such a constant, careful husbandry of stimulation from parents, schools, books, computers and – in some countries with decent children's programmes at least – television.

Poor schooling lowers intelligence and handicaps children intellectually for life. In schools that give inadequate education, children may learn so little that they steadily fall behind in academic performance and on tests, when compared to all other children of the same age in their country. In other words, their intelligence is steadily eroded because the synapses in their brain are inadequately tuned and shaped by the planned and structured experience that good teachers provide.

This is precisely what happened in some rural school systems in the southern states of America during the 1970s. Education was so poor in some of these systems that intelligence was more badly eroded the longer children stayed in the system. As a result, the IQs of the older children in a family who had been in the school system longer were routinely lower than those of their younger brothers and sisters whose brains had not yet suffered the great synaptic hunger which comes from poor education.

In the 1950s, before desegregation in the southern states of America, poor education of this type was the rule rather than the exception. In one study, black children who had moved from the south to Philadelphia had their IQ scores raised more than half a point for every year they spent in this better school system.

Some prominent academics believe that intelligence is very largely genetically determined. Such a view simply does not fit with this evidence that IQ rises and falls depending upon the type of stimulation to which children's brains are exposed. But the interactions between genes and environment are so complex that this evidence is not quite conclusive in showing that environment has a major effect on intelligence.

A critical test of the importance of experience and environment would be this. You would have to take babies from poor – low socio-economic status (SES) – families and have them adopted into high SES families. Then you would have to take babies born of high SES families and adopt them into low SES families. In fact, just this study has been done in France, giving the critical piece of evidence to show that intelligence is shaped by environment.

People who argue that genes are the main determinant of intelligence think that poverty and socio-economic status are to a very large extent determined by genetically inherited intelligence. Their prediction for the French adoption study would therefore be that biology should win out in the competition with environment. They would predict that the intelligence of babies born with the 'good' genes of the high SES parents would be relatively unaffected by the more impoverished environment provided by the low SES parents adopting them. Similarly, those babies with the 'less intelligent' genes would not, in their view, benefit particularly from the greater opportunities, stimulation and learning offered in the high SES families.

The French researchers studied two groups of children at around the age of fourteen who fell precisely into these two critical categories – namely, poor natural parents and well-off adoptive parents versus well-off natural parents and poor adoptive parents. In support of the geneticists' view of things, children of well-off natural parents had a higher IQ at the age of fourteen than those of low SES natural parents.

However, in support of the brain-sculpture environmentalist view, an equally large difference appeared between children reared in well-off versus poor adoptive families – a very significant 12 IQ points. In other words, environment had as big an effect on intelligence as did inherited biology. This is exactly what you would predict if the trembling web is as yielding to the sculpture of experience as I have been arguing.

Of course, SES is a very crude indicator of how stimulating a home is. Some very poor families provide very stimulating environments for children and pay close attention to providing brain-shaping stimulation for them. Conversely, some wealthy households can be neglectful of the synaptic hunger in their children's brains.

In this light, the French adoption results are very impressive. They would probably have been even more impressive had the researchers been able to study the actual interactions and stimulation in these homes. When researchers *have* measured the quality of stimulation at home, they have often been able to detect even greater influences of environment on intelligence than are possible when measuring only SES.

However, this is not to deny a genetic component to intelligence: indeed, scientists in London have recently identified a gene which is linked to intelligence, called IGF2R, located on the long arm of chromosome 6. In fact, it would be inconceivable that genetic factors did not influence mental functioning; but it is equally inconceivable that environment does not shape mental functioning.

The problem with measuring how much genes affect a particular behaviour is that you can only measure that effect in a particular environment. Suppose, for instance, that several thousand children were all given absolutely no stimulation in their infancy and childhood. In such a situation, genes would probably have a huge effect in determining the differences in the way that the children's mental abilities developed.

Then take the converse: imagine a situation where these thousands of children were all given the best stimulation that parents, schools and technology could give them. In such a situation, the measured effects of genes on intelligence would be much less and the quality of the environment would have a much bigger effect in determining who was more intelligent than whom.

So, with complex human behaviour it is never possible to say with any certainty exactly how much of that behaviour is genetically caused. Any number you care to come up with will be the hostage of the particular environment within which these genetic effects are measured. This includes the IGF2R gene for intelligence. Whether this accounts for 10 per cent or 90 per cent of the spread in intelligence between different people can never be established as a universal constant, because the number depends on the environment in which it is measured.

In this book about brain sculpture, therefore, we need not look over our shoulders all the time, fearing that our attempts to sculpt the brain are about to hit the genetic buffers. These genetic buffers are to all intents and purposes extremely elastic, and not until many other studies are done can we know exactly what the limit of their elasticity is.

It is the human brain's huge potential for sculpture by experience and training that should concern us, and there is no immediate genetic veto on continually raising our sights about what brain sculpture is capable of. Governments, societies, schools and parents can do much to change the brains of children.

Only when we have perfected and exhausted the resources of environmental stimulation will we be in danger of collision with the genetic buffers. Nowhere on this earth has this so far happened, and so we should be very optimistic about the possibilities for engineering the performance of our own brains. But to explore these possibilities we need to know exactly what it is about the environment that affects intelligence and other human capacities. That is the next question.

Releasing the brain's potential

Children deprived of some or many of the millions of brain-shaping learning experiences that families and schools bring them consequently have poor mental functions. Poverty is one major reason why children may be deprived of these experiences: poverty corrodes mental abilities. Of course, other factors linked to poverty, like poor diet, low expectations and many others can reduce brain function.

We know, however, that the type of sensitive interaction that Sam had with his father in the scene described at the beginning of this chapter is critically important in nurturing and strengthening brain connections. If this is so, then we should be able to improve intelligence by providing this kind of stimulation to poor children whose homes and communities have not been able to give it.

In the United States, the 1960s saw a great initiative to remedy these types of problems among hundreds of thousands of young children living in poverty. The project, 'Head Start', consisted of a whole range of programmes throughout the country, some intensive and lasting years, others much briefer and taking weeks or months.

This great effort was pronounced a failure by many people, but in fact the best programmes within project Head Start produced some remarkable improvements. Some of its positive effects lasted for years after the end of the project, with gains of 10 IQ points not being unusual.

Think for a moment, however, about the 10 million words per year spoken to the average middle-class baby for the first three years of life. Contrast this with the 3 million or so words spoken to the average child from the family on welfare. Multiply this number of brain-changing interactions by the number of years of childhood, and you are faced with a staggering shortfall in stimulation to the brain. Even the most comprehensive educational and stimulation programme provided by institutions will have great difficulty in substituting for more than a relatively small proportion of this experience. In spite of such enormous inertia, however, many studies show that remedial programmes *can* substitute for at least some of this shortfall in brain stimulation.

But what about the child who is not in poverty? Can above-average mental ability be increased still further with the right kind of stimulation? Let's turn to this question now.

A recipe for genius?

'Geniuses are born, not made.' Nonsense. At most they are born *and* they are made – but the scientific evidence suggests in fact that geniuses may be more made than born. Take Mozart, for instance, whose father had him touring to Paris and London when he was just six years old, displaying his musical genius to the adulation of sell-out audiences. Mozart's father was coaching his precocious son in music almost before he could speak. Bobby Fischer, one of the world's greatest chess players and an international grand master at the age of fifteen, was coached from the age of seven on a weekly schedule by the president of the Brooklyn chess club. Judit Polgar, who also achieved this status at the same age, was tutored by her father from the age of four, did not attend regular school and was allowed to spend all her time with her parents, who were both teachers.

Two scientists have surveyed all the world research on high achievement and have come up with one, startling conclusion: the major secret of international success and achievement is practice! Not only did they find that the published research pointed to this conclusion, but they also discovered it to be the case after studying élite violinists and pianists at the internationally esteemed Music Academy of West Berlin.

They compared the best of these students with a group of their high-achieving but less excellent peers. These were further compared with international professional violinists on the one hand, and on the other a group of more mainstream players who were likely to become music teachers rather than professional musicians. What distinguished the students at the music academy and the professional violinists from the music teachers? The answer was the total amount of practice they did. The music-academy students practised for almost three times longer than did the students destined to be music teachers.

They also calculated the total amount of practice done before the age of eighteen. This turned out to be the same for the international professional musicians and the top students at the music academy. The second group at the music academy had accumulated fewer hours of practice by the age of eighteen than their élite classmates, but had practised more than the 'music teachers'.

The researchers concluded that it takes a minimum of ten years of regular practice to achieve the highest level of expertise – not just in music, but in most areas of human endeavour, ranging from chess to science, writing to art. Their laborious research led them to 'reject any important role for innate ability in expert performance'. 'Talent' for them cannot explain expertise and eminence; rather it is the minimum ten years of effortful, deliberate practice which produces the highest levels of human achievement.

Now this is not to say that all children are born equal. Of course genes play their part in many abilities, including intelligence. But intelligence, as measured by IQ tests, is only good at predicting people's performance early on in learning new skills. After this preliminary phase of learning, how well you perform increasingly depends on how much you practise.

If you look at the world's most eminent people over the last few centuries, you will find that those who reach the pinnacle of achievement in their fields were usually not the highest performers in academic and intellectual tasks at school. Albert Einstein was one such notable example, as was Sir Winston Churchill. Though high intelligence was needed for their achievements, it was not the highest levels of intelligence that produced genius, in general. Persistence, motivation and effort in a particular field seem to be better harbingers of genius once a given level of intelligence is in place.

It may well be, however, that some of these very characteristics – motivation, capacity for hard work and the ability to sustain attention for long periods of deliberate practice – may themselves be innate, though it seems highly unlikely that environment does not have a very big effect on these factors also. There is no doubt that some children's brains simply develop differently from others, leading to problems with particular types of mental ability, ranging from concentration to memory

Though there are some limits imposed by the brain on how well a skill can be learned, the fact is that almost every human skill – including those measured by IQ tests – can be improved by training and practice. Take memory for numbers, for instance, a task that is included in some of the most widely used IQ tests. The scientists studying expertise showed that students could be trained to improve substantially their ability to remember strings of numbers – in one case by 1000 per cent. Quite amazing memory feats can be achieved by the average person if he or she is taught to use a small number of memory strategies. Mental calculation – another common constituent of intelligence tests – can also be trained to spectacular levels of achievement.

But are these effects not just confined to a rather strange minority of nerdy genius types, obsessed by their musical instruments, chess pieces or tennis rackets? Surely for the majority of people, these questions of training and practice become much less important? Not so. According to research on teaching methods, individual tutoring produces hugely better academic performance than does general teaching by standard classroom methods.

In fact, the *average* individually tutored student performs better than 98 per cent of students who are given standard teaching – and this has little to do with prior ability. In the tutored group, what determined success was practice and training, with the pre-existing academic abilities playing a relatively small part. Only when training was rather poor – as is the case in most standard classroom teaching – did prior abilities play a part in predicting who achieved well and who achieved badly.

It is difficult to underestimate the importance of this fact. Take any school subject – algebra, geography, English, for instance. Put 100 children into the standard classroom and measure their achievement after a course of normal classroom teaching. Now take another 100 children of the same average range of abilities and intelligence and give them individual tutoring in the subject. No matter what their abilities at the beginning of the course, the *average* individually tutored pupil will be better than ninety-eight of the children in the standard classroom group.

What then is the importance of pre-existing abilities in this kind of tuition? Trivial, according to the researchers. This isn't terribly good news for parents who think they can sit back and let their children's genes lift them to high achievement! While good genes help, the type of training and teaching a child gets has a huge impact on the development of mental abilities. So what is one is supposed to do to unlock this potential?

The keys to unlocking brain potential

Does this mean that all children should receive one-to-one tutoring? No, it doesn't, because changing the way that classroom group teaching is done can achieve almost as much as individual one-to-one tutoring. To do this, teachers have to give standard tests of the subject they are teaching. They then give feedback to each pupil about what mistakes they are making, and they show the individual and the class how to avoid these errors in future. More tests are given, then more, until as many of the children as possible have mastered the subject.

When ordinary teachers in ordinary classrooms use this feedback method, the *average* pupil in their classes now does better than 84 per cent of pupils in classes whose teachers do not use the method. Many good teachers no doubt use this method already: they are the teachers whose children will learn and achieve the most in school. Teachers who don't 'diagnose' the errors that individual children make in a subject are failing their pupils by starving their brains of the individual feedback that is needed to shape their trembling webs. For it is this reshaping of the neural web that is the basis for learning.

Further modest changes in the way teachers teach can get the average pupil to levels of achievement better than 95 per cent of those in classes using more standard teaching methods. This involves adding one other element to the testing-based feedback method.

One problem with learning a new subject – say probability and statistics – is that you may not have mastered the basics of other subjects that you need to understand the new subject. So, for instance, someone whose arithmetic or algebra was weak would have difficulty with statistics and probability. No matter how excellent the teaching of these new subjects, the pupils would find it hard to learn them because they lacked the basic prerequisites from other, more fundamental subjects.

Teachers can, again using standard tests of these basic subjects, diagnose whether and what these missing prerequisites are in individual children. They can then use remedial teaching to bring the pupils up to scratch on these basics before embarking on the new course. When this is done, followed by the feedback-based teaching of the new subject, then the average pupil does better than 95 per cent of his less fortunate peers in a standard teaching class.

In the interaction between Sam and his father, you can see most of the ingredients for unlocking brain potential and shaping the trembling web. Were Sam's father to devote his life to it – as Mozart's father did, for instance – he would have a reasonable chance of developing, with the help of excellent teachers in the subject, some special skill in Sam to a very high level of expertise. That might be music, mathematics, chess, tennis or any one of a thousand other skills that can be shaped and trained.

Of course there are biological limits to all this. Many children have aptitudes in one area more than another. But it is hard to overestimate the importance of sheer effort and practice – those ten years of intensive training and careful coaching by good teachers – in building expertise of the highest level.

Research shows that the following elements are critically important in fostering that expertise. Take, for example, Sam's knitted brow and intense concentration as he struggled to read each letter of the word 'cat'. Here we have the first condition for expertise: motivation and effort. Sam won't learn very much of anything without these. Encouragement and example are major sources of motivation, as is confidence in oneself and self-esteem. Sam's father's attention and encouragement made up the fuel that kept Sam going through the labour of learning.

A second thing to notice about Sam's training was this. His father first got him to read a simple word that he already knew by sound and which he would understand. In other words, the coaching was tailored precisely to Sam's level of ability and to what he understood already. This is the second ingredient for learning: paying close attention to the child's existing knowledge and abilities and tailoring the coaching to these.

Anyone who has had a bad, insensitive sports coach – say a ski instructor – will know how critically important it is that the teacher has a good grasp of what it is you can and cannot do. If you think back on teachers you have had, you will probably be able to remember one who completely overestimated your level of understanding of the subject. As a result, much of the subsequent teaching would have been wasted. Sometimes this can lead to people believing that they are 'no good' at a subject – say science or mathematics – and that they are incapable of learning it. In most cases, this can be put down to inadequate teaching, perhaps combined with a belief that acts like a self-fulfilling prophecy. It can happen simply because the teacher hasn't troubled to tailor his or her teaching to a person's existing knowledge and understanding of the subject.

Nevertheless, good teachers do manage to work wonders on the brains of large numbers of students and one critical way of doing this is through *feedback* – the third ingredient in the recipe for unlocking brain potential. Think of Sam's father, saying 'Well done, Sam' when his son produces the right sound for the squiggle on the page. And when Sam says 'tac' instead of 'cat', his father gives him immediate feedback about his error.

Knowing whether what you have said or done is correct or not is critically important for learning and a key ingredient for the shaping and strengthening of synapses in the neural web. Some types of class-room education – even with large numbers of pupils – are very good at providing feedback of this type. In certain countries in recent years, however, teaching fashion has dictated that children should not be 'discouraged' by having errors pointed out to them.

One of my friend's little boys, for instance, was able to read before going to school, much at the level that Sam was reading. In school, however, the philosophy was that children should 'explore' books and they were encouraged to guess words by looking at the pictures that surrounded them. As a result, the child completely lost the habit of trying to decode the squiggles on the page and his father could see his eyes darting for the pictures whenever he tried to read a word. His wild guesses were only occasionally corrected, simply because the teacher could not possibly supervise the reading of every child. So not only was the feedback very limited, but the little boy had been taught to use a strategy for reading which inevitably resulted in many more errors than one where he had painstakingly to decode each word letter by letter.

Children can also be taught to think abstractly in a more general way, so that they become better at a whole range of school subjects and not just in the particular subject they are being taught. One study looked at the effects of just one lesson, once a fortnight over a period of two years, begun with several classes of twelve-year-olds in London schools. Though the lessons were within the science curriculum, they were much more about teaching the children how to think than they were about teaching them specific scientific principles. They were, for instance, encouraged to look at a group of objects and figures and say what the dimensions or variables were on which the objects could be classified – size, colour, use, shape, etc. They were also encouraged to think about their own thinking. For instance, rather than just saying to themselves after a difficult problem, 'That was difficult', they were taught to ask themselves questions like 'What was difficult about that problem, and how did I overcome it?' This was all done in the course of carrying out scientific experiments and solving scientific problems.

The effects, however, spread beyond science ability into mathematics and even English examination grades. Two years after the *end* of the special course, the children who had been in these special, once-per-fortnight classes on average outstripped other children by a very significant amount. In the case of science, the effect was one standard deviation: in other words, the average child who attended the science classes outstripped 84 per cent of children who did not when it came to scores on formal examinations four years after the course started. Almost as big effects appeared in mathematics and English.

The last ingredient in the recipe for learning and expertise is plain simple practice. Asian-Americans in the United States have outstripped most other cultural groups in academic achievement and are over-represented in careers such as science and medicine. The evidence is that this achievement occurs in spite of their IQs being equivalent to those of lower-achieving fellow students from other cultural groups.

What causes this difference, it seems, is the amount of effort and labour that they put into their studies.

This is exactly in line with the evidence from the German musicians and other groups – namely that years of regular, hard labour and effort are required to build up expertise and to excel in a skill or subject. Sam will have many millions of trials of reading words throughout his life, and this practice will be essential in training up the brain networks that will allow him to read fluently and effortlessly as an adult.

But what about those people who do not learn to read fluently? Let's briefly consider a problem that has become prominent in many countries in the last few years – dyslexia. Let's see whether brain sculpture has anything to do with this.

The burden of dyslexia

At the age of ten, Simon was a very skilled woodworker. But he certainly hadn't read anything on the subject, because he 'wasn't keen' on reading – not like his brother, who was top of the class in everything. Simon left school without qualifications and now, aged thirty-six, he works as an odd-job man, rueful about the fact that he earns half of his younger sister's salary.

School left Simon with a raw sense of personal inadequacy. His teachers saw him as a 'dunce' and treated him as such; he reacted by kicking against the system and was labelled a troublemaker. His low self-esteem was made lower by the contrast with his older brother, academic star of the school; the resulting tensions irrevocably poisoned their relationship. In fact, Simon and his brother were both very bright, but Simon had an unrecognized problem with reading and spelling. Known as 'developmental dyslexia', Simon's problem sapped his self-esteem, soured his relationships and, ultimately, blighted his whole life.

As many as one in twenty-five of the population – 2 million people in the UK, for instance – may suffer from Simon's problem. This number, however, could be reduced considerably – maybe to as few as one in

100 – if appropriately timed brain-sculpting intervention in the early years of schooling were available.

Children who learn to read like Sam, breaking down words into their phoneme sounds, become better readers than children who don't learn this way. They read more fluently and understand more of what they read. Teaching children to break down words into their sounds, and then giving them practice in 'blending' together the sounds to form parts of words, puts them far ahead in reading ability.

But Simon's reading difficulties may be partly inherited: his father had reading problems, as did his grandfather before him. Genetic research confirms that in some cases dyslexia can be inherited – indeed, some genetic markers have already been identified. There is also evidence that the brains of some dyslexics are different, in that the left and right halves of their brains are more symmetrical than is the case in non-dyslexics.

As with intelligence, however, quite how important this genetic difference is, is totally unclear. It may be, for instance, that where children are given the right kind and amount of stimulation by parents, and proper reading training by teachers, then the genetic effects on how well they learn to read could be very small indeed. The genetic effects may only begin to be major players in explaining differences in reading ability in a situation of poor stimulation and inadequate teaching.

Such a situation has pertained for many millions of children in the USA and UK for periods during the last two decades. A great number of parents seldom read to their children, tending to leave them to watch videos or TV on their own. When many of these children have gone to school, many teachers have, for obscure reasons, refused to teach them how to break up words into their constituent sounds. Under such circumstances, where the brain is starved of the right stimulation, it may well be that genetic differences between the children begin to have a much greater effect in determining who learns to read well and who does not. This is because a central problem with dyslexia appears to be with the so-called 'phonological' aspects of language – that is, the ability to break down speech into its sound segments. This was one difficulty the illiterate Portuguese women had. Phonological problems cause great trouble with spelling as well as reading. In fact, phonological tests can let you predict which three- and four-year-old pre-readers will have difficulty with reading once they are six and seven.

Among other things, the poor readers are not able to repeat the first couple of lines of several nursery rhymes before they learn to read. Furthermore, the pre-readers are poor at so-called 'phonemic segmentation' – just as the illiterate Portuguese women were. In one test of this ability, for instance, children are asked to tap with a stick for each phoneme in a word that they hear. So, for instance, they hear Sam's word 'cat', and they tap three times for the phonemes /c/, /a/ and /t/. The study found that the ability to do this task in six-year-olds strongly predicted their reading levels a year later. Dyslexics can also have a range of other cognitive difficulties, but the scientific evidence locates the core of the problem firmly in the ability to make sense of language, particularly its sound structure or phonology.

As with almost all mental abilities, how well you can break down words into their sounds probably depends partly on what kind of brain you have inherited and partly on how your brain has or has not been sculpted by experience.

Many people with reading and spelling difficulties simply haven't been taught well enough – by parents as well as by teachers. If parents are more inclined to put on a video than to read to their children, then the thousands of hours of 'phonological awareness' training – containing the millions of brain-shaping interactions – which grow out of daily nursery-rhyme and story reading is lost, and they start school at a disadvantage. Sam is one of the lucky ones.

During the 1970s and 1980s, teacher-training colleges in the UK were strongly influenced by a theory of how children learn to read developed in North America. These educational theorists put forward scientifically unproven theories maintaining that teaching children to read in structured programmes by sound – 'phonically' – was actually *harmful*. Instead, children were supposed to learn reading by guess-work and unstructured experience. This was part of the influence that held back my friend's little boy once he went to school. As a direct consequence of this theory, at least one generation of teachers in the UK received virtually no training in how to teach children to read. Yet it turns out that these *laissez-faire* theories of reading were totally wrong. Research shows quite clearly that the children who learn to read well are the ones who have been taught the alphabet and whose brains have learned to break up words into their different sounds.

Some words in English can't be read by sounding out individual phonemes. The word 'tough', for instance, has to be learned as a single unit and locked straight into the lexical-semantic system of the brain. If you tried to apply a pronunciation rule for 'tough', you would run into problems the moment you tried to teach the child to read 'plough'. So, for irregularly spelled words like this, teaching children to 'look and say' some words directly is necessary. Brains are complicated organs, and you need different types of sculpting methods for different situations, if you are to get the best out of them.

Bright children can often get by reasonably well using the 'look and say' method, but having never been taught to chop up words into their sounds, they are to some extent similar to the illiterate Portuguese women. It may well be that their brains too have developed differently because of this, though there is no direct evidence for this yet.

Putting all your reading eggs in a single basket, however, is a pretty risky strategy. Reading words without being able to sound them out will get you through the first few years of school, but what about later on, when you have to start mastering words like 'hydrochloric acid' or 'differential equation'. As schools start to throw technical terms like that at you, then you will really struggle to be able to read them using the direct, lexical 'look and say' method. No, for words like this you really need to be able to break them up into their sounds. Without this ability, you are like the illiterate Portuguese women who couldn't properly repeat words they didn't know.

In fact, research in England shows exactly this happening among children let down by an education system that rather irresponsibly largely abandoned phonology in teaching reading. Researchers in Oxford pointed to the existence of just such a group of pupils whose academic problems only began to show once they have reached their teens. The scientists hypothesized that these were children who had learned to read by looking and guessing without having the ability to sound out unfamiliar words.

Schooling and education, without doubt, physically change the brains of children. It matters enormously how, and how much, children are taught. Using the best methods, the vast potential of children's brains can be unlocked. Many dyslexic children would not be dyslexic if their trembling webs had been sculpted in the right way by the right kind of teaching. With the proper input, many children with reading problems could overcome their difficulties in the first two or three years of school.

But it isn't just in teaching reading that we sculpt our children's brains more or less skilfully. In everything they do, their brains are being moulded by experience, the trembling webs pruned, some connections saved, others discarded. The ability to pay attention – to concentrate on something – is one thing that we teach our children every moment of every day.

Attention-deficit disorder is a very commonly diagnosed problem in the United States, Australia and The Netherlands, though it is less often identified in Britain. In the US, up to one in twenty children is prescribed the drug methylphenidate – often known as Ritalin – to try to improve their inattentive and disruptive behaviour. Some of these children really do have differences in their brains that make it harder for them to hold their attention to any one thing for more than a few minutes, but many more simply have not had their brains' attention systems coached and trained into working well.

Just as Sam's father was sculpting parts of his son's brain into being able to break up words into their sound parts, so he was also training Sam to use his brain's attention systems to stick to a task, even when the task is difficult and at times boring. In my work with people who have suffered brain damage, I can train them to keep their attention on a task and not let it drift off randomly. This is what parents do with their children all the time, coaxing them to finish the picture they are drawing, talking them through the TV programme to help them keep their attention on the story, etc. Some parents, however, allow their children's attention to be at the mercy of what's going on in the world. Rather than sit with the child and help her build the model toy she has started to construct, the parent lets her drift off when she comes to a difficult part and watch television.

Watching television is a case of your attention being passively massaged by the sounds, stories and colours on the screen. As we saw earlier in the book, attention is one of the keys to brain sculpture. Without attention to what we are doing, our brain will not be sculpted to anything like the degree that it will if we give our full attention to what is happening. This means *actively* attending, rather than passively letting your attention be drawn along by whatever happens in the world or on the television. Parents are the main sculptors of their childrens' brains in this respect, teaching them what to attend to and training their brains to override the tendency always to pay attention to whatever is new and exciting, rather than to the task they started out with.

So, just as with dyslexia, there are many children diagnosed as having attention-deficit disorder who are being given strong drugs to change their brain function to help them pay attention. While some of these children have abnormal brains from birth others could pay attention if their brains had been given the right training and brain sculpture. But just as sculpting the brain requires effort, attention and practice by the child, so it need the same things from busy parents who have their own worries and preoccupations.

So let's hothouse our kids?

Most brains have enormous potential to be tuned and sculpted into performing much better than they currently are. The temptation is to go hell-for-leather into boosting our children's expertise and intelligence so that we can help them get on in the world. It can be done, so why not do it?

Well, you only have to look at young sporting protégés whose expertise is built by hundreds of thousands of hours of practice in special schools from their earliest years. In their teens they become world champions, until they are knocked off their pedestal by an even younger champion. What now? They may be one-dimensional human beings, interested in only one thing, able to do only one thing. Is that what we want for our children?

The same is true for academic achievement. If we really devote thousands of hours of practice to just one part of life, where does that leave other aspects of our personalities and lives? What about fun, what about being freed from the endless treadmill of goals and achievement, just to play? Most importantly, what about learning the most vital and difficult of life's tasks: handling your emotions and relating to other people?

If you look at how well people do in the world outside the rarified atmosphere of world championships and international concert halls, then intelligence is far from a perfect predictor. Yes, you need intelligence to get to the top in most fields, but even more important in many cases is your ability to get on with other people, to read and understand them, and to respond appropriately to them. This ability in turn depends on your ability to understand, express and control your emotions.

Emotional intelligence may be an even more important goal for our children than intellectual achievement and expertise. Let's turn to that now.

9

Fear and Loathing in the Brain

It had been a lovely holiday. The boot was packed with French wine, pungent cheeses and the detritus of a warm and relaxing two weeks in the Dordogne. Alone in the front car, he tapped his fingers on the wheel in time to the Emmylou Harris tape: Jill and the boys would never have allowed him this luxury if they had all been together in the one car. So here at least was one advantage of the mad Friday-night rush two weeks earlier, when he had abandoned the company car at the ferry terminal and just made it on to the boat before it pulled away for France.

He checked in the mirror. Jill was 100 yards behind and he could just make out Rob's and Peter's heads bobbing up and down in the back seat, at least as much as their safety harnesses would let them. Jill was obsessed with safety, and even though the boys were nine and ten, she still insisted that they wear special seatbelts.

Only 10 miles to go. The summer sun bathed the Cotswolds in a soft English light; coming home was not so bad after all. He rounded a bend, suddenly braking hard as a trailer piled high with newly cut grass loomed into view. He glanced in the mirror but he need not have worried – Jill had slowed for the corner as usual, ever-vigilant for the unexpected danger

167

round every bend. If he had been on his own, he would have been home an hour ago.

The roads were strangely empty. Only a single car edged towards them in the distance on the long, straight stretch before the last hill that separated them from home. Emmylou Harris was singing 'These Sleepless Nights' and he had a sudden image of playing this the night Peter was born. This memory fused with the glow spread across the luminous green fields by the setting sun to produce in him a sense of intense if nostalgic happiness.

The song was coming to an end and the road, as if in sympathy with his quietly joyful mood, was still empty, save for the single red car – he could see that it was an old Vauxhall Cavalier – coming towards him. He found his attention strangely captured by the car. As it approached it seemed to be accumulating a strange significance, like a slow recognition of a long-forgotten face.

The whole expanded world telescoped to this one approaching object. Time seemed to slow as he watched it drift across the central line. The solid hedge loomed to his left, but his eyes were fixed on the dirty red half-ton of metal hurtling towards him on the wrong side of the road. He wrenched the steering wheel to the left and felt his car lurch on to the narrow, sloping bank, simultaneously aware of the red car flashing by his right window.

His car bounced and skidded to a halt. In that second's silence the single bang behind him seemed to last for whole minutes. Panic rose in his chest like something physical and alive. He fumbled for the door-handle, stumbling from the car and staring wildly down the road behind him. The red car was upside down on the road, its wheels still spinning. Just beyond it, Jill's car sat crumpled and smoking, nose down in the ditch.

Tim began to run and shout at the same time, trying to sprint on leaden legs. As he neared the car, he noticed small flames licking out from under the sills. He heard a shout that rose to a scream, but it took ten steps before he realized it was his own voice.

As he reached the car he was met with silence and the smell of petrol. The noiseless flames were hypnotic, and behind them were the ghostly, pleading faces of Jill and the boys. He stood, mesmerized, frozen in a dream. Only when he heard a shrill, keening cry of 'Daddy!' was he released from paralysis, leaping for the back door, pulling at it frantically. It wouldn't give. Through the flames he yanked the front doorhandle. The door flew open. He reached in, bundling a screaming Jill out on to the road, crawled into the back seat, tore at the boys' safety harnesses as their fingers clutched him and their screams mixed with the crackling of the no-longer-silent flames.

At last the buckles gave and he dragged the boys by their collars over the seats and out through the flames on to the tarmac. As they scrambled and rolled away, with a muffled 'whoomph', the car erupted into an inferno.

Emotional scars

Tim, Jill and the boys weren't badly hurt. Physically, that is. After two days they were discharged from hospital. Rob and Peter insisted on sleeping in their parents' bedroom when they went home that night, but after a week that had to stop, because no one slept: at most hours of the night, one of them gave a terrified shout from the middle of disturbed sleep.

It was not long before Tim and Jill were sleeping in separate rooms, and a raw, acidic atmosphere of nerves and emotion ate into the formerly secure family bonds. Worst affected was the relationship between Tim and Jill. To Jill, Tim had become cut off and distant from her and the boys, to the extent that he almost seemed like a stranger. They were all irritable, but Tim's outbursts of temper sawed away at their relationships more surely than anything else.

To Tim, it was as if he had been locked into a bad dream since the accident. He felt cut off from everyone and everything by a dismal screen. He could concentrate on nothing, neither books nor television nor work, and the smallest unexpected noise would startle him, sending his heart racing and a clammy sweat crawling across his skin. It seemed that his memory had abandoned him: at work he forgot clients' names, missed appointments and left important tasks uncompleted.

Life had lost its meaning for Tim, and there seemed to be no future – neither for him nor for his family. Nothing seemed secure or predictable any more. Life had been reduced to a set of bleak intervals between flashbacks by day and nightmares by night.

The flashbacks could be triggered by the smallest reminder of the accident: a red car on the road, the squeal of tyres, a child's cry of 'Daddy' on the street. Sometimes they came out of nowhere, drenching him in sweat, making his heart race to impossible levels and hijacking his brain with cruelly vivid sights, sounds and smells of that August evening.

The nightmares were worse: his children burning, Jill clutching at his sleeve, immovably trapped in a burning car, the feeling of running down a road towards them but unable to move forward as the road turned to a swamp.

But the smells were the worst. He could no longer go into a garage to get petrol, as the smell of it took hold of his brain more surely than any drug could have done. He couldn't drive on country roads any more, and this, together with his tattered concentration, hole-filled memory and strange, avoidant detachment, lost Tim his job, his marriage and his family.

In this chapter, we will tell you how the emotion produced by the accident changed Tim's brain and caused this disastrous cascade of events. For among the different types of experience we can have, all of which change our brains to some extent, emotional events can have the most dramatic effects on the trembling web. But first, a little about the brain and emotion.

Hijacking the brain

You are conscious of only a fraction of what is going on in your brain, and even when you become aware of that fraction, consciousness often stumbles far behind your brain's reactions, like an infant trying to keep up with a pack of ten-year-olds.

Just as well, really, or else we – like the dinosaurs – would have become extinct aeons ago. Just imagine relying on your conscious mind when you find the truck bearing down on you as you are halfway across the road: you would be pulp in milliseconds. In fact – if you are lucky – you will find yourself panting and sweating at the side of the road, having flung yourself out of its path.

Like a Special Forces hardman elbowing aside the dithering civilian policeman, an older, tougher part of the brain takes over in emergencies and rescues you from death. Deep below the cortex, two almond-shaped parts of the brain – the 'amygdala' – detect danger in a split second and take command, forcing you to jump and escape.

The amygdala is part of the brain's emotional system – the limbic system. When you hear, see, feel or smell something, this information passes both to the cortex and to the amygdala. In fact, it gets to the amygdala before it reaches other parts of the brain; and if what you sense has been linked with danger, the amygdala springs into action.

This is because the amygdala functions as a storehouse of emotional memories. However, the amygdala is no Einstein, and it is pretty crude in the way it interprets the information it gets. In fact, the amygdala is a major source of 'gut feeling' – and, as everyone knows, gut feelings are hard to ignore. Lagging behind this direct-line information to the amygdala comes further information from the higher brain centres in the cortex. Though slower, this information will be based on a more cerebral analysis of what has been heard, seen or smelt.

For instance, you open the drawer to find an enormous hairy tarantula. Your amygdala triggers a cry in your throat and coils your muscles ready to jump away, but then your cerebral cortex registers: 'Oh, don't worry, it's a toy spider your son left there to scare you.' Though you are still a bit frazzled, this knowledge calms you down, enabling you to pick up the beast and march purposefully down the stairs to settle an old score.

The crude features of the hairy beast triggered an ancient fear, programmed into your amygdala by evolution, and set off a survival 'fight or flight' reaction of racing pulse, cold sweat and bristling hair at the back of your neck. These reactions were so quickly and automatically triggered that, caught unprepared, there wasn't much you could do about them. This was due to their being triggered by the 'direct line' between your senses and the amygdala. In less than a second, however, your much more clever but less quick-off-the-mark cortex detected the hoax and sent 'don't worry, it's just a toy' reassurances from the higher brain centres down to the amygdala.

Without these hair-trigger reactions to danger, the human race would never have survived and evolved as it has. The great evolutionary biologist Charles Darwin was well aware of these primitive but vital reactions. He once described a visit to the reptile house in London Zoo, where he put his face close up to the glass in front of a puff adder, determined that he would not flinch if it struck at him. When the snake did strike at him behind the glass, however, he leapt backwards, propelled by ancient and automatic brain circuits. No amount of reason and rationality could stop this primitive reaction, which had helped Darwin's genetic predecessors survive in the snake-infested forests hundreds of thousands of years ago.

The amygdala is a major source of these involuntary reactions. It is genetically programmed to respond to certain so-called 'prepared' stimuli, such as snakes, because the genetic ancestors who were less well endowed with these snap reactions tended to die out and hence not pass on the genes underlying the brain circuits responsible for the reactions.

The ancestral fear of snakes still earns its keep in some parts of the world. In rural India, for instance, between 10,000 and 20,000 people per year die from cobra bites alone. But most of you reading this book will live in cities where there are no snakes, and so such reactions make no sense.

Sense, however, has only limited ability to rein in the excesses of the ancient emotional brains which are the cause of so much pain – and such exquisite pleasure – in our lives. If we relied too much on sense, then we would soon be pulp under the wheels of a juggernaut. Our lives, therefore, are a constant dance between these surges of ancient emotion and their impulsive behaviours on the one hand, and the slower cogitations and admonishments of the evolutionarily later developed cerebral cortex on the other.

For the cortex – and in particular the frontal lobes – can exert some control over our emotional reactions. Connecting fibres from the middle surfaces of the frontal lobes down to the amygdala can dampen down its excitability. They can also trigger it into action where the threat is complex and subtle, and detectable only by the clever cortex.

After the Chernobyl nuclear-reactor explosion in 1986, for instance, milk supplies in many parts of Europe were contaminated by radiation. To the parents of small children at that time, a bottle of milk could arouse a sense of dread as surely as any snake. The rather dull-witted amygdala, however, could never have picked up this threat from its direct connections to the sensory parts of the brain. Rather, the cortex computed the invisible threat and nudged its action-man downstairs neighbour into alertness.

That being said, there are many more connections from the amygdala to the cortex than vice versa. So, while the more sophisticated parts of the brain can exert some control over their at times unruly emotional compatriots, the emotional brain has a much greater potential to overrule the higher-brain centres. At the risk of sounding trite, no single fact about the brain is more relevant to explaining war, conflict and environmental recklessness in the human race.

Programming the unconscious mind

It is not just snakes that scare us, though. Things – sounds, sights, tastes, smells – that our brains *link* to fear can become triggers for terror. To Tim, for instance, red cars and country roads were pretty neutral things before the accident. Now they strike fear in his heart more surely than any puff adder.

Fear of a bottle of Chernobyl-contaminated milk is rational. Terror at the sight of a red car on a country road is not. The chances of harming your children by feeding them the milk are significant. The probability of a red car on a country road hitting Tim's family again is infinitesimally small.

But emotions are not necessarily rational. Tim is terrified of red cars and of the smell of petrol because these were linked in time to blind terror at the prospect of his family burning to death before his eyes. This link is seared into his brain like a hot brand on the hide of a bull.

The coarse-grained sensations of red car and petrol fumes picked up by Tim's amygdala are welded to the nerve cells there which trigger terror. Cells that fire together, wire together – Hebbian learning again.

This, however, is an especially brutal kind of Hebbian learning – almost indelible, in fact. Under the coarse logic of evolutionary survival, danger should not have to be constantly relearned. Once bitten, twice shy. Keep away from dogs – and red cars – that is what our amygdalas impel us to do. So the embroidery of emotions in the trembling web is a special kind of sewing – it is stitching with steel thread.

Pavlov's famous dogs would look curiously but neutrally at his ringing bell at first. Then, whenever the bell rang, he would waft meat powder under their noses. Dogs like the smell of meat, and it makes their mouths water. After a while, the ringing bell and the meat powder became linked together in the dog's trembling, hungry web.

This is called conditioning. If someone whistles and then immediately blows a puff of air into your eye, you will blink automatically. Blinking to a puff of air is a natural, genetically programmed defensive response to protect your eye. If this happens a few times, then if the person whistles but doesn't blow in your eye, you will still blink.

Blinking to a whistle is not genetically programmed. You blink to the whistle because your brain has been changed – changed by the linking together in time of whistle and blink. Cells that fire together, wire together. Every day of your life your brain is shaped and sculpted by experience like this. You are blissfully unaware of most of it.

When I was a boy, I always used to have a desperate urge to go to the toilet whenever I started searching for a book to read in the local public library. It didn't seem to matter whether I had gone before leaving home or not. Some psychoanalysts would spin exotic tales to explain this, but reality is more mundane. On a few occasions, I had in fact desperately needed to go to the toilet while searching for a book. Being a rather indecisive lad, however, I had engaged in this perilous hopping dance between the desire for a good read on the one hand and the desperate urge for relief on the other. At the last possible moment I would flee the toilet-less library for home, book in hand.

Such was the conflict-ridden poignancy of just a few such experiences, that the very sounds, smells, sights and sensations of searching for a book in any library would induce, for many years, intestinal anguish. I was, of course, at the time completely unaware of how my brain had forged a link between libraries and the need to go to the toilet. But forged it it had, as surely as Pavlov linked a tinkling bell to the ache of hunger in his underfed Alsatians.

Fortunately for me, in my career as an academic doomed to roam the aisles of libraries, this link in my brain has gradually dissipated. The undoing of such conditioned links is called 'extinction'. Extinction tends to happen when the 'conditioned stimulus' – whistle, bell, library – repeatedly turns up without its biological partner – puff of air, meat powder, full bladder. When cells fire apart, wires depart.

Not completely, though. Traces remain of these links, even after they are apparently wiped out by extinction. You can tell this because it is often easier to re-establish the link a second time than it was the first; and some types of conditioning are near-indelible.

I know this because when I was at Boy Scout camp once, I ate an entire packet of Abbey Crunch biscuits in ten minutes. Even after an hour of projectile vomiting, the mere thought of an Abbey Crunch biscuit could induce retching. Thirty-five years later, I am still unable to contemplate an Abbey Crunch biscuit without a feeling of mild nausea.

Though Abbey Crunch biscuits were not easily available in the forests where our hunter-gatherer ancestors roamed, poisonous plants and berries were. Projectile vomiting was not a good re-commendation for a berry. People whose brains made them feel sick for a long time after eating a berry were less likely to eat it again. Such individuals were more likely to survive long enough to pass on their genes.

So my brain – and yours – has inherited this propensity to develop easily an aversion to something that makes us sick. Because this type of learning is particularly favoured by our genetic make-up, it is much less easy to undo than is, say, the link between the whistle and the puff of air in the eye.

And so it is, unfortunately for Tim, for his fear. The reasons are the same – it makes sense to weld steel threads in the trembling web where danger is concerned. So, while the brain is genetically prepared to fear certain stimuli, such as snakes, it can also learn to be frightened of almost anything, provided that that anything has become linked to extreme anxiety.

For instance, as a clinical psychologist I have seen people who have become phobic – paralysed with fear – at the prospect of encountering birds, moths, caterpillars, dogs, elevators, supermarkets – even vomit – as well as scores of otherwise innocuous things, animals or places. Just as Pavlov's dogs were conditioned to salivate to the bell, so these patients of mine were conditioned to experience anxiety when they met the object of their fear.

Sometimes the fear became conditioned for obvious reasons. One man, for instance, had been locked accidentally and briefly in a cupboard as a young boy. Any small enclosed space, such as a lift, made him very anxious after that, even as an adult.

Sometimes, though, the conditioning happens less directly. One woman I saw was very stressed because her mother was terminally ill. One day she went into her bedroom to find that a blackbird had become trapped there and was flapping panicstricken around the room. She was seized with a terrible anxiety which led to a phobia of birds so severe that eventually she found it difficult to leave the house for months on end.

Now this woman had been a stable person who wasn't prone to anxiety. Her nerves, however, were raw because of the stress of her mother's illness, and so a small extra increase in anxiety – the shock of finding a bird flapping round her bedroom – had a disproportionate effect on her emotional state. The surge of fear was big enough that they became bound together with the immediate apparent cause of the fear – the blindly fluttering bird.

This fear conditioning takes place in the amygdala. Animals with a damaged or disconnected amygdala don't show fear conditioning, but – more persuasively in our search to understand how Tim's life fell apart after the accident – scientists have actually studied such programming of the unconscious mind as it takes place in the human brain.

Volunteers were shown photographs of two angry faces. Whenever one of these faces appeared, a very loud, startling noise blared out from a speaker beside them. This was repeated again and again, until one of the faces was able to trigger an anxious, startled response even without the noise. The same volunteers were then placed in a PET scanner to study what their brains were doing as they looked at the pictures, but the pictures were shown to them so quickly and in such a way that they were not conscious of having seen a face – i.e. they appeared subliminally. In spite of the fact that their conscious minds saw nothing, whenever the face was shown their right amygdala became active. Here was the unconscious mind in action, reacting to something to which the conscious mind was oblivious. The brains of these people had been changed physically, sculpted by the experience of seeing a face and at the same time hearing a frightening noise.

Tim's brain function was almost certainly changed in a similar but much more dramatic way by his terrible experience. When the brains of Vietnam War veterans – suffering, like Tim, from post-traumatic stress disorder – were studied in action, they showed a similar kind of activation. If they were asked to imagine scenes of combat, for instance, the right amygdala became active, just as it did in the conditioning study with the angry faces.

So, throughout our lives, our brains are shaped by experience, with emotional events sculpting the connections in the trembling web in a particularly potent and at times indelible way. Many of the changes in our attitudes and preferences are made without our being aware of what is going on: in fact, such persuasion is usually more effective if people are not aware that they are being persuaded. Advertisers know this well, and use it to mould and sculpt our brains every hour of every day.

They have to do it surreptitiously, however. Why? Because some types of emotional learning happen best if we aren't aware that it is going on. If advertisers are trying to do anything, they are trying to bind our emotions to the products they are selling, so they must try to hide what they're doing to get the best effects.

Ad-people intuitively know quite a lot about how the human brain ticks. You can see the progress in this learning over the last fifty years by flicking through the ads in old magazines.

Advert, 1922. Words: 'Drive our impressive new Sedan, and you will feel important and powerful, attracting the admiration of your companions, particularly those of the opposite sex.' Images: A smug-looking young man in louche suit leaning against gleaming sedan, waiting for forthcoming admiration of members of opposite sex.

Advert, 1992. No words, just images: A black car racing through a field of burning sugar cane. Danger, excitement, exotic location, mystery. Fleeting camera shot of the car-maker's insignia.

The secret is to link emotions to the brand image – subliminally if at all possible. It won't work with everyone, but a successful advertisement will sculpt the brains of enough people to make it worthwhile. People who notice the link between their emotional response and the brand name at the time will be less likely to have the connections sculpted into their brains. People who don't notice the link, on the other hand, are more likely to have it unconsciously embroidered into their trembling webs. Because of this, the brand name will be more likely to trigger the advert's emotions when they come across the product in the future. These emotions are likely to be a more potent prod into buying it than reasoned argument would be.

If you need one final piece of evidence that the unconscious brain can be programmed without any conscious memory, then Dr Edouard Claparede, a French physician, provided it in 1911. One of his patients, a woman, had suffered brain damage which meant that she could not lay down new memories. This problem – the jargon term is 'anterograde amnesia' – meant that she could meet you one minute and then a few moments later greet you as a stranger whom she had never met before.

One day, Claparede introduced himself to her as he had done many times previously. But this time, he rather cruelly hid a pin in the palm of his hand. When she took his hand – in her mind meeting this eminent doctor for the first time – she quickly drew back her hand with a gasp at the painful prick of the pin. The next time the doctor came back, she still had no memory of him, and treated him with her normal politeness. She showed no signs of wariness or anxiety, but when he held out his hand as usual, she wouldn't take it. Nor could she tell him why.

Claparede had sculpted her unconscious mind, linking his hand to a painful, startling event. Though she could not consciously remember this event, the emotional memory centres in the brain – almost certainly involving the amygdala in this case – were sculpted by the experience.

Fear and cruelty

If the amygdala is so important in binding our emotions to the outside world, what happens when this part of the brain is damaged or destroyed? In some cases, the amygdala is removed as part of the treatment of intractable epilepsy. Does this affect the patient's ability to experience emotions such as fear?

Indeed it does. One woman in the UK who had this operation lost her sense of danger. For instance, on one occasion her husband just managed to stop her before she plunged her hand into a pot of boiling water – and, rather than feeling anxious when she realized what she had nearly done, she laughed and shrugged. This woman cannot follow the plot of thrillers where understanding the story means appreciating the fear and danger involved.

Damage to the right amygdala also means that you startle much less readily. You are also less likely to learn to bind fear to some innocuous stimulus. In other words, if Tim had suffered from epilepsy and had had such surgery before his accident, his brain would not have so readily conditioned fear to the smell of petrol or the sight of a red car.

Nor, incidentally, would Tim have been very good at recognizing fear in other people's faces, for this part of the brain seems to be crucial not just for linking fear with events in the world, but for the whole experience of fear and the recognition of it in the faces and voices of other people. This can have effects far beyond the individual.

Every day you read about acts of casual or calculated cruelty inflicted on men, women and children. Almost every country in the world has its infamous killer. What perplexes us as we read about the unspeakable cruelties that these people have committed is that they are not held back by compassion, by fellow-feeling for their victims and the terror they must have seen in their faces before they killed them.

Or did they? It seems that some psychopaths' brains don't respond to signs of distress in other people the way our brains do. When you or I are startled, or see some distressing film or picture, our brains generate a physiological response in the body which includes a slight clamminess on the skin. This moistening of the skin reduces its electrical resistance, and it can be measured – it is called the 'electrodermal response'. When psychopaths are shown distressing pictures, however, they don't show such a skin change, proving that they have not reacted emotionally to the signs of distress in other people in a normal way.

Not that this in any way excuses or explains away cruel behaviour. We usually choose what we do, amygdala or no amygdala. Epileptics who lose this part of the brain don't usually turn into psychopaths. Evil behaviour is too complex and multi-caused to be explained in terms of one little part of the brain. On the other hand, how the amygdala develops or does not develop may play a part in the making of monsters.

Not that the brain develops in a vacuum, of course. It is shaped and sculpted by experience even before it has left the womb. The amygdala can hardly be an exception to this. For instance, children learn to be fearful of things simply because they see their mothers or fathers being frightened of them. Phobias can be contagious, in other words.

Therefore if a child grows up in an environment where the adults around show no anxiety at the prospect of hurting others, then that child's brain won't make some of the connections needed for a social conscience. Children who do see their parents and other adults responding with anxiety to distress in others will develop stronger connections in the trembling web, linking the experience of anxiety to the sight of the suffering of others.

An army, of course, strives to undo some of these connections and hence to change the brains of its young recruits. If it does not do so, it will be a lousy army. All soldiers must be able to kill on command. If they can't do this, they will be useless soldiers (I happen to think that civilized nations need armies, so this is not a moral position – it is simply a statement of fact). Soldiers are therefore trained to try to master the surge of anxiety generated by the amygdala at the prospect of killing someone – and for that matter at the thought of their own death or mutilation. Not that they can do anything more than dampen it down in most cases, but their training does limber up the – albeit rather weak – downward links from cortex to amygdala.

Roughly a quarter to a third of people who encounter a very severe trauma will develop post-traumatic stress disorder the way Tim did. However, differences in the extent to which individuals' brains respond with fear are almost certainly determined by nurture and nature interacting in complicated ways. These factors would then explain why one person suffers psychological breakdown following a traumatic event, while another does not.

Not that any father could have escaped mentally unscathed after what Tim went through; there are, however, lesser incidents which will cause long-lasting traumatic stress in one person, but not in another. It isn't fully understood why one person reacts with prolonged stress while another does not, even though they have been in the same event. A previous history of psychological problems, their relationships before and after the accident, and their attitudes and beliefs about the accident make up just a few of the factors which explain this.

Post-traumatic stress does not boil down simply to conditioning in the amygdala, though this almost certainly plays a part. Things are much more complex, and your response to trauma will depend on many things – for instance your attitude to death and the degree to which you feel that the world has suddenly become unpredictable and uncontrollable.

When hate is burned into the brain

Just as phobias can be contagious, so can hate. The child who sees his father show fear at the sight of a dog may well himself become frightened of dogs. This can happen even though the boy has never been bitten by one, the way his father may have been. Similarly, if his father is prejudiced against some racial, social or religious group, so the boy will have this prejudice embroidered into his trembling web. This can happen without the boy's ever having met a member of the despised group.

Such programming of the brain is all the more indelible because it happens unconsciously, accessing directly the emotional brain and shaping its circuits during the first years of life. For prejudice works like advertising – emotions are more easily linked to objects or people when you are not consciously aware that the connection is being made.

I remember once talking to a colleague – a friend, in fact – with whom I had worked for a couple of years. She was a lovely, bubbly, intelligent woman, university educated, liberal and witty. She came from Northern Ireland, from the Protestant tradition, but was living in the UK, married to an Englishman. A group of us were relaxing over a few drinks one evening at a conference, when she suddenly turned to me, her face completely changed and charged with loathing: 'I *hate* Catholics, you know, Ian. I can't help it – I hate them so much they make me shudder.' And she actually *did* shudder as she said it. Her face was contorted, suddenly ugly with hate and disgust. I was shocked by this transformation as much as I was by the sentiments. All at once I had to reassess a person whom I thought I knew and understood reasonably well. Clearly she was not the decent, tolerant and intelligent person that for the last two years I had assumed her to be.

Now, years later, I realize that I was wrong. She *was* all these things. She was, for instance, as opposed to the racism of pre-Mandela South Africa as anyone. The visceral hate which had erupted from her that evening had been programmed into her brain since infancy. Connections had been made – possibly, among other places in the brain, in the amygdala – which were as near indelible as the most deep-seated phobia.

Just as phobias are sculpted into a part of the brain to which rationality has little meaning, so it was for her hatred of Catholics, learned at the knee of the father she adored. This apparent schism in her personality was not actually a pathological aberration in her brain. It was simply the natural consequence of the way the brain is organized, into the rather coarse-grained, knee-jerk emotional brain on the one hand and the more sophisticated cerebral cortex on the other.

Her brain was no different from mine – I too have my store of involuntary likes and dislikes, embroidered with their steel thread into my emotional brain, and I bring these reactions to bear on certain categories of human beings to whom I have been programmed to react in a certain emotional way. The difference between me and my former friend is the strength of these reactions.

Throughout the world, this type of brain sculpture is at the root of many vicious conflicts, in places as far apart as Ruanda and Bosnia. Of course, some politicians harness these automatic, programmed emotional responses in the brain for their own sinister purposes. In doing so, they deliberately create circumstances which will strengthen the brain circuits underpinning these emotional reactions, by provoking massacres, setting up rivalry and conflict over housing and land, and by promoting stereotypes through the mass media. Thus whole political systems are constructed to shape the most primitive emotional reactions in the brains of their constituents.

That brings me to the critical question about this type of brain sculpture: can it be reversed?

Unpicking the steel thread

Pavlov's dogs kept salivating to the bell long after he had stopped giving them the meat powder. Eventually, however, the bell lost its power to trigger this physiological response. This is known as 'extinction'. The dogs' brains had learned that the bell no longer predicted the smell of food.

Extinction can be used to treat some types of phobias which have been etched into the brain. Take the woman who had become frightened of birds, for instance. In her brain – and in particular in the amygdala – strong connections between fear and the sight of birds had been formed. When I treated her, I used the same principles as Pavlov;

in other words, I tried to make sure that she saw the 'conditioned stimulus' – bird – many times without making the 'conditioned response' – fear.

How did I do this? Well, first, I had to make sure that my patient was relaxed, and this I did by just talking to her and reassuring her. Sometimes, a more formal relaxation training can help, but it wasn't needed in this case. I then got her to look at some very innocuous cartoon-like drawings of birds in a children's book. Even these lifted her anxiety levels, however, and I had to keep her looking at the pictures for several minutes before she stopped feeling anxious. We then moved on to more realistic pictures, but of small, colourful birds not normally found in Britain, such as humming birds. After she got used to these, I had her look at pictures of birds similar to the type she was particularly frightened of. By the end of our first meeting, she could look at pictures of birds without any problem. However, when I brought in a small stuffed bird for the second session, it took a full hour before she could hold it without feeling intense fear.

I then had her watch videos of nature programmes about birds, before getting her to go to a small aviary in the local park with her husband. This she had to do several times before she felt unanxious. But the real challenge for her was to face up to a situation where birds were flapping freely and unpredictably about her. It was this aspect of the panicky fluttering of the trapped bird in the bedroom which had particularly terrified her.

To tackle this, I had the woman and her husband visit a local butterfly farm, where, in a large conservatory, butterflies of all sizes – some as big as small birds – fluttered about freely. From there, she moved on to a park with lots of birds flying about and people feeding them. Each time she moved on to a new stage, she felt a new surge of anxiety, but, with the help of her husband, she stuck it out until the fear died down.

The final goal was a trip to Trafalgar Square in London, where pigeons in their hundreds flutter about and often land on the heads of the tourists who are feeding them. After half an hour here, the woman's phobia was conquered. As in all the other experiences I had put her through, as she got used to the situation her anxiety died down. Thus we reached the point where the conditioned stimulus – bird –

appeared without the conditioned response – fear. In other words, we had extinction.

The way of life into which my patient had fallen since her encounter with the trapped bird was now changed completely. Even though in an average day she might not encounter many birds, the phobia had made her constantly vigilant, and her anxiety could be triggered by a fluttering shadow glimpsed out of the corner of her eye. As a result, her life had been completely disrupted by a pervasive anxiety that she might come up close to a bird – particularly a trapped, fluttering bird. She avoided going into empty rooms, enclosed spaces or anywhere where there might be the possibility of encountering birds. Though she had just about held on to her job, her social life had been eliminated, her children's lives severely constricted and her marriage placed under very great strain indeed. These problems in themselves generated more anxiety, which of course acted like petrol poured on the flames of her phobia. The original bad experience with the trapped bird, coming on top of her bereavement, had changed her brain, but so did the subsequent extra anxiety and stress. It was these brain changes which my therapy had to tackle.

The woman became able to lead a normal life again because her brain no longer went into emergency mode when she saw, or thought she saw, a bird. In other words, therapy almost certainly changed the brain again. But did this involve simply unstitching the steel threads woven into the amygdala by the initial trauma? Possibly not.

It seems that extinction is caused by higher areas of the brain learning to inhibit the unruly amygdala. In particular, the middle surface of the frontal lobes of the brain seems to be important in policing riotous emotions. If this part of the brain is damaged in animals, for instance, then extinction tends not to happen.

The woman gradually got used to the stuffed bird eyeing her beadily from my desk because the relatively relaxed situation allowed her frontal lobes to gain control over the amygdala's panic reaction. In other words, the frontal lobes prevented the panicky amygdala from always ringing the brain's fire alarms when it thought it saw a bird.

What happened, however, to the steel threads in the amygdala? Though almost certainly weakened with disuse, it seems that they do lurk there for a very long time indeed. Pavlov noticed this with his dogs, for instance. Sometimes, long after the bell had ceased to predict the smell of food, its ringing would, out of the blue, make the pooches' mouths water. This must mean that the connection between bell and salivation was still woven into the brain connections, and that extinction had – possibly through the frontal lobes – simply gagged the memory, preventing it from triggering its response. This is a little worrying for my patient, as it suggests that the brain wiring of her phobia is still in place.

Sure enough, a few months after she had apparently completely lost her fear of birds, she was made redundant and the anxiety caused by that reawakened the phobia to its former, disabling glory. Fortunately, however, with a couple of further sessions of therapy, she recovered again, possibly because the synaptic connections between frontal lobes and the 'phobic' cells in the amygdala were restrengthened by the extra therapy.

One reason why such emotional connections can be burned so indelibly into the amygdala has to do with Hebbian learning. The amygdala cells that fire when the bird is seen are well connected with neighbouring cells in the amygdala. As the phobic cells fire again and again, so these neighbours tend to be triggered – and, of course, 'cells that fire together, wire together', so the pattern spreads.

In other words, a group of neurones in the trembling web become attached to this general response pattern, even though these particular brain cells are not directly connected with the object of phobia. These connections may stay in place even after treatment when the previously frightening object no longer triggers anxiety. This may in part explain why such phobic-type reactions can erupt spontaneously long after they have apparently been cured.

That being said, this type of treatment of straightforward phobias is in general pretty effective, even in the long term. Though post-traumatic stress disorder is more difficult to treat, this type of extinction therapy can work, as part of a package of treatment. In Tim's case, he might start by getting used to driving along the stretch of road where the accident happened. At first, this would be very disturbing for him, but, if correctly handled, he would probably eventually stop feeling particularly anxious. Similarly, he might be encouraged to go into petrol stations until the smell of petrol no longer triggered anxiety.

Though this study has not yet been done, you would expect that successful treatment of Tim would see a reduction in activity in his right amygdala when he smelled petrol or saw a red car approaching. Indeed, such studies have been done with therapy for another type of disorder – obsessive compulsive disorder (OCD).

People who suffer from OCD feel a compulsion to perform repetitive rituals at certain times. For instance, a person may feel compelled to wash his hands again and again – even until the skin is raw – if he feels that they have been contaminated by touching some object which he believes is dirty. This sense of having been contaminated can expand to such an extent that life reduces to making good contamination arising from anything ranging from touching a doorhandle to going to the toilet.

One treatment for OCD is quite similar to the treatment of phobia: it involves exposing the person to the stimuli which trigger the rituals – for instance, touching a 'dirty' object. During this 'behaviour therapy', the therapist stops the person from carrying out the washing (or other) ritual which he would normally feel he had to do. At first this is really stressful and difficult for the person. With time, however, if again and again they are dissuaded from performing their ritual, they become less distressed by the 'contamination' and often show big improvements in everyday life. In practice, this means a sharp reduction in their rituals and a new freedom in their lives to do the normal things which the rest of us enjoy.

This behaviour therapy changes the brains of people with OCD, and these brain changes go hand in hand with the improvements in their mental functioning and behaviour. PET scans of brain activity in a group who had behaviour therapy showed reduced activity in another part of the brain that we know is involved in OCD – the 'caudate nucleus'.

Therapy which involves no drugs or physical treatment, then, can change your brain and help you recover from disabling conditions. This has been shown directly only in the treatment of OCD, in the parts of the brain linked to this condition. It is very likely, though, that amygdala changes would follow treatment for phobia.

Tim suffered from depression as well as all his other problems. People under long-lasting stress often become depressed. Depressed people tend to have reduced activity in parts of the frontal lobes of the brain, which is one reason why they have such problems concentrating. However, depression can be treated successfully by a type of therapy called 'cognitive therapy', which is a method of training people to change the way they feel by altering their thinking patterns.

It is very likely that successful talking therapy of this type actually changes the brain activity in the frontal lobes of depressed people, though again this has not yet been tested. Not all types of psychotherapy work with depression, and it is probable that those that don't work will not change the brain.

Psychological therapies can be seen as a way of reprogramming the thoughts, emotions and behaviour of a person. When you reprogramme a computer, the silicon chips inside the machine are made to fire at different rates, in different combinations, at different times. So it is for the brain's hardware – the trembling web of neurones. New programmes make these neurones fire in different ways, and we can measure such changes by studying the brains activity.

Drugs can also make these changes in the brain, but we don't take drugs lightly and governments are very careful about what drugs are allowed and who is permitted to prescribe them. Only drugs which have passed rigorous tests of their effectiveness can be used. But psychotherapy and counselling can change the brain as much as drugs can, and, as is the case for drugs, therapy can harm if used wrongly or if given for the wrong condition. Yet more or less anyone can set themselves up as a psychotherapist and most psychotherapists offer treatment which is scientifically unproven.

If I become depressed, I know that certain types of psychotherapy may make me worse. I only want to be treated by therapies which have passed the kinds of tests which drugs have to undergo. If I have repeated panic attacks, for instance, there are particular types of talking therapy which work. Don't let me be treated by some other method which may well harm me!

Tim went through many different types of therapy as his life disintegrated around him. Some helped, most did not. Some increased his anxiety and deepened his depression. Others simply made him feel more of a failure because he didn't benefit from them.

He did manage to overcome his phobias to some extent. He was helped to break the link between stimuli connected to the trauma and the choking fear which they produced. But Tim's problems were much more wide-ranging and complicated than just this phobia.

The short-circuits of terror

In the stem of the brain, just above where it tapers into the spinal cord, there is a tiny bunch of cells known as the 'locus coeruleus'. If you electrically stimulate this part of the brain, then the reaction is fear, extreme alertness and all the bodily symptoms associated with these states, such as a pounding heart.

The locus coeruleus produces one of the brain's chemical messengers, noradrenaline. Whenever you encounter something surprising, shocking or frightening, it sends noradrenaline streaming into the higher areas of the brain. If you think of the last time a loud noise startled you, you should remember the way you froze, listened and watched intently, and for a moment forgot everything else that had been preoccupying you. This happened because of a temporary change in your brain chemistry designed to force you to attend to possible danger, and if necessary to flee. During this state, your brain is more sensitive to faint sounds, touches or movements. This means, for instance, that if you have just been startled, a subsequent innocuous tap on the shoulder can make you jump out of your skin.

Film makers use this principle to scare you stiff. You know the scenario: young woman on dark staircase, eyes wide, chest heaving, edging her way away from the leering psychopath with the butcher's cleaver. Long silence, soft thud, suppressed scream, spins around to see kitten that has jumped down from a window.

This state of hyper-alertness, where anything makes you jump and you are constantly scanning around you for danger can be quite

exciting for a few minutes while watching a film. Even so, most film-
makers know that they have to calm you down after a scary scene with
some lighthearted shots. And if we think we hear a burglar in the
house at night, then this heart-pounding state of high alertness is anything but pleasant.

People who have been involved in major disasters show changes in
their brains' levels of arousal many years after the traumatic events. In
1988, for instance, there was a terrible earthquake in Armenia.
In Spitak, the city closest to the epicentre of the quake, half the city's
schoolchildren were killed. Even five years after the disaster, large
numbers of the surviving children were still traumatized – haunted by
the screams of victims entombed in collapsed buildings, highly
stressed and easily startled. There was evidence that their brain
chemistry had changed because of their traumatic experience, causing
the hypervigilance and many other symptoms of post-traumatic stress
disorder.

This was what happened to Tim. This was how his brain reacted
every day for months and even years after the accident. Deep in the
brain stem, the locus coeruleus kept pumping the noradrenaline up
into his brain, keeping him in a state of exhausting hypervigilance and
edginess. This tendency was what most corroded his relationship with
his wife. He could never really relax and enjoy her company. For him,
it was as if a burglar were constantly in the house. And if you believe
such a thing, then facing up to this threat takes priority over everything else. If, like Tim, you feel in continuous danger, then you have
little time for the relaxed companionship on which every successful
marriage depends.

One reason why Tim and people like him seem to feel vulnerable
most of the time is that the trauma they have suffered fatally under-
mines their assumption that the world is predictable and reasonably
controllable. In most westernized countries we are cushioned from
many threats, from illness and from death, and many people reach
middle-age without encountering any major adversity. When something dreadful happens, it is completely out of kilter with everything
we have come to expect from the world. Trauma may therefore change
the brain at the very highest level of complex assumptions and beliefs,

embroidered into the trembling webs of the cortex, as well as profoundly altering the electrochemical activity in the brain's emotional and arousal circuits.

Even more destructive of Tim's marriage, however, was the way in which he both seemed and felt cut off and detached from the world, and even from those closest to him. To his wife, it was as if she had lost him. Even his children felt rejected by his detachment. For Tim, it was as if he was in a glass bubble. Everything had a sense of unreality about it – he felt 'depersonalized' and emotionally numb. If you have ever been in an accident or witnessed some traumatic event, you may have felt something like this. Time seems to slow down, and it feels as if you are someone else watching yourself as events unfold. I remember once as a child pulling a large pot of hot liquid over myself. I heard myself cry out, but it was as if someone else was making the noise. The liquid spilled out in a slow, graceful cascade, and I did not really feel its heat – again, it was as if someone else's skin was being touched. My sense of rather dreamy detachment soon passed, however, to be replaced by distress, but people like Tim can be so trapped in this sense of detachment that their life can end in ruins. It is as if the brain's emotional centres are locked into 'danger mode', the amygdala continually primed to react to a world which has become uncontrollable. Indeed, severe stress can cause, under certain circumstances, permanent and damaging changes to the brain.

Blown fuses and burned-out wires

The dramatic way in which a single shocking experience can change the brain is shown in this case in Germany. A twenty-three-year-old man who worked in an insurance company discovered a fire in the cellar of his house one evening. He fled the house and called the fire brigade; he suffered no injuries and inhaled no smoke. He remembered everything that had happened, but seemed dazed and frightened.

Next morning, he didn't know where he lived or what his job was. He barely recognized his girlfriend of three years, and could remember hardly anything of his life after the age of seventeen. When his brain activity was studied using a PET scanner, it was seen to be greatly reduced, particularly in the parts of the brain responsible for memory, in a region known as the 'hippocampus'. Not surprisingly, he also did very badly on tests of memory and learning.

Eight months after the fire, his brain functions had not improved. How could such a relatively minor trauma produce such devastating and long-lasting effects on the brain? An answer to this question came after three weeks of psychotherapy. During one of these sessions, he told his therapist about one of his earliest childhood memories.It was truly horrifying. As a four-year-old, he recalled seeing a road accident which set on fire one of the cars. He watched the driver dying in the flames, screaming, with his head pressed against the windscreen. The young man's mother confirmed that this had in fact happened.

This terrible memory was burned into the child's amygdala. When, nineteen years later, he found a fire in his own house, his emotional brain reacted violently because of the indelible memory of terror linked to fire.

Part of the stress reaction triggered by the amygdala – storehouse of these terrible emotional memories – is to release steroid stress hormones into the blood. Too much of this stress hormone can damage brain cells, particularly in the hippocampus, an area that is critically important for our day-to-day memory and for new learning. We need the hippocampus to remember what we did this morning, to learn the name of a new acquaintance or to recall what we were told five minutes before.

Stress, if it is severe or prolonged, can cause the neurones in the hippocampus to shrink. They usually spring back into shape again once the stress is lifted, but sometimes the connecting wires between cells – dendrites – can be permanently shrivelled by the stress.

Consequently, some very stressed people may notice that their memories are not as good as usual. In the majority of cases of relatively normal stress, this will be due simply to the distraction of worry, rather than to any changes to the brain. Where the stress is very severe or prolonged, however, the neurones in the hippocampus may shrink and hence reduce the ability to remember things. When the stress lifts, though, in the majority of cases the brain cells will expand again to their normal size.

Very bad stress, though, can make the brain change permanently. Some survivors of firefights in the Vietnam War who suffered post-traumatic stress were later found to have shrunken hippocampuses, and poor memory to go with it. People who have undergone repeated abuse as children can also suffer the same kind of brain change because of their traumatic experiences.

This damage to the brain in turn makes it harder to cope with new stresses and difficulties that life throws up. In turn, this generates more stress and may shrink the trembling web of the memory system even further. For young children brought up in harsh, stressful environments, the corrosive effects of stress on the brain can sap their ability to learn and prevent their intelligence developing fully. Children who are neglected and/or physically abused, for instance, tend to have brains that are abnormally developed. The frontal lobes, the emotional brain and the fibres that join the two halves of the brain (the so-called 'corpus callosum') can all be significantly altered by the lack of stimulation that goes with neglect, as well as by the stress that comes with physical and emotional abuse.

Taken together with other factors, such as poor diet, lead and other pollution, these facts make one very sceptical about claims that the difference in intelligence levels found between races are genetically determined. Black people generally live in very high-stress environments, whether in the poverty of many African countries or in the inner-city ghettoes of the USA.

Change your brain now!

Trauma and stress change the brain. But so do you, every hour of every day, by what you think and do. Everyone has moods. The ups and downs of emotional tone one day can make us feel optimistic and carefree. A day – or even an hour – later, we can feel lethargic, pessimistic and negative about ourselves.

These changes in mood are gently rolling hills in some people, plunging Alps in others. Some change very little, some are locked perpetually in a fog of gloom, while others skip interminably through a sunshine of ho-hum cheerfulness. Both are difficult to live with. The human brain needs some change at least.

What brings on these changes in mood? While such physiological processes as hormones, hunger or tiredness play their part, so the rough and tumble of daily life imprints itself on to the firing patterns of the trembling web. The driver who aggressively cuts us up at the junction, the word of praise from a senior colleague, the belittling aside of an acquaintance can all quite suddenly change our mood. Or your mood can tip because of some unbidden memory that erupts in awareness.

Changes in mood happen because of changes in brain activity, and vice versa. You change your brain as much as your brain changes you. In the laboratory, psychologists can easily manipulate your mood. They can make you depressed (with your permission, of course) by having you read a series of statements like this: 'Looking back on my life, I wonder if I have accomplished anything really worthwhile . . .'; 'There are things about me that aren't very attractive'; 'I feel a bit disappointed at the way things have turned out . . .'. Once you have read through a few dozen of these cheerful ditties, you may not feel like slitting your wrists, but life definitely loses some of its zizz for a while. You can similarly tilt people into a happy, elated mood by getting them to read sunny sentences like 'All in all, I'm pretty pleased with the way things are going'; 'Life is pretty good at the moment'; 'Everything looks good the way I feel right now'.

Music can also help. In one study, people who had read the gloomy sentences also had to listen to Prokofiev's brooding music *Russia under the Mongolian Yoke* – played at half speed! Those who had read the cheerful sentences listened to Delibes' *Coppélia*, or to an anodyne compilation of popular classics.

Perfectly normal volunteers can be tipped from elation to sadness and vice versa by these techniques. Of course, such mood changes are only temporary, but the changes in the brain that go hand in hand with them are very real. Brain activity changes significantly, particularly in the frontal lobes, and when the brain changes in this way with your mood, it is not just how you feel that alters. The whole functioning of your brain is changed. In a happy mood, for instance, you are actually better at solving intellectual and practical problems.

In one experiment, some volunteers were put into a happy mood by watching a funny film, while others watched a neutral film and were left in their normal mood. Everyone then had to solve a problem. They were given a candle and a box of tacks and told to fix the candle to a wall. The candle was too thick for the tacks to pass through, so it couldn't be pinned directly to the wall. Think about this for a moment before reading on.

The solution to this problem is to empty out the tacks and pin the tack box to the wall as a candleholder. Only 20 per cent of those who had been watching the neutral film found the solution within 10 minutes, while 75 per cent of those who had been watching the funny film solved it!

If the activity in the frontal lobes of the brain changes with mood, then of course your thinking ability changes with it. Business people use gifts and entertainment to lift the mood of clients, knowing that in the full flush of a good meal their brains are more open to persuasion.

Moment by moment, our brains are changed by what we experience, think and remember. Our moods can even be affected by which side of the body we move. Try this exercise. Find a rubber ball, soft toy or bunched-up cloth. Take it first in your right hand and squeeze it for roughly 45 seconds. Take a break for 10 seconds, then squeeze it again for another 45 seconds. Repeat this twice more, taking a 10-second break between each bout of squeezing. Now, after a rest, do the same with your left hand. Did you notice any differences between the two?

Well, in one study, people were more likely to come up with positive statements when describing an ambiguous picture if they were clenching their right hands than when they clenched their left hands. There was also some suggestion that the right-hand movements made them feel more positive. This, though not yet fully understood, is thought to be due to the fact that the right hemisphere of the brain may be specialized for negative emotions, while the left hemisphere has a greater role in positive emotions.

When you clench your left hand, it increases activity in the right hemisphere of the brain, which in turn tends to produce more negative emotions. There is some evidence to support the view that the right hemisphere may play a particular part in negative or avoidant emotions. Some babies are more clingy to their mothers and inhibited than others, particularly in strange situations such as a playgroup. Babies who are most like this have more electrical activity in the right sides of their brains than do children who are less inhibited. People watching funny films show more brain activity in the left frontal lobe of their brain while they are making happy expressions. The same people watching gruesome scenes of burn victims show more activity in the right frontal lobe while grimacing, on the other hand.

Even changing the expression on your face can change your mood. Try pulling your eyebrows together and down and holding that expressions for a minute or to. You may notice that your mood gradu- ally changes to fit your expression. Now try fixing your face into a smile and hold that for a minute or two. On average – though there are always many exceptions to these average rules – you should notice a slight improvement in your mood through holding the muscles of the face in a facsimile of happiness.

In German, there is a version of the vowel 'u', written 'ü', which requires a tight pursing of the lips, somewhat like the response to biting into a sour lemon. Pronouncing an 'ü' gives you an expression of pursed-lip disapproval. In one study, some native German-speakers were asked to read aloud a page of normal German, followed by a page of prose abnormally peppered with 'ü's. Debriefed afterwards, the volunteers said that they had enjoyed the story without the 'ü's much more than the one with them! This was in spite of the fact that the stories had very similar content, with nothing to make one more enjoy- able than the other.

'Just put on a happy face' isn't such anodyne advice as it seems then. The reason for this is that the brain circuits which control particular facial expressions are closely linked to the brain circuits for the experiencing of these emotions themelves. Just as being reminded of past unhappiness by some fragment of music can bring on sadness, so particular body sensations – even the feelings that come from holding your lips pursed – can evoke echoes of the emotions with which they are associated.

The feeling in your face as it sets itself for a frown or smile is just one way in which bodily feelings can trigger emotions. So can tiredness or hunger, for instance. These physiological states can have quite a lot in common with emotions such as sadness and fear – at least as far as the brain is concerned. When you are very hungry, for example, your legs can get shaky; similarly, your knees tremble when you're scared of something. So if you are someone with a history of anxiety, sometimes you can get panic attacks that 'come out of the blue' without any obvious cause.

Sometimes the cause can be a bodily event that has nothing to do with fear – like shaky legs brought on by hunger. As far as the emotional brain is concerned, with its lowbrow 'hair-trigger' responses, shaky legs are a sign of danger. At least they are in people who have had a lot of panic attacks, for in the course of these bouts of anxiety they have sculpted the emotional brain into linking its emergency routine to a wider and wider range of stimuli, some outside the body, some inside.

As a result of Hebbian linkage between emotion and rather non-specific bodily feelings, one can become a trigger for the other. So, for instance, people prone to depression might have a bout of low mood triggered by fatigue. This is because the bodily symptoms of fatigue are quite similar to those of depression and in the brain's trembling web overlapping patterns of connections tend to activate each other.

Hence the dangers of overwork. You may start off the week in a good frame of mind, but end it in a state of exhaustion and low morale. Your low mood could be switched on simply because your brain links the body feelings of extreme tiredness with those of depression. This low mood can cast a grey tinge over your thinking, making you pessimistic, and liable to ruminate over past failures rather than to reminisce about your achievements. Of course, you are probably also going to be poorer at problem-solving when you're in a gloomy mood like this, so your work might suffer. Then you realize you are not doing your best at work and this deepens the gloom. So a vicious circle can develop, spiralling you into a state of mind which would not have arisen had you not exhausted yourself by overwork early in the week.

Of course, most of us quickly snap out of these blue interludes – a good night's sleep or a relaxing drink is often enough. Many of the brain changes I have talked about in this chapter are based on temporary alterations in the trembling web that are quickly reversed as circumstances change. Others are linked to more long-lasting changes, though. Hence some people's brains are more vulnerable than others to a self-defeating downward spiral of transient mood into more enduring depression. This can often be because of previous bad emotional experiences in life, which have become embroidered in the trembling web, making the brain more susceptible to this sort of emotional cascade.

This is what happened to Tim, complicating his already complex problems. He was exhausted not only by the overwork in which he took refuge from his personal problems, but also because of his extremely disturbed sleep, disrupted by nightmares and depression. The ensuing fatigue, masquerading as depression, would trick his brain into moody bouts of hopelessness.

Tim's depression drove friends and family away from him. Part of the reason for this is that emotions – including depression – are contagious. Students, for instance, who start off term light of heart, will end up significantly more depressed if they have been sharing a room with a gloomy roommate. Fear is contagious too – parents pass on phobias to their children. This is true also for anger and aggression, which can be transmitted like viruses through whole populations.

With the right kind of therapy most people like Tim can be helped to reshape their trembling webs and at least partly to overcome their emotional problems. In such severe cases as Tim's, reshaping the brain may need a combination of drugs along with the therapy. But what about whole generations, entire cultures? With depression and other emotional disorders becoming more and more common in most westernized countries, how do we try to prevent the threads of emotional and intellectual damage being embroidered into the brains of whole generations of infants? This is a question for the next chapter.

10

Faith, Hope and Love in the Brain

Claire kicks her bare legs in the air and fixes her mother with a bright-eyed smile. 'Hi there,' her mother replies delightedly, taking a foot in each hand and pedalling it gently back and forwards. The baby gives a squeal of pleasure and kicks her legs free, thrashing them wildly, giggling breathlessly and gazing intently at her mother for a reaction. 'Hey!' comes the laughing response. 'What are you up to?' The baby squeals again, acknowledging the joke and celebrating the shared emotion. She thrashes her legs again, but catches one of them on a bar of the cot, cries out in pain and begins to sob. Her mother picks her up at once and Claire clutches her, still crying. 'There, there, did you hurt your foot, did you hurt your foot?' her mother croons, rubbing the baby's back and kissing that periphery of her face which is not pressed into her neck. As the sobbing subsides, a bird lands on the windowsill outside. The infant raises her head and stares. Sensing her movement, her mother looks at her and follows her gaze. 'Look, it's a birdie,' she whispers, in conspiracy with the rapt attention of her child. In silence they stare together for a few seconds, the baby breaking off to look excitedly at her mother, checking she is with her. 'Yes, I can see it!' whispers her mother, the emotion in her voice perfectly in tune with her baby's animation. The bird flies away and the baby snuggles close to her mother again, suddenly aware once more of her sore foot. 'That's right, your foot's getting all better now, isn't it,' murmurs her mother in response between kisses, rubbing the foot.

The baby is sitting on her mother's lap as the train sets off. She looks up at her mother and says 'Baba.' Her mother glances out of the window. The baby stretches backwards, arching her back. 'Sit still, Lucy,' her mother says, turning the baby round, her back towards her. Lucy gives a cry, kicks her legs and struggles to twist back round. 'Stop wriggling!' her mother says in an irritated voice. Thwarted, Lucy begins to howl. She cries and cries, but her mother sits inert and switched off, staring at the window. Other passengers glance over, some irritated, others sympathetic. In response to a sympathetic comment, the mother raises her eyes in martyred resignation. Still Lucy howls. An elderly American tourist comes down the aisle and begins to talk to Lucy. 'Oh dear, someone is upset, what's the matter?' Lucy has stopped crying. 'Don't you like the train?' Lucy looks at the woman intently as she chats to her for the next few minutes. The woman goes on to talk to Lucy's mother, who responds in an animated and friendly way, before making her way back to her seat. For the rest of the journey, Lucy is quiet.

The parents are sitting at the table, talking. Little Peter, their three-year-old, toys with a coloured pencil, occasionally doodling on a piece of paper. 'Here's a doggy,' he murmurs, half to himself. His father is now on the phone, his mother reading the newspaper. 'Mummy, I've drawn a doggy,' he calls out. 'Mmm,' his mother replies, dreamily, from somewhere in the centre pages. Peter scribbles over the drawing, beginning to drum his feet on the crossbar of his chair. 'Peter, stop that, please,' his father breaks off from the phone to admonish him. Peter stops for a few seconds, but starts again as soon as his father returns to his conversation. 'Peter, stop it!' his mother snaps at him over the top of the broadsheet. Peter stops. He gets down noisily from his chair and wanders to the window. 'There's a black cat in the garden!' he calls out excitedly. There is no reply. His father finishes the phone call and settles down with another newspaper at the table. Peter knocks on the window. 'Pussy cat, pussy cat,' he calls. 'Don't knock on the window, darling,' his mother says, not looking up. Peter wanders back over to the table, takes up a crayon and begins to doodle on the bare tabletop. 'Peter! What are you doing? Don't you dare mark the table like that!' his father cries out. 'That's very naughty!' his mother snaps. Peter throws down the crayon and howls, drumming his feet against the chair. 'Now, just stop that, Peter!' his mother says, throwing down her paper; both parents are standing over him now – he has their full attention.

'Mark, come here!' Mark, aged eight, trudges down the stairs towards his mother. 'How did this happen to your jacket?' She points to the long tear in the lining. Mark shrugs, avoiding looking at it. 'I'm asking you, how did this happen?' Her voice is raised. He shrugs again. 'Open your mouth! Have you lost your tongue?' she shouts, pushing him roughly. 'I dunno,' he mutters, head lowered further and scowling. 'Don't you give me that look!' she hisses through gritted teeth. She tries to push him again, but he steps back nimbly and she lurches forward, stumbling to the side and knocking her shoulder against the wall. Her voice rises to a hysterical pitch. 'How dare you! How dare you!' She lashes out at him, catching him with a slap on the side of the head. He ducks the next blow and darts into the kitchen. 'Paul! Paul!' she shouts shrilly. 'What is it?' a hoarse male voice responds. A man appears at the top of the stairs. 'You'll have to come and deal with him!' His footsteps are heavy on the stairs. 'Why, what's going on here?' 'COME HERE!' she screams at Mark, who is fumbling to open the garden door. Paul pushes past his wife and strides over to where Mark is now desperately tugging at the doorhandle. Paul seizes him by the collar and yanks him away from the door. 'When your mother tells you to do something, you do it! Understand?' Mark wrenches himself free, but he is grabbed again before he can get two steps away. Paul gives the boy a stinging slap across the back of the head. 'You do as you're told, understand?' Another slap, this time duller as it is with the back of the hand. Still Mark has not cried out. 'You understand?' The hand returns, this time the fingers fisted to make a dull thud on the side of Mark's face. 'YOU UNDERSTAND?' The hand returns, fully fisted, smashing into the other side of the boy's head. 'PAUL! STOP IT! THAT'S ENOUGH!' Mark's mother screams, tugging at Paul's raised arm. He spins round and

punches her viciously away. 'If you bring me into something, you let me finish it my way, OK?' He wheels round, fist high over the cowering boy, who finally, this Monday morning, finds words for his mother: 'Mum, please, Mum, stop him!'

The infuriating optimist

In the more northerly parts of North America, where winters are harsh, it is not uncommon for perfectly healthy elderly people to move out of their own homes and into residential, semi-institutional accommodation for entirely practical purposes, such as not having to clear snow from their driveways. Compared with very similar people who have chosen to stay in their own homes, on average the residents of such communities deteriorate mentally over the months and years, in terms of memory and general intellectual abilities. This is just the average, however. In fact, some people who make this move keep up a good level of cognitive function, while others go downhill quite markedly, thus dragging down the average ability of the residential group.

What distinguishes these two groups? One key factor is the degree to which people feel as if they have control over their own lives and destinies. People who feel a sense of control tend to be optimists. You know the type, because sometimes they can be quite infuriating. A man phones up for tickets for a show, to be told that there are none left. He tells his optimist friend, who says, 'I bet they do have some – call them back and ask what they do with cancellations.' The fatalist groans. 'There won't be any, it's a waste of time – the tickets are all sold.' The never-say-die optimist responds impatiently, 'Oh, you always give up – give me the phone and I'll sort it out!' Nine times out of ten, the optimist's first try doesn't work, but nine times out of ten, the unsuccessful first try yields other leads which *do* end up in a problem eventually solved; for instance, the theatre box office may not resell cancelled tickets, but it turns out that a ticket agency in town does. The fatalist/pessimist would never have discovered this fact, because he or she would have stopped at the first hurdle through a belief that there was nothing he could do to change brute reality.

Optimists who feel that they have control over their lives, not surprisingly, tend to be happier than pessimists, and their rosy outlook on life means that they engage with it more. Elderly people who gave up their own independent homes for a residential life fared well mentally if they were of such a cast of mind. Even though the objective reality is that they have less control over their own lives now that they are in an institution, they do not feel at the mercy of this external reality.

Those who don't feel in control of their lives, on the other hand, do feel at the mercy of external circumstance. Because of this, the objective reality of the institution intrudes into the trembling web of their brains: 'I am in an institution, therefore I must be failing mentally and physically,' might be, one could speculate, the kind of deduction that a fatalist brain could make.

Such a conclusion is very likely to be a self-fulfilling prophecy. If you believe that you have little control, then there is not much point in squaring up to problems. After all, what's the point, if there's nothing much you can do about them? Once you take this position, then it is highly likely that there will be a reduction in activity in the synapses of the trembling web. This is particularly likely to be true in the frontal lobes of the brain, which is where the machinery for problem-solving and active anticipation resides. Once you start starving the trembling web of the nourishment of stimulation, the synapses may begin to shrink and contract. Hence, one could speculate, the loss of mental function that follows institutionalization among people not protected by the shield of optimism and personal control.

It is not just mental functions that suffer when you don't feel in control. Pessimists tend to have poorer health than optimists, and they are also more likely to become depressed. In turn, depression weakens the immune system and makes people more vulnerable to disease.

The job that you do also affects how much you feel in control of your life. Ultimately, such a feeling of control can determine not only your health, but also how long you live. This is the conclusion of a study of over 10,000 civil servants in London. These in the lowest, clerical grades had *three times* the death rate of the highest, administrative grades over a ten-year period. This was not due to differences in rates of smoking, obesity or high blood pressure: these factors explained only about one-third of the death-rate difference between low- and high-status jobs. The prime suspect for the difference was having control over your working life. This seems to reduce your risk of suffering a wide range of illnesses. The civil servants with low job control would, for example, report the following:

- 'I don't have much choice in deciding what to do at work.'
- 'Other people take decisions concerning my work.'
- 'I can't decide when to take a break.'
- 'I don't have much say in planning my work environment.'
- 'I don't have a say in choosing with whom I work.'

People who reported that their jobs had these and other similar characteristics were much more likely to go off sick and to suffer a wide range of illnesses. Vulnerability to illness may arise in part because feelings of powerlessness depress the immune system and disrupt the cardiovascular system.

We can see a similar process in rats who were put into the established territories of a group of other rats. The new rats were defeated by the top rats in the group, and not surprisingly they showed signs of submissiveness and stress. The lower their status in the group, the more the efficiency of their immune systems was eroded. This was shown by the number of antibodies in their blood compared to other rats.

The same thing happens to monkeys who make it to the top of the hierarchy: they have more vigorous and efficient immune systems, allowing them to fight off disease and to live longer. The same thing happens to us: stress changes the brain, which in turn depresses the body's battery of immune defences against infection and disease. Many types of stress have been shown to lower immunity and resistance to disease, including rows with our partners, taking an examination and long-lasting unemployment.

One major source of stress is feeling that you have little control over your life – and the job you do takes up a big part of that life. But where else does this sense of control – this faith in oneself – come from? The question brings us back to the first months and years of life.

Lessons from the cradle

Baby Claire has started life with a psychological silver spoon in her brain. Her changing states of mind – playful delight one moment, intense curiosity another, followed by sudden pain – are all sensitively reflected in her mother's moment-to-moment reactions to her. From each of these responses comes the shaping of the emotional circuits in the brain. After all, to a baby, experience is something of a confusion of blurred sensations. These feelings can be brought into focus only by the reactions the baby sees, hears and feels to what it does.

When Claire's mother stops everything to share her daughter's rapt attention to the bird, she is strengthening the connections in the trembling web of the brain's underlying curiosity, as well as those involved in attentiveness. Such sensitivity to the child's mental state is linked to better mental functioning and better behaviour in children once they go to school, as we saw in Chapter 8.

A friend was in hospital with her first child. She told me that she was the only mother in her room of four beds who talked to her day-old baby. The other mothers talked to each other, but – to my mind perfectly understandably – did not 'talk' to their apparently un-comprehending babies. What I didn't understand, but my friend did, was that 'talking' to a day-old baby is not about the meaning of words, but rather about learning to detect and respond to the changing mental and emotional states in the baby's brain.

Babies who spend their early months in nurseries with a succession of different nursery nurses looking after them during the day show relatively delayed language development later on, compared to, for instance, babies who are looked after by the same childminder each day. This is probably because no one nursery nurse came to know, understand and respond to the individual baby's temperament and moods in the way, for instance, that Claire's mother had learned to do. After all, babies can learn in the womb – learning, for example, to recognize their mothers' voices. Learning is a type of brain sculpture, so it is not surprising that what a baby experiences in the early days and months of life also shapes its developing brain connections.

Moods are contagious and babies catch them

Young babies whose mothers are depressed 'catch' their mothers' moods. Depressed people tend to be sad and irritable, and babies whose parents often show these emotions are much more likely to show sadness and irritability themselves – up to thirty times more than normal, one study has shown.

Babies whose mothers are depressed also behave differently towards other adults than do babies with non-depressed mothers. In one study, for instance, babies were watched playing with their mothers and then with a stranger, who did not know that some of the babies' mothers were depressed. Babies playing with their own depressed mothers tended to look away from their mothers much more often than the other babies, and generally behaved much more negatively. This was also true when they interacted with the stranger. In other words, even as young infants, they had learned a particular way of responding to the world and to other people.

These early experiences may, together with inherited temperament, determine who will get life's theatre tickets and who will not. Lucy, the baby I watched on the Cambridge train, might end up as one of life's 'giver-uppers'. Of course, this is pure speculation – her poor mother probably had a blinding headache and just wanted some peace. If her lack of responsiveness to Lucy was typical, however, then what Lucy might have learned about life is that things happen to you and that what you do yourself doesn't have much influence.

School for moods

By now, at least some of you must be raising your eyebrows and muttering about namby-pamby psychologists preaching indulgence and fostering a generation of spoiled brats. If you are, then you have a point – success in life depends on knowing when and how to express emotion, and in soldiering on sometimes even when your emotional brain wants you to stop. Without this ability to tame and sometimes overrule our emotions, then we are very likely to be doomed to a life of aimless under-achievement and emotional turmoil. I can certainly think of people whom I have met whose brains have not formed the connections to control emotions triggered in the emotional brain. These connections – almost certainly between parts of the frontal lobes of the brain and parts of the limbic system – are made partly by parents, teachers and friends as they school the moods of young children.

Of course, genetic factors play a part – emotionality is almost certainly partly heritable. But, as with intelligence, environment is also crucial, weaving in complex ways with the inherited biology to determine whether someone is a Scandinavian-style stoic, a volatile Mediterranean type or a brooding Slav character. (I hasten to add that I have met emotionally volatile Swedes, utterly impassive Italians and incurably cheerful Russians. However, one only has to travel to realize that different cultures tend to shape – statistically speaking only – the emotional brains of their children in certain ways. The culture of the English upper classes, for instance, places a premium on keeping emotional expression to a minimum – the 'stiff-upper-lip' approach to life.)

It is very likely that these different ways of bringing up children actually affect the way their brains develop emotionally, though this has not been shown scientifically. However, the logic of brain sculpture is that if you are taught never to express emotion, then the emotional circuitry of your brain will wither through disuse.

After all, we know that you can change your brain state by setting the muscles of your face in the facsimile of a particular mood. It seems very likely that doing this again and again might shape the trembling web's connections in a more enduring way. Conversely, if you never allow yourself to experience a particular emotion, then connections may be lost, making it harder to produce this mood in future.

Of course, we mustn't mistake the outward signs of emotions for the inward experience. Everyone can think of the apparent robot who is in fact a bubbling cauldron of emotions inside. Nevertheless, we know that the brain can learn to damp down experienced emotions, and this may be done too much in some people. Indeed, there is a recognized psychiatric syndrome known as 'alexithymia', sufferers of which barely express – or indeed experience – emotions. In fact, these people are more vulnerable to illness, suggesting that too ruthless a dampening-down of the emotional brain circuits might not be desirable.

The happy medium, then, lies somewhere between unfettered indulgence of emotional whim on the one hand and potentially harmful emotional constipation on the other. One study of young children shows vividly how important it is to embroider connections in the trembling web to hold back the impulses of the emotional brain.

Pre-school children seated at a desk were presented with a choice between having one or two things that they liked – for instance, marshmallows. Now clearly, any self-respecting child would go for two marshmallows rather than one, but things were not that simple. They were told that the psychologist had to leave the room for a while. While he was gone they could ring a bell that sat on the desk beside the tempting marshmallows. Ringing it would bring the adult back immediately, but would mean they could have only one marshmallow, not two. If, on the other hand, they didn't ring the bell but held out for the full – to a four-year-old interminable – 15 minutes, then they could have the two marshmallows.

Some children cracked more or less immediately, rang the bell and wolfed down the single marshmallow. Others sat in varying degrees of mental torment, some covering their eyes while others distracted themselves with songs or rhymes. For those who managed to avoid ringing the bell, holding out for the full 15 minutes, their torture was ended with the reward of an extra marshmallow, to the mouth-watering chagrin of their low-self-control classmates.

These young children were followed up ten years later when they were adolescents. The differences between those who could resist the temptation to go for the single marshmallow sitting in front of them and those who could not were dramatic. The longer children had been able to control themselves and prevent themselves going for the easy gratification of the single marshmallow, the better adjusted they were as adolescents. Those who had poor self-control in the marshmallow experiment were, ten years later, poor at coping with stress, were less self-confident and showed less initiative. These children also showed more social difficulties in getting on with classmates, tending to be bad tempered, and were poor at coping with frustration. Generally, they were rather emotionally vulnerable and immature. What's more, the children who had poor self-control as four-year-olds performed much worse in academic standard assessment tests (SATs) when they were in their teens.

On reflection, perhaps these results are not so surprising. It's hard to get anywhere in life if you can't stave off immediate reward in favour of more distant, future prizes. Education is one big exercise in not taking the marshmallow in front of you, so that you can get two marsh-mallows some time later. Hardly anyone enjoys studying for exams, but they do so partly because they want to build their skills and knowledge so that they can find personally and financially rewarding jobs later on. Some adolescents – even though they may have the intellectual potential to continue their education – leave school at sixteen because they want money and the freedom that goes with it. Like the children with the marshmallows, they can't – or won't – postpone immediate pleasure and replace it with short-term pain.

Genes and temperament play a part here, but learning is also critical. You can see this even in people whose ability to control their emotions and impulses has been affected by brain damage. Brain damage of this type is unfortunately very common after bad car accidents, where some-one's head has smashed against the windshield or steering wheel. The frontal lobes of the brain, particularly the under-surface of the lobes just above your eyes, are very vulnerable to this type of impact, and can become torn and bruised by the blow. Damage to this part of the brain can often lead to a person changing from a stable, mature adult into someone who is impulsive, erratic and emotionally unstable.

As a practising neuropsychologist, I have seen this many times in people whose brains have been damaged in road accidents, falls or fights. One of my patients – John – was at university, studying medicine. He was very clever and had a glittering career ahead of him. Tragically, though, John was hit by a car when he was out jogging one evening and his brain was damaged. Amazingly, his academic intelligence was largely unaffected. He could still understand the complex topics of his course, and he could learn and remember new facts as well as he could before the accident. But in spite of this miraculous sparing of his intellectual faculties, John had to abandon his studies and leave university.

The reason for this was that he had lost much of his emotional control, becoming impulsive and unpredictable in his behaviour. He would lose his temper with fellow students, tutors and lecturers. Without warning he would flare up, and if he had taken any alcohol at all, he could also become physically violent. In fact, one evening he punched a complete stranger in a pub for a trivial reason, and only the intense conciliatory skills of his friends got him out unscathed. Sadly, this kind of behaviour gradually alienated loyal friends and he ended up quite isolated, living in a small apartment on his own, unemployed and with his career in ruins. John felt quite unable to explain how he came to act as he did – out of the blue he would find himself doing things that he would never have done before his accident.

One day, for instance, he was walking aimlessly down the street when a woman walking in front of him – a complete stranger – stopped and bent over to fix something in her shopping bag. As the former medical student passed her by, he found himself giving her a slap on the behind. The woman was understandably upset, believing that she had been deliberately sexually assaulted, and the alarm was raised. John stood meek and bemused, waiting until finally the police arrived and he was taken away and formally charged with indecent assault.

He had never done anything like this in his life before, and he had not even known that he was going to slap the woman until he felt his hand hitting her. For someone else, the thought of slapping the woman, had it occurred, would just have been a fragment of thought among the hundreds of ideas which go through the brain every second. There would have been little chance of this thought being realized into action, because the act would have been suppressed and inhibited in a fraction of a second by the frontal lobes of the brain.

In John's case, however, the very apparatus of the brain that curbs the impulse before it can be turned into behaviour had been damaged. A brain scan confirmed this, showing that the under-surface of his frontal lobes had been scarred and torn, leaving his intellectual intelligence relatively unaffected while devastating his ability to control his impulses and emotions.

However, just because his behaviour was caused by brain damage, it didn't mean that learning some control over it was necessarily impossible. In fact, I did manage to help John overcome the worst excesses of his newly acquired impulsivity.

First, I taught him to become a student of his own mental life. He kept a diary of all the significant things he did each day – particularly the really stupid things! In his diary, he had to note down what he was doing, where he was and how he was feeling immediately before some problem arose. We met regularly to discuss his diary, and I encouraged John to try to remember the fine details of what was going on in his mind and what he was feeling immediately before he did something impulsive. At first this was very difficult, but gradually he acquired the habit of monitoring his own mental state, and slowly became better at sensing when he was about to do something stupid. The problem now was, though he often knew a few seconds in advance that he was going to do something stupid, he still did it!

What we had to do then was to find a way of helping John 'short-circuit' the impulse in that critical second or two between realization and action. In the end, I taught him a mini mental-relaxation strategy, involving slowing down his breathing and for a few seconds just focusing attention on his breath. At first, John had great difficulty doing this in the heat of the moment, but gradually he learned the habit not only of monitoring his own mental life, but also of remembering to relax – and distract – himself briefly in that fraction of time between feeling and action.

Though John never got back to medicine, he did manage to find a job in a computer shop – he loved computers and was an Internet addict –

and gradually built up a new life which was relatively, though never completely, free from the most damaging manifestations of his impulsivity.

Now if John could regain some control over emotion and impulse after this control had been so cruelly damaged by the accident, so a child with an inherited impulsive temperament should relatively easily be helped to acquire such control, if parents handle him or her in the right way.

When parents teach their children to wait until mealtimes before they have a biscuit, they are teaching them habits of self-control. So are they when they won't give in to the tantrums demanding that the toy in the shop be bought RIGHT NOW! Similarly, when parents encourage their children to persist with a difficult task without giving up at the first hurdle, they are sculpting their brains, embroidering threads of emotional control into the trembling webs.

It is hardly surprising, then, that the little children who had not learned to resist temptation by the age of four fared so much worse than their more self-controlled friends over the next decade or so of life. After all, getting on successfully with our fellow human beings depends critically on our ability to hold back from the first flare of emotion and to soften our reactions with tact and patience.

If we don't learn to overrule the first urge, then we can too easily end up slumped in front of the television, postponing indefinitely the work, studying or chores that we should be doing. In fact, many young people who have the intellectual potential for university never even get beyond school-leaving exams because their brains have not acquired the necessary connections for delaying the immediate pleasure for the long-term benefit. The marshmallow study demonstrates this fact dramatically.

Perhaps even more importantly, learning to control urges and emotions is critical for a person's own emotional stability. If your brain has not been taught to damp down anger or overrule fear, for instance, then you will be at the mercy of these emotions when they are provoked in everyday life. So, for instance, if parents give in to the temperamentally timid child who at the last moment doesn't want to go to the party, then they are reinforcing the brain's fear-induced avoidance tendencies. Not only that, but they are also missing the opportunity to help embroider threads of emotional control into the brain. Similarly, when the child's rages and tantrums are constantly indulged and given in to – rather than being ignored until they pass – parents are encouraging this style of responding in the child's life. Not only that, but they are also missing the chance to help embroider in the child's brain control circuits which will help him or her master emotions, rather than become their victim.

That is precisely the price of a failure to nurture emotional intelligence – lifelong victimhood and slavery to one's emotions. In the marshmallow study, for instance, the emotionally impulsive four-year olds were as adolescents much more likely to go to pieces under stress. They were also more likely to lack self-confidence and to be bad tempered and generally difficult. It seems very probable that these children would also have tended as adults to end up with chronic psychological problems blighting their lives.

Peter, for instance, the three-year-old boy described at the beginning of this chapter, is in danger of learning that the best way of getting attention is to misbehave. This, of course, assumes that his parents behave like this most of the time and were not just taking a well-deserved Sunday-afternoon break from parental duties.

An epidemic of moods?

It has been estimated that, by the year 2020, depression could be the major cause of illness in the industrialized world. In many countries, suicide rates among young men in their teens are rising disproportionately compared to other groups. Furthermore, in many westernized countries, there has been a dramatic rise in the number of children with psychological problems, ranging from bad behaviour to depression and anxiety. Problems of paying attention and poor impulse-control are also on the increase.

Boys are particularly vulnerable. In British schools, for instance, there has been a steady widening of the gap between academic achievement in girls and boys, with girls outstripping boys significantly. Boys are having more reading problems than twenty years ago and there is also a steep rise in the diagnosis of attention deficit disorder.

What is the cause of this malaise? One reason may be a decline in the quality of education for the emotional brains of our children, leading to the kind of emotional inadequacy of the type that the four-year-olds who couldn't resist eating the marshmallow eventually showed in adolescence.

In some families, parents talk to their children about emotions and feelings. For instance, a mother might talk to her daughter about the nervousness she feels about going to a party; or a father might talk with his son about how miserable he feels because some of his former friends at school suddenly won't play with him. In talking about emotions, children learn to put words to the confusing feelings inside them; and putting words to them is part of the process of linking up the connections between parts of the frontal lobes and the emotional brain. Just as teaching a child to read involves reshaping connections in the brain, so teaching them to recognize and label their emotions entails shaping the brain's trembling web.

One way of making sure that children *don't* learn to understand and recognize their own emotions is physically to hit them for doing something wrong, rather than taking the trouble to explain what they have done and why it is wrong. Not only is hitting an inarticulate and uninformative response, but punishment is one of the least effective ways of making anyone learn – not only human beings, but even rats and pigeons!

Children who are hit tend to hit out in turn. What they learn then is an 'easy' quick-draw response to dealing with difficult human situations. What do they learn from these interactions? Nothing much, except about their own strength or lack of it. Hitting children, therefore, can make them emotionally and socially dumb. And it can make them intellectually dumb too. Children whose parents regularly hit them have lower IQs than those whose parents don't often physically punish them. This is true even with social and economic factors taken into consideration.

Not that the odd smack is going to have much bad effect, providing there is a loving relationship and plenty of 'explaining' of emotions going on along with it. The danger is, though, that exhausted and busy parents might gradually slip into using the slap to sanction the intricacies of social behaviour, rather than engaging in the more demanding business of explaining what's right, what's wrong and why.

Many families, however, seldom discuss feelings – either positive or negative – with their children. Three-year-olds whose parents talk with them a lot about the various feelings they have are better able as six-year-olds to judge and gauge the emotions shown by an adult stranger. This is a pretty critical skill to have in life – maybe even more important than intellectual ability.

It is important, though, not to burden parents with all the responsibility for sculpting the emotional circuits in their children's brains. After all, if you think back to your own childhood, you will no doubt remember pretty powerful emotional lessons learned while playing with other children – and other children, of course, become increasingly important in children's lives as they get older. In this rough school of life, you learn about friendship, aggression, jealousy, attraction and a sackful of other complex emotions. The problem is that more and more children are sitting on their own at home after school, rather than being out on the street undergoing emotional and social brain sculpture. Playing mathematical games over the Internet will almost certainly stimulate the intellectual abilities and very likely improve exam results in the long term. If this happens at the expense of learning the social ropes, however, then the child may end up as a social incompetent, unable to read other people's emotions and even more incapable of knowing how to respond to them.

This type of emotional intelligence is almost certainly as important – if not more important – than intellectual intelligence in predicting success in life. Yet, for many different reasons, children throughout the industrialized world are being increasingly deprived of the opportunity for unstructured, free-ranging play with other children.

Children are also spending less time with their parents and other relatives. Computers, television and other solitary activities have steadily eroded the time available for the family chat in which so many informal, brain-shaping emotional lessons are learned. Both parents are often working long hours, leaving little time for this.

Take Peter, for instance, the three-year-old at the beginning of this chapter. He may not get any more attention from his parents than he would have had he been born fifty years earlier; fifty years ago, however, Peter would have had much more contact with other adults – neighbours and extended family – and he would also have played much more with other children in the neighbourhood.

Perhaps as a consequence of all of this, many children grow up with insufficiently educated emotional brains. This makes them emotionally vulnerable as they grow into adulthood, thus contributing to the epidemic of psychological problems that is plaguing the industrialized world.

But there is another big change in western culture that is damaging the emotional functioning of children's brains – family strife and break-up.

Strife in the brain

Parents often worry what will happen to their children if one of them dies. They know that children above a certain age never forget the death of a mother or father, and appreciate that this may affect them for the rest of their lives. However, most parents probably worry less about what will happen to children if they divorce or separate. This is a pity, because research has shown that children can be damaged more by the strife leading up to divorce and its subsequent effects than by parental death.

In some industrialized countries, a situation is approaching where almost as many children come from broken homes as from homes where the parents stay together. In Britain, children of middle-class parents who were born in 1958 and whose parents divorced before they were sixteen were twice as likely to leave school without any qualifications as those whose parents remained married. They were also much less likely to go to university, and similarly less likely to be in a job when they were twenty-three years of age. They were four times more likely to be living in subsidized social housing and were much more likely to be smokers than were other middle-class people whose parents had not split up.

Children whose parents had divorced were on average also less emotionally stable, left home earlier and themselves divorced or separated more frequently later in life. As children, they showed more behaviour problems in school, were more likely to be unhappy and worried, and were behind their schoolmates at reading and arithmetic.

In other words, strife between parents and the divorce it often leads up to affect some children very badly indeed. Of course, in families that stay together, conflict and emotional turmoil also take their toll on children. Emotions are contagious: babies whose mothers display more anger or sadness than usual will by the age of six months themselves show these emotions to an abnormal degree. And children – particularly boys – whose parents frequently argue angrily with each other will themselves be much more likely to be aggressive. One experiment showed that children playing together would become more aggressive with each other if they saw two strange adults having an angry verbal argument.

More generally, the emotional tone in families shapes the emotional brains of babies. In one study, for instance, infants were studied at three months and then again at nine months. As we all know, some babies are 'difficult', crying a lot and generally showing negative emotions, while other babies are 'easy', being happy, smiley infants. Inherited temperament and biological factors probably play a big part in these differences. In this study, though, by the age of nine months some babies had changed in their emotions from negative to more positive, and vice versa. Others stayed the same. In the group who changed from being 'easy' to 'difficult' – that is, from showing more positive to more negative emotions over this six-month period – there were more problems in the parents' marriage. In particular, there was conflict in these families between parents about how much involvement the father should have with the baby, and the fathers themselves were less positive about their marriage before their babies were born. In contrast, the babies whose emotions changed from being relatively negative to relatively positive over the six months tended on average to live in less troubled families. Their mothers were likely to have experienced less conflict in their marriages and had higher self-esteem. Their mothers were also more responsive to their babies and had a more harmonious relationship with them.

In other words, even very young babies can change their emotional responses in line with the emotional tone of their families. Of course, temperament – which is partly inherited – also plays a role here. Some babies really are 'difficult', and can remain so even within very harmonious families. As with almost all behaviours, however, there is a delicate and complex dance between nature and nurture in shaping the trembling webs of the brain's emotional circuits.

Families can therefore shape the trembling webs governing the emotions of their babies and young children. Seldom is this more dramatically demonstrated than in cases of abuse.

A cradle for cruelty

Mark – the boy described earlier being beaten by his stepfather – suffered badly from the physical and emotional abuse he had endured ever since his mother had remarried when he was a baby. Severe neglect and physical abuse in childhood physically changes the brain, stunting connections in the trembling web, as we saw in the last chapter. There is, however, another penalty that many abused children have to pay for the cruelty that has been inflicted on them. This penalty is that abused children are much more likely to abuse others in turn. Parents who hit their children are programming into the children's brains the tendency to physical aggression. The same is true for sexual abuse – the majority of infamous sex offenders you read about in the newspaper have themselves been sexually abused as children. The vast majority of people who have suffered such abuse do not go on to commit such hideous crimes, however. But the stark fact is that the experience of being abused as a child may break down critical barriers in the brain.

One such barrier is the experience of 'fellow feeling', or empathy – the ability to put yourself in someone else's emotional shoes. Like much else, we learn to empathize to a considerable extent from our parents.

You only have to watch toddlers at play to see how they often act out what they themselves have experienced. The little girl who has been given a telling-off will very likely reprimand her doll in a similar way. The boy who has been comforted when he has been hurt may well similarly comfort his toy dog's notional injury. So it is for young children who are abused by the adults who are supposed to be caring for them. Children exposed to violence and aggression often learn to behave like this towards other people – including, eventually, their own children.

Like many other emotions, therefore, insensitive brutality can be programmed into the trembling webs of the emotional brain. And if this is true, then violence and aggression can take root among groups of people, even whole societies, like a virus. In Washington, DC, for instance, 9 per cent of six- and seven-year-olds in one deprived neighbourhood had personally witnessed someone being shot. A further 13 per cent had seen someone being stabbed, while a staggering 16 per cent had seen a dead body on the street. Witnessing muggings was commonplace – a quarter of these little children had seen one.

Little wonder, then, that violence and aggression can take root in the brains of whole societies of people. The problem is, once aggression is established in the brain, it is almost as enduring over time as is intelligence. In other words, the little children who behave aggressively in nursery school are very likely to be the ones who are aggressive as teenagers and adults.

In one study, for instance, boys and girls whose playmates rated them as particularly aggressive when they were eight years of age were the ones who were most aggressive as thirty-year-old adults. As adults, they were more likely to have a police record, to hit their children and to be violent towards their spouses.

Next time you wince at the sight of a parent roughly hitting a child on the street, you can be pretty sure that that parent experienced similar treatment as a child. So it will be for Mark, victim of his violent stepfather. Though it is not inevitable, he is much more likely than other children to get into trouble at school and on the street because of bad behaviour and violence to others.

However, though this aggressive tendency is woven into the brain's connections from an early age, it doesn't mean that these connections cannot be at least partially undone later in life. The problem is, however, that aggression can often pay off and be a rather useful way of getting on in the world. So many aggressive, violent people have no desire to overcome it. Where they do wish to, however, some training and therapy programmes can help them gain control over their violence. This may involve, among other things, teaching them to put themselves into the shoes of their victims, nursing empathy in their untutored emotional brains years after this should have happened in the family.

We are, of course, almost certainly born with different propensities to aggression. As with most of our behaviours, there is a delicate dance between genes and environment in determining how we behave. In other words, even if there were such a thing as purely inherited aggression, it could be tempered by experience.

At its extreme, cruel indifference to the suffering of others emerges in the emotional deserts of the psychopath's brain. Emotions make up the glue that holds relationships together, so it is not surprising that psychopaths drift from relationship to relationship, from job to job, inflicting suffering and bewilderment in their wake.

As we saw in the previous chapter, one way of detecting an emotional response is to measure how well the skin on the hand conducts a trickle of electricity. This is called 'galvanic skin response' (GSR), and is a reasonable indirect measure of a sudden emotional or startled reaction to some event. Psychopaths differ from the rest of us in that a distressing image of suffering leaves them unaffected, and hence their skin resistance changes much less in response to a shocking picture. It seems that, for whatever reason, the emotional brains of psychopaths – and in particular the amygdala – may be much less responsive to emotional stimuli than normal. This is the case when they cruelly manipulate trusting friends for their own selfish ends, or inflict physical pain on stranger, spouse or child. Errol Flynn was reputedly a psychopath who was nevertheless charming and socialized – at least when it suited him. Psychopaths often commit bizarre acts of cruelty to animals in childhood, and this was certainly true of Flynn. They may also enjoying starting fires, and generally they are unpopular and feared by their playmates and schoolmates.

Whether psychopaths are born or made is probably not a sensible question, as almost everything we do is both genetically influenced and shaped by experience. In fact, the very expression of genes is shaped by experience. Errol Flynn certainly had a poisonous relationship with his mother, and this may have had a major influence on a wild and remorseless life.

Some psychopaths can be very successful – for a while at least. Some politicians rise to starry heights on the basis of ruthlessly trampling over others, including their families, even in democratic countries such as Britain. They lie remorselessly, but often their recklessness and lack of caution catches up with them in the end. Sometimes, however, it takes the diligence of journalists threatened by crippling libel actions to unmask these people.

Unfortunately, however, in undemocratic countries that lack a free press and appropriate political balances, it can be impossible to curb the rise to power of psychopaths. Their brutality can become sewn into the very fabric of society, woven into the brains of the most susceptible children of that society. So, not just individuals, but whole cultures can become infected by this emotional programming which may engender casual cruelty and lack of concern for others on a disturbingly wide scale.

Even in the most brutal of societies, however, empathy and decency survive. Just as cruelty can dissolve connections in the brain, so love can grow them.

Love grows the brain

When young rats are regularly stroked gently on the back with a soft, dry paintbrush, their adult brains develop differently to those of baby rats that don't get this stimulation. As adults, the stroked rats are cognitively more able, and this mental advantage is strongly related to how much their brains have changed. Stroking alters the trembling web, and with these brain changes comes better brain functioning.

It should not be surprising, therefore, that children who are deprived of cuddles and a close emotional relationship to one or more adults show brains and bodies that are stunted. In recent years our television screens have been filled with images of terrible Romanian orphanages, a legacy of the appalling Ceauçescu regime. The pictures of row upon row of dull-eyed orphans sitting in bare, dirty rooms certainly haunts me. In Romania's better orphanages, the children are reasonably well fed, clean and are allowed access to the fresh air. What they often lack, however, is much more important – namely, the brain-nurturing interchange with a loving adult who learns to understand and respond to their highly individual responses.

At the beginning of this chapter, we saw how even a baby a few months old communicates in sophisticated ways with an adult – usually the mother – who learns to understand the baby's individual moods and expressions. This sensitive responding by the adult sculpts and shapes the brain of the baby, fostering connections, building intelligence and – most importantly of all – fostering a sense of self-worth.

Even within the rich and privileged westernized countries, though, variations in how sensitive parents are to their babies may influence their emotional, social and intellectual development. Compared to all but a tiny minority of the most deprived Western countries, however, most Romanian orphans have virtually none of this brain-nurturing loving attention. The heartbreaking fact is that if these children stay in these grim institutions, then the experience will permanently stunt their brains, their bodies and their emotions. Is there nothing that can be done about this?

Fortunately there is – at least for some of the children. As we all know, children are incredibly resilient. Just as the deprivation of loving attention can shrink a child's brain and emotions, so the discovery of loving attention can grow them again.

In the 1980s, a group of researchers in London followed up children who had gone into institutional care before the age of two and left again some time over the next five years. Though these institutions provided very good physical care, as well as decent mental and verbal stimulation, what the children did not get was a close relationship with one or two adults. Rather, they were looked after by an army of different staff – fifty on average over the course of their stay.

It is, of course, impossible for fifty different people to form the close relationship that a young child needs, so it is not surprising to find that, in one study, a third of women who had been in institutions as children were psychiatrically ill by the time they were adults. In contrast, only one in twenty women who hadn't been in institutions as children were psychiatrically ill.

Depressingly, the women who had experienced such poor emotional care as children tended themselves to be poor mothers, lacking in warmth, harsh with their children, showing inconsistency and poor control over them. In short, before our eyes we see not only the faulty sculpture of brains within a generation, but also between generations.

Now for the good news. Some of the women who had had terrible early experiences actually became good parents themselves. So there is hope for the children in the Romanian orphanages if they can be adopted into a loving family. Going back to the London children in the 1980s who were in institutions before the age of two, those who had been adopted into a family were doing well. Though they did have more problems at school than children who had not been in institutions, at home they mostly had good, intimate relationships with their families.

The picture was not quite so rosy for children who had been restored to their original families. These families tended to be plagued by more problems than the adoptive families, and were also ambivalent about having the child back in the family. The children, not surprisingly, had many more problems at home, including difficult and less warm relationships. They also had more emotional problems than the children living with adoptive parents who really wanted them.

The resilience of children and their ability to recover from the effects of years of deprivation and neglect is even more dramatically demonstrated by the story of a pair of twins in Czechoslovakia. In 1979, seven-year-old twin boys were discovered locked in squalor in a windowless room. For most of their lives, they had been brought up in almost total isolation. They lived in a small, unheated cupboard, where they had been kept by a stepmother who favoured her own children over them. For almost five and a half years they were frequently beaten by their stepmother, and for long periods would be locked up in the cellar, sleeping on the floor on a plastic sheet.

The twins' mother had died shortly after giving birth, and they had lived in a children's home for almost a year before being taken to live with their father and stepmother when they were eighteen months old. When they were discovered at the age of seven, they could hardly walk and had a mental age of three years. They suffered from rickets, and were frightened and astonished to see everyday objects such as a moving toy, television or cars on the street.

This true, latterday Hansel-and-Gretel tale of cruelty and deprivation did, however, like the fairytale itself, have a happy ending. The twins were moved to a children's home for about eighteen months, before going to live with a foster family with whom they stayed until they were adults. Even within a few months of rescue, their brains showed a rapid recovery of mental abilities, and the four-year gap between their mental and chronological ages steadily narrowed. This improvement accelerated, however, when they moved in with the foster family, and the two boys ended up as adults with above-average verbal and mental abilities. They also were emotionally quite well adjusted.

So, while deprivation and neglect can cause trembling webs to shrink and mental and emotional faculties to wither, at least some of this loss can be made good by stimulation, attention and – most importantly of all – love.

The crossed wires of love

Like any other human relationships, those between parent and child are complex and variable. Even within well-off middle-class families where there is no hint of physical cruelty or neglect, and where parents provide everything for their children, sometimes the relationship between parent and young child can become knotted and difficult.

In roughly one in every eight North American middle-class families with a young infant, that child showed a confused and troubled relationship with his or her parent – usually the mother. You could see this most clearly when the child was separated from the parent for a few minutes and left with a stranger. Normally in such situations, when the mother comes back, the infant reacts with pleasure and relief at seeing her again. In this substantial minority of infants, however, their reaction on seeing their mothers again was ambivalent and confused. It seemed almost as if they hadn't learned to see their mothers as a beacon of security in times of stress. Year-old infants would swing between clinging to their mothers on reunion, closely followed by a rejecting avoidance. They might freeze in her company, slow their movements, or do things in a confused, out-of-sequence way. Sometimes they would look sad and even apprehensive when reunited. In short, even in the first year or so of life, they showed uncertainty and ambivalence in their relationships with their mothers.

Infants of around twelve to eighteen months who have this type of confused relationship with the parent who mainly looks after them are much more likely to be troublesome and psychologically troubled when they are five years of age. And this type of relationship between parent and child – emotional ambivalence and confusion – is more common the poorer people are.

Poverty and depression go together like hand and glove, so it is not surprising that more than half of low-income North American mothers who are suffering from depression show this knotted, disorganized emotional relationship with their infant children. If you take abused children, then the majority – over 80 per cent – show this style of attachment to their mothers.

Poverty, therefore, may have some of its most corrosive effects on human potential through its destructive influence on human relationships. These relationships make up the crucibles within which the connections in growing brains are shaped and nurtured. Where poverty, neglect and deprivation are endemic, brains literally wither from lack of stimulation, and in particular in the absence of the nourishment of loving attention from parents.

The type of attention that baby Claire gets is much harder to give in the midst of stress, poverty and endemic depression. Yet this type of attention is critical for the brain to grow and develop properly, both intellectually and emotionally. What's more, as we saw earlier, severe stress can physically shrink the brain – and this is as true for children as it is for adults.

Taken together, then, a knotted, difficult relationship between parents and child, taking place within stressful, impoverished circumstances, can take a terrible toll on the brain's trembling web. Loving relationships and the sense of self-worth that they bring can, however, redeem at least some of this corrosion of human potential.

Love heals

It is not only children's brains and bodies that thrive on love. It is just as true for adults like you and me. Take the women who had been brought up in institutions as children. Many ended up as poor mothers themselves, inflicting on their own children a version of the emotional deprivation that they had endured. Some, however, escaped this vicious cycle and became good mothers. What had happened to them, to stop the emotional virus contaminating their relationships with their own children? The answer is straightforward: love. Those women who had met a partner they could count on to help them, and in whom they could confide, ended up becoming good parents themselves.

The healing effects of loving relationships was also clear among the 10,000 London civil servants I mentioned earlier. Those in low-status jobs with little control over their work got sick and died much more often than those in higher-status jobs with more control. Quite independent of the job they did, however, how healthy these men and women were was strongly affected by the quality of their close relationships. Lack of emotional support and not feeling able to confide in a partner damaged their health, as did the feeling of putting much more into a relationship than they were getting out of it.

Conflict with a partner is a stressful business, and this stress can reduce the number of antibodies in our blood available to fight disease. Conflict can also make you depressed, and that involves changes to the brain, including a drop in activity in the frontal lobes. Such depression can numb you into mental inaction, making it very hard to muster the resources to solve some of the problems making you depressed. And depression changes the brain, reducing synaptic activity in the frontal lobes in particular. So, given that a twenty-five-fold increased risk of depression was found in both men and women who said they had an unhappy marriage, then you can see clearly how lack of love affects the brain.

Love heals both body and mind, buffering us against the worst effects of life's slings and arrows. After the Three Mile Island nuclear power-station disaster, for instance, where large amounts of radio-activity were released into the atmosphere, parents were particularly stressed and anxious about the effects on their young children. Quite a number of the mothers became depressed as a result, but whether or not they became depressed in response to this stress depended heavily one one important factor: whether they had a close and intimate relationship with someone in their life, usually their partner. Of the women who had a good, loving relationship, roughly one in eight became depressed; but among those with much less intimate relationships more than one in five became depressed.

Love does indeed heal both body and mind. And love means the triumph of 'we' over 'me'.

The electric 'we'

You – the electric 'you' – exist in the trembling web of connected brain cells. What and who you are has been sculpted by your interactions with the world, by your relationships with other people and by buffeting winds of fate. This sculpture of experience has, in league with nature's genetic recipe for your brain, moulded 'you' into what you are now.

This utterly unique and impossible-to-replicate creation is in constant flux, second by second. For even as you read this, somewhere in your brain a synapse is being strengthened, another withering. By an act of will – or whimsy – you could decide to change the state of your brain this moment: by choosing to summon some sweet memory into consciousness; by dwelling on some moment of shame or failure; by recalling a success that may have powerfully shaped your trembling web.

Should you wish to, you could train yourself vastly to improve your memory. You could learn to solve problems much better than you can now and thus improve your intelligence. You could learn to play any musical instrument you like. You are free to train your eye to detect the subtlest nuances of colour in a Vermeer painting, or to recognize the complexities of mathematical beauty in a Bach concerto. For 'you', though embroidered into a trembling web, are also in command of it – in charge of a fragment of the universe that has more connections than there are stars in our galaxy.

Any of these things that you might want to do will sculpt these connections and in turn be engraved within them. It is sometimes said that we use only 10 per cent of our brain. Though this particular figure is baseless, it is nevertheless true that our brains have a great untapped potential for developing and improving their function. It doesn't matter whether you are eight months or eighty: until the very end the trembling web is hungry for the nourishment of experience.

Your trembling web, however, will not achieve its potential if the 'you' within it does not have faith in itself. This faith comes in turn from the people who have sculpted 'you' into the trembling web – your parents, brothers, sisters, teachers, friends and lovers. In effect, the electric 'you' is actually an electric 'we'.

It is this very inter-connectedness of our trembling webs that is the source of both the wretched withering and stunted potential of some, and the superb achievements of others, among the billions of human brains that have ever existed. Mind can sculpt brain, but only if other minds in families and societies join together to make this possible.

11

Unlocking the Brain's Potential: Mind's Coming of Age

Evolution's gift to us is that we are no longer slaves of our biology. Very little of the important things we do are pre-programmed and preordained in our genes. The cultures we create through the meeting of human minds, the societies that emerge from this culture – these are what make us do what we do.

Minds sculpt the human brain, and how they sculpt it determines the measures of love and cruelty, intelligence and stupidity, creativity and slavish habit, that we dispense to the world. Yes, biology can bequeath a limited intellect, a propensity for aggression, butterfly attention, a faulty memory. It can endow us with these tendencies and a thousand others. But along with these, it has bestowed on us the gift to shape the trembling webs in which these inclinations are embroidered, and to modify them.

The intelligence of the human mind has discovered – using the science it invented – the principles and the technologies to engineer its own substratum: the human brain. Our evolutionary success is based on our ability to learn. What we learn moulds the soft plastic of the brain. That yielding plastic is evolution's parting gift to us – a parent's coming-of-age present to a young mind stepping out to a self-determining future.

So please let our poor parent off the hook, here. We are cast out from the Garden of Eden and must make our own way. As individuals, as families, we can – if we are allowed – mould our brains in a near-infinite number of ways. Mind can in many ways learn to make brain yield to its intentions. Always within biological limits, of course: the mind is impotent in facing the ravages of brain disorders like Huntingdon's, Parkinson's or Alzheimer's Disease, for instance.

It is not impotent, however, when it comes to disorders such as depression, to take just one example. Even though depression can have its roots partly in the malfunctioning of brain chemicals, mind can help to reshape these malfunctions and restore a normal mood – for instance, through inventions of the human mind such as cognitive therapy.

Even though dyslexia may in part arise from a quirk of biology, the human mind has devised ways of teaching itself to tame the faulty brain into acquiescence. So it is for intelligence. Even though age gnaws at the biological roots of our intellect, mind's inventions can stem this tide and preserve a portion of that intelligence. And give us a child whose brightness poverty and neglect have dulled, then we human beings can polish that intelligence – if we have the will.

That is the crux of it: if we have the will. The problem is that will is often sapped by distortions of Darwin's theory and the fatalism they induce. When a gene is discovered that is correlated with some complex human attribute – say intelligence – some think that this means that the environment cannot then be a factor in determining intelligence. Not so, of course. That gene may only explain a small percentage of the variation in human intellect; and, of course, the expression of many genes is only possible given the right kind of experience. The same is true for scores of other complex human behaviours for which genes apparently have been discovered.

So let us not be so meanspirited as to blame that benign parent evolution for the ills that beset us. Violence and murder can no more be blamed on that parent than Hitler's father and mother can be blamed for the Holocaust. Nor can we shift responsibility for the corrosive effects of poverty on intellect on to our biological progenitor. Darwin shuddered at his magnificent theory being so wrongly applied: in our culture, there is no such thing as natural selection in humans any more, now that the human mind has had its freedom.

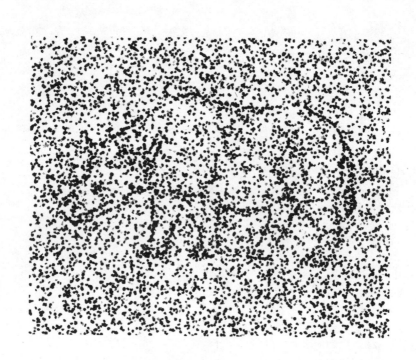

Notes

Chapter 1

p.2 ... *known as the hippocampus*. Eriksson, P.S., *et al.*, 'Neurogenesis in the adult hippocampus', *Nature Medicine*, 4, 1998, pp. 1313–17.

Chapter 2

p. 9 ... *spring into life*. This exercise is loosely based on a study carried out at the Wellcome Functional Imaging Laboratory in London. Volunteers were asked to look at degraded pictures of faces, while bloodflow in their brains was studied. They were then shown a clearer pictures of faces, followed by the degraded pictures again. As you probably found, they were much better at seeing the faces among the blobs after having seen the clearer picture. Comparing the brain's bloodflow before and after this learning, it was found that part of the temporal lobe known to be involved in perceiving faces became active. Even though they were looking at the same blobs each time, the fact of having seen the faces in the mean time moulded the synaptic connections so that the face area became active on the second look. (Dolan, R.J., *et al.* 'How the brain learns to see objects and faces in an impoverished context', *Nature*, 389, 1997, pp. 596–9.

p. 11 . . . *recall her name.* This observation was published in the *British Medical Journal*, December 1985, by Ian Deary of Edinburgh University.

p. 12 . . . *with other neurones.* See Purves, D., and Voyvodic, J.T., 'Imaging mammalian nerve cells and their connections over time in living animals', *Trends in Neuroscience*, 10, 1987, pp. 398–404, and Cotman, C.W., and Nieto-Sampedro, M., 'Brain function, synapse renewal and plasticity', *Annual Review of Psychology*, vol. 33, 1982, pp. 371–401.

p. 16 . . . *hand has changed.* See Mogilmer, A., *et al.* 'Somatosensory cortical plasticity in adult humans revealed by magnetoencephalography', *Proceedings of the National Academy of Sciences USA*, 90, 1993, pp. 3593–7.

p. 17 . . . *over a long period.* See Wang, X., Merzenich, M.M., *et al.*, 'Modelling of hand representations in adult cortex determined by timing of tactile stimulation', *Nature*, 378, 1995, pp. 71–5.

p. 18 . . . *part of the brain.* Spengler, F., and Dinse, H.R., 'Reversible relocation of representational boundaries of adult rats by intracortical microstimulation', *NeuroReport*, 5, 1994, pp. 949–53.

p. 19 . . . *it also weakens.* Fitzsimonds, R.M., Song, H., and Poo, M., 'Propagation of activity-dependent synaptic depression in simple neural networks', *Nature*, 388, 1997, pp. 439–48.

p. 21 . . . *ruefully tell you.* See Anderson, M., 'On the status of inhibitory mechanisms in cognitive memory retrieval as a model case', *Psychological Review*, 102, 1995, pp. 68–100. These studies were not based on famous people, but on various semantic categories. A similar principle is, however, likely to apply to the category of famous people.

Further reading
Kandel, E.R., Schwartz, J.H., and Jessell, T.M., *Essentials of Neural Science and Behaviour*, Prentice Hall International, 1995.

Chapter 3

p. 27 . . . *over three weeks.* Karni, A., *et al.*, 'Functional MRI evidence for adult motor cortex plasticity during motor skill learning', *Nature*, 377,

1995, pp. 155–8.

p. 28 . . . *how much they responded.* Elbert, T., *et al.,* 'Increased cortical representation of the fingers of the left hand in string players', *Science,* 270, 1995, pp. 305–7.

p. 29 . . . *benefiting other faculties.* Chan, A.S., Ho, Y-C, and Cheung, M-C, 'Music training improves verbal memory', *Nature,* 396, 1998, p. 128.

p. 30 . . . *affected in this way.* Byl, N., *et al.,* 'Sensory dysfunction associated with repetitive strain injuries of tendinitis and focal hand dystonia – a comparative study', *Journal of Orthopaedic and Sports Physical Therapy,* 23, 1996, pp. 234–44

p. 31 . . . *parts of the body.* Byl, N.N., *et al.,* 'A primate model for studying focal dystonia and repetitive strain injury: Effects on the primate somatosensory cortex', *Physical Therapy,* 77, 1997, pp. 269–84.

p. 31 . . . *such as the trunk.* Scheibel, A.B., *et al.,* 'A quantitative study of dendrite complexity in selected areas of the human cerebral cortex', *Brain and Cognition,* 12, 1990, pp. 85–101.

p. 31 . . . *of different ages.* Jacobs, B., and Scheibel, A.B., 'A quantitative dendritic analysis of Wernicke's area in humans. I. Lifespan changes', *Journal of Comparative Neurology,* 327, 1993, pp. 83–96.

p. 32 . . . *has been found.* Pascual-Leone, A., and Torres, F., 'Plasticity of the sensorimotor cortex representations of the reading finger in Braille readers', *Brain,* 116, 1993, pp. 39–52.

p. 33 . . . *by Hebbian learning.* Sterr, A., *et al.,* 'Changed perceptions in Braille readers', *Nature,* 391, 1998, pp. 134–5.

p. 33 . . . *days off work.* Pascual-Leone, A., *et al.,* 'The role of reading activity on the modulation of motor cortical outputs to the reading hand in Braille readers', *Annals of Neurology,* 38, 1995, pp. 910–15.

p. 34 . . . *with their hands.* Sadata, N., *et al.,* 'Activation of the primary visual cortex by Braille reading in blind subjects', *Nature,* 380, 1996, pp. 526–8.

p. 34 . . . *area had shrunk!* Liepert, J., *et al.,* 'Changes of cortical motor area size during immobilization', *Electromyography and Motor Control – Electroencephalography and Clinical Neurophysiology,* 97, 1995, pp. 382–6.

p. 35 ... *less interesting quarters.* Kolb, B., *Brain Plasticity and Behaviour*, Hillsdale, NJ, Erlbaum, 1996.

p. 36 ... *being in space.* Black, F.O., *et al.,* 'Vestibular plasticity following orbital spaceflight – recovery from vestibular postflight postural instability', *Acta Oto-Laryngologica*, S520 S10, 1995, pp. 450–54.

p. 36 ... *now-silent fingers.* Rossini, P.M., *et al.,* 'Short term brain plasticity in humans – transient finger representation changes in sensory cortex somatotopy following ischemic anaesthesia', *Brain Research*, 642, 1994, pp. 169–77.

p. 37 ... *of training sessions.* Yue, G., and Cole, K.J., 'Strength increases from the motor program – comparison of training with maximal voluntary and imagined muscle contractions', *Journal of Neurophysiology*, 67, 1992, pp. 1114–23.

p. 38 ... *changing the brain.* Pascual-Leone, A., *et al.,* 'Modulation of muscle responses evoked by transcranial magnetic stimulation during the acquisition of new fine motor skills', *Journal of Neurophysiology*, 74, 1995, pp. 1037–45.

p. 39 ... *imagined themselves moving.* Stephan, K.M., *et al.,* 'Functional anatomy of the mental representation of upper extremity movements in healthy subjects', *Journal of Neurophysiology*, 73, 1995, pp. 373–86.

p. 40 ... *the other hand.* For a good review of several of these mental imagery studies, see Jeannerod, M., and Decety, J., *Current Opinion in Neurobiology*, 5, 1995, pp. 727–32.

p. 41 ... *Nancy Kerrigan.* See Moran, A.P., *The Psychology of Concentration in Sports Performers*, Hove, Psychology Press, 1996.

p. 41 ... *recording of it!* The source of the information about the training of doctors and surgeons, as well as the anecdote about Glenn Gould, is in Des Coteaux, J.G., and Leclere, H., 'Learning surgical technical skills', *Canadian Journal of Surgery*, 38, 1995, pp. 33–8.

p. 43 ... *areas of the brain.* Drevets, W.C., *et al.,* 'Bloodflow changes in human somatosensory cortex during anticipated stimulation', *Nature*, 373, 1995, pp. 249–52.

p. 44 ... *to that stimulation.* Recanzone, G.H., *et al.,* 'Plasticity in the frequency representations of primary auditory cortex', *Journal of Neuroscience*, 13, 1993, pp. 87–103.

p. 47 . . . *effortless – learning.* Karni, A., *et al.,* 'Dependence on REM sleep of overnight learning of a perceptual skill', *Science*, 265, 1994, pp. 679–82.

Chapter 4

p. 50 . . . *unconvincing reassurances.* The first case was described by Dr Peter Halligan, John Marshall and colleagues at the University of Oxford (Halligan, P. W., Marshall, J. C., and Wade, D. T., 'Three arms: a case study of supernumerary phantom limb after right hemisphere stroke', *Journal of Neurology, Neurosurgery and Psychiatry*, 56, 1993, pp. 159–66.) The second case was described in Ehrenwald, II., 'Verändertes Erleben des Korperbildes mit konsekutiver Wahnbildung bei linkseitiger Hemiplegie', *Monatschrift für Psychiatrie und Neurologie*, 75, 1930, pp. 89–97.

p. 51 . . . *experiences of losing a limb.* Carlen, P.L., *et al.,* 'Phantom limbs and related phenomena in recent traumatic amputations', *Neurology*, 28, 1978, pp. 211–17.

p. 51 . . . *its proper place.* Mitchell, S.W., *Injuries of Nerves and their Consequences.* Philadelphia, J.B. Lippincott Co., 1872.

p. 52 . . . *fell on it.* See, for instance, Ramachandran, V.S., 'Perceptual correlates of massive cortical reorganization', *NeuroReport*, 3, 1992, pp. 583–6; and also Ramachandran, V.S., 'Phantom limbs, neglect syndromes, repressed memories and Freudian psychology', *International Review of Neurobiology*, 37, 1994, pp. 291–333.

p. 53 . . . *nothing in between.* Op. cit.

p. 54 . . . *of the phantom.* Op. cit.

p. 54 . . . *used to give him.* Op. cit.

p. 55 . . . *of the body strip.* Kew, J.M.J., Halligan, P.W., *et al.,* 'Abnormal access of axial vibrotactile input to deafferented somatosensory cortex in human upper limb amputees', *Journal of Neurophysiology*, 77, 1997, pp. 2753–64.

p. 55 . . . *side of the body.* Appenzeller, O., and Bicknell, J.M., 'Effects of nervous system lesions on phantom experience in amputees', *Neurology*, 19, 1969, pp. 141–6.

p. 56 . . . *above the elbow.* Halligan, P.W., *et al.,* 'Sensory disorganization and perceptual plasticity after limb amputation: a follow-up study',

NeuroReport, 5, 1994, pp. 1341–5.

p. 59 . . . *pain people experienced.* Birnbaumer, N., *et al.,* 'Effects of regional anesthesia on phantom limb pain are mirrored in changes in cortical reorganization', *Journal of Neuroscience*, 17, 1997, pp. 5503–8.

p. 59 . . . *with great effort.* Ramachandran, V.S., and Rogers-Ramachandran D., 'Synaesthesia in phantom limbs induced with mirrors', *Proceedings of the Royal Society*, B, 263, 1996, pp. 377–86.

p. 60 . . . *to this question.* Op. cit.

p. 61 . . . *ten years earlier.* Op. cit.

p. 61 . . . *phantom had changed.* Op. cit.

p. 63 . . . *do after amputation.* Op. cit.

p. 63 . . . *or even years.* Donoghue, J. P., 'Plasticity of adult sensorimotor representations', *Current Opinion in Neurobiology*, 5, 1995, pp. 749–54.

p. 64 . . . *came and went.* Cacace, A.T., *et al.,* 'Anomolous cross-modal plasticity following posterior-fossa surgery – some speculations on gaze-evoked tinnitus', *Hearing Research*, 81, 1994, pp. 22–32.

p. 64 . . . *in his mind's eye.* Harrison, J., and Baron-Cohen, S., 'Acquired and inherited forms of cross-modal correspondence', *Neurocase*, 2, 1996, pp. 245–9.

p. 65 . . . *such strange sensations.* Paulesu, E., *et al.,* 'The physiology of coloured hearing. A PET activation study of colour-word synaesthesia', *Brain*, 118, 1995, pp. 661–76.

Chapter 5

p. 69 . . . *in an accident.* Grafman, J., 'The relationship of brain tissue loss volume and lesion location to cognitive deficit', *Journal of Neuroscience*, 6, 1986, pp. 301–7.

p. 72 . . . *fibres are torn.* Sabel, B.A., 'Unrecognized potential of surviving neurons: Within-system plasticity, recovery of function, and the hypothesis of minimal residual structure', *The Neuroscientist*, 3, 1997, pp. 366–70.

p. 72 . . . *nigra have died.* Hornykiewicz, O., and Kish, S.J., 'Biochemical Pathophysiology of Parkinson's Disease', *Advances in Neurology*, 45, 1986, pp. 19–32.

p. 74 . . . *as Kirk Douglas.* Weiller, C., *et al.,* 'Recovery from Wernicke's

Aphasia: A Positron Emission Tomographic Study', *Annals of Neurology*, 37, 1995, pp. 723–32.

p. 75 ... *movement-control areas.* Seitz, R.J., *et al.,* 'Large-scale plasticity of the human motor cortex'. *Neuroreport*, 6, 1995, pp. 742–4.

p. 76 ... *from Parkinson's Disease.* Anglade, P., *et al.,* 'Synaptic plasticity in the caudate nucleus of patients with Parkinson's Disease', *Neurodegeneration*, 5, 1996, pp. 121–8.

p. 77 ... *hand twitched obediently.* Heald, A., *et al.,* 'Longitudinal study of central motor conduction time following stroke: 1 – Natural history of central motor conduction', *Brain*, 116, 1993, pp. 1355–70.

Heald, A., *et al.,* 'Longitudinal study of central motor conduction time following stroke: 2 – Central motor conduction measured within 72 h after stroke as a predictor of functional outcome at 12 months', *Brain*, 116, 1993, pp. 1371–85.

p. 78 ... *activity in the other.* Meyer, B.U., *et al.,* 'Inhibitory and excitatory interhemispheric transfers between motor cortical areas in normal humans and patients with abnormalities of the corpus callosum', *Brain*, 118, 1995, pp. 429–40.

p. 79 ... *St Louis, Missouri.* Buckner, R. L., *et al.,* 'Preserved speech abilities and compensation following prefrontal damage', *Proceedings of the National Academy of Sciences of the United States of America*, 93, 1996, pp. 1249–53.

p. 80 ... *to brain stimulation.* Turton, A., *et al.,* 'Contralateral and ipsilateral EMG responses to transcranial magnetic stimulation during recovery of arm and hand function after stroke', *Electroencephalography and Clinical Neurophysiology – Electromyography and Motor Control*, 101(4), 1996, pp. 316–28.

p. 80 ... *was only twelve.* Sabatini, U., *et al.,* 'Motor recovery after early brain damage – a case of brain plasticity', *Stroke*, 25, 1994, pp. 514–17.

p. 81 ... *of his brain.* Vargha-Khadem, F., *et al.,* 'Onset of speech after left hemispherectomy in a nine-year-old boy', *Brain*, 120, 1997, pp. 159–82.

p. 81 ... *one of them:* Op. cit.

p. 83 ... *in most cases.* Vargha-Khadem, F., and Polkey, C. E., 'A review of cognitive outcome after hemidecortication in humans', in Rose, F.D., and Johnson, D.A. (eds), *Recovery from Brain Damage: Reflections and Directions*, New York, Plenum, 1992.

p. 85 . . . *on the left side.* Goodale, M.A., *et al.*, 'Kinematic analysis of limb movements in neuropsychological research: subtle deficits and recovery of function', *Canadian Journal of Psychology*, 44, 1990, pp. 180–95.

Chapter 6

p. 98 . . . *pub darts team!* Halligan, P. W., and Marshall, J. C., 'Left neglect for near but not far space in man', *Nature*, 350, 1991, pp. 498–500.

p. 99 . . . *from unilateral neglect.* Robertson, I.H., *et al.*, 'Phasic alerting of right hemisphere neglect patients overcomes their spatial deficit in visual awareness', *Nature*, 395, 1998, pp. 169–71.

p. 101 . . . *second or two.* Robertson, I. H., *et al.*, 'Sustained attention training for unilateral neglect: theoretical and rehabilitation implications', *Journal of Clinical and Experimental Neuropsychology*, 17, 1995, pp. 416–30.

p. 102 . . . *of a therapist.* Hesse, S., *et al.*, 'Treadmill training with partial body weight support compared with physiotherapy in nonambulatory hemiparetic patients', *Stroke*, 26, 1995, pp. 976–81.

p. 103 . . . *style of training.* Bütefisch, C., *et al.*, 'Repetitive training of isolated movements improves the outcome of motor rehabilitation of the centrally paretic hand', *Journal of the Neurological Sciences*, 130, 1995, pp. 59–68.

p. 104 . . . *by electronic sensors.* Hummelsheim, H., Arnberger, S., and Mauritz, K. H., 'The influence of EMG-initiated electrical muscle stimulation on motor recovery of the centrally paretic hand', *European Journal of Neurology*, 3, 1996, pp. 245–54.

p. 104 . . . *and arm improves.* Taub, E., *et al.*, 'Technique to improve chronic motor deficit after stroke', *Archives of Physical Medicine and Rehabilitation*, 74, 1993, pp. 347–54.

p. 105 . . . *the damaged area.* Nudo, R. J., *et al.*, 'Neural substrates for the effects of rehabilitative training on motor recovery after ischemic infarct', *Science*, 272, 1996, pp. 1791–4.

p. 106 . . . *from other children.* Merzenich, M., *et al.*, 'Temporal processing deficits of language-learning impaired children ameliorated by training', *Science*, 271, 1996, pp. 77–81.

Tallal, P., *et al.*, 'Language comprehension in language-learning impaired children improved with acoustically modified speech', *Science*, 271, 1996, pp. 81–4.

p. 107 . . . *of this training*. Op. cit.

p. 108 . . . *two years later!* Robertson, I. H., *et al.*, 'Motor recovery after stroke depends on intact sustained attention: a two-year follow-up study', *Neuropsychology*, 11, 1997, pp. 290–95.

Robertson, I.H., *et al.*, 'Sustained attention training for unilateral neglect: theoretical and rehabilitation implications', *Journal of Clinical and Experimental Neuropsychology*, 17, 1995, pp. 416–30.

p. 108 . . . *movements could have*. Smania, N., *et al.*, 'Visuomotor imagery and rehabilitation of neglect'. *Archives of Physical Medicine and Rehabilitation*, 78(4), 1997, pp. 430–6.

p. 109 . . . *accelerated physical recovery*. Crisostomo, E. A., Duncan, P. W., and Propst, M., 'Evidence that amphetamine with physical therapy promotes recovery of motor function in stroke patients', *Annals of Neurology*, 23, 1988, pp. 94–7.

p. 110 . . . *damaged brain's recovery*. Mayer, E., *et al.*, 'Striatal graft-associated recovery of a lesion-induced performance deficit in the rat requires learning to use the transplant', *European Journal of Neuroscience*, 4, 1992, pp. 119–26.

Chapter 7

p. 113 . . . *any particular fact*. Schacter, D., *et al.*, 'Preserved and impaired memory functions in elderly adults', in Cerella, J., *et al.*, (eds), *Adult Information Processing: Limits on Loss*, Academic Press, New York, 1993.

p. 116 . . . *and your eighties*. Gomez-Isla, T., *et al.*, 'Neuronal loss correlates with but exceeds neurofibrillary tangles in Alzheimer's Disease', *Annals of Neurology*, 41, 1997, pp. 17–24.

p. 117 . . . *trees gradually withering*. Anderson, B., and Rutledge, V., 'Age and hemisphere effects on dendritic structure', *Brain*, 119, 1996, pp. 1983–90.

p. 117 . . . *than younger people*. Gur, R.C., *et al.*, 'Age and regional cerebral blood flow', *Archives of General Psychiatry*, 44, 1987, pp. 617–21.

p. 118... *in fifty-year-olds*. Buell, S., and Coleman, P., 'Dendritic growth in aged human brain and failure of growth in senile dementia', *Science*, 206, 1979, pp. 854–6.

p. 118... *which were new*. Grady, C.L., *et al.*, 'Age-related reductions in human recognition memory due to impaired encoding', *Science*, 269, 1995, pp. 218–21.

p. 119... *scores goes up*. Rabbitt, P., 'Does it all go together when it goes?' *Quarterly Journal of Experimental Psychology*, 46A, 1993, pp. 385–434.

p. 119... *who did not*. Sihvonen, S., *et al.*, 'Physical activity and survival in elderly people: a five-year follow-up study', *Journal of Aging and Physical Activity*, 6, 1998, pp. 133–40.

p. 119... *stronger brain responses*. Bashore, T.R., and Goddard, P.H., 'Preservative and restorative effects of aerobic fitness on the age-related slowing of mental processing speed', in Cerella, J., *et al. Adult Information Processing: Limits on Loss*, New York, Academic Press, 1993.

p. 120... *five years' education*. Bonaiuto, S., *et al.*, 'Education and occupation as risk factors for dementia: a population-based case-control study', *Neuroepidemiology*, 14, 1995, pp. 101–9.

Bonaiuto, S., *et al.*, 'Survival and dementia: a 7-year follow-up of an Italian elderly population', *Archives of Gerontology and Geriatrics*, 20, 1995, pp. 105–13.

p. 122 *and mature way*. Blanchard-Fields, F., and Abeles, R.P., 'Social cognition and aging', in *Handbook of the Psychology of Aging*, New York, Academic Press, 1996 (4th edn).

p. 122... *were younger contestants*. Maylor, E.A., 'Ageing and the retrieval of specialized and general knowledge: Performance of Masterminds', *British Journal of Psychology*, 85, 1994, pp. 105–14.

p. 123... *bag be stolen*. Giambra, L.M., and Quilter, R., 'Sustained attention in adulthood: a unique, large-sample, longitudinal and multi-cohort analysis using the Mackworth Clock-Test', *Psychology and Aging*, 3, 1988, pp. 75–83.

p. 124... *to catch up*. Baron, A., and Cerella, J., 'Laboratory tests of the disuse account of cognitive decline', in Cerella, J., *et al.* (eds), *Adult Information Processing: Limits on Loss*, New York 1993, Academic Press.

p. 125 . . . *caused by ageing.* Swaab, D.F., 'Brain aging and Alzheimer's Disease, "Wear and Tear" versus "Use it or Lose it"', *Neurobiology of Aging*, 12, 1991, pp. 317–24.

p. 125 . . . *younger professional colleagues.* Krampe, R. T., and Ericsson, K. A., 'Maintaining excellence: Deliberate practice and elite performance in young and older pianists'. *Journal of Experimental Psychology: General*, 125(4), 1996, pp. 331–59.

p. 125 . . . *effects of ageing.* Shimamura, A. P., *et al.*, 'Memory and cognitive abilities in university professors: Evidence for successful aging'. *Psychological Science*, 6, 1995, pp. 271–7.

p. 126 . . . *to decline cognitively.* Gruberbaldini, A.L., *et al.*, 'Similarity in married-couples – a longitudinal-study of mental abilities and rigidity-flexibility', *Journal of Personality and Social Psychology*, 69, 1995, pp. 191–203.

p. 126 . . *an intelligent spouse* Op. cit.

p. 127 . . . *of mental workout.* Stigsdotter-Neely, A., and Bäckman, L., 'Long-term maintenance of gains from memory training in older adults: Two 3½ year follow-up studies', *Journal of Gerontology: Psychological Sciences*, 48, 1993, pp. 233–7.

Baltes, P.B., *et al.*, 'Cognitive training research on fluid intelligence in old age: What can older adults achieve by themselves', *Psychology and Aging*, 4, 1989, pp. 217–21.

p. 128 . . . *mistakes during learning.* Wilson, B. A., *et al.*, 'Errorless learning in the rehabilitation of memory impaired people', *Neuropsychological Rehabilitation*, 4, 1994, pp. 307–26.

Chapter 8

p. 135 . . . *repeating spoken words.* Castro-Caldas, A., *et al.*, 'Learning to read and write during childhood influences the functional organization of the adult brain', *Brain*, 121, 1998, pp. 1053–63.

p. 139 . . . *are on welfare.* Hart, B., and Risley, T., *Meaningful Differences in Everyday Parenting and Intellectual Development in Young American Children.* Baltimore, Brookes, 1995.

p. 139... *childcare were assessed.* Melhuish, E.C., *et al.*, 'Type of childcare at 18 months – I. Differences in interactional experience', *Journal of Child Psychology and Psychiatry*, 31, 1990, pp. 849–60.

p. 140... *day-care was studied.* Melhuish, E.C., *et al.*, 'Type of childcare at 18 months – II. Relations with cognitive and language development', *Journal of Child Psychology and Psychiatry*, 31, 1990, pp. 861–70.

p. 142... *as it is born.* Fifer, W.P., and Moon, C.M., 'The role of mother's voice in the organization of brain functions in the newborn', *Acta Paediatrica*, 83, 1994, pp. 86–93.

p. 143... *responded to them.* Murray, L., *et al.*, 'Depressed mothers' speech to their infants and its relation to infant gender and cognitive development', *Journal of Child Psychology and Psychiatry*, 31, 1993, pp. 1083–1101.

Murray, L., *et al.* The cognitive development of 5-year old children of postnatally depressed mothers', *Journal of Child Psychology and Psychiatry*, 37, 1996, pp. 927–35.

p. 145... *periphery of vision.* Neville, H.J., 'Neurobiology of cognitive and language processing: Effects of early experience', in Gibson, K.R., and Petersen, A.C. (eds), *Brain Maturation and Cognitive Development: Comparative and Cross-cultural Perspectives*, Amsterdam, Aladine de Gruyter Press, 1991.

p. 147... *at these tests.* Haggard, M., and Hughes, E., *Screening Children's Hearing*, HMSO, London, 1998.

p. 148... *from poor education.* Ceci, S.J., *On Intelligence ... More or Less: A Bio-ecological Treatise on Intellectual Development*, Englewood Cliffs, Prentice Hall, NJ, 1990.

p. 149... *better school system.* Op. cit.

p. 149... *shaped by environment.* Capron, C., and Duyme, M., 'Assessment of effects of socio-economic status on IQ in a full cross-fostering study', *Nature*, 340, 1989, pp. 552–4.

p. 152... *not being unusual.* Ramey, C.T., *et al.*, 'The plasticity of intellectual development: Insights from preventitive intervention', *Child Development*, 55, 1984, pp. 1913–25.

p. 153... *but practice!* Ericsson, K.A. *et al.*, 'The role of deliberate practice in the acquisition of expert performance, *Psychological*

Review, 100, 1993, pp. 363–406.

p. 155 . . . *standard classroom methods*. Bloom, B.S., 'The 2 sigma problem. The search for methods of group instruction as effective as one-to-one tutoring', *Educational Researcher*, 13, 1984, pp. 3–16.

p. 156 . . . *use the method*. Op. cit.

p. 159 . . . *mathematics and English*. Adey, P., and Shayer, M., 'An exploration of long-term transfer effects following an extended intervention program in the High School science curriculum', *Cognition and Instruction*, 11, 1993, pp. 1–29.

p. 160 . . . *into their studies*. Flynn, J.R., *Asian-American IQ: Achievement beyond IQ*, Hillsdale, NJ, Erlbaum 1991.

p. 161 . . . *in reading ability*. Johnston, R.S., and Watson, J., 'Developing reading, spelling and phonemic awareness skills in primary school children', *Reading*, July, 1997, pp. 37–40.

p. 162 . . . *structure or phonology*. Adams, M.J., *Beginning to Read*, London, MIT Press, 1994.

p. 163 . . . *out unfamiliar words*. Bryant, P.E., and Bradley, L., 'Why children sometimes write words which they do not read', in Frith, U. (ed), *Cognitive Processes in Spelling*, Academic Press, New York, 1980, pp. 355–72.

Chapter 9

p. 171 . . . *jump and escape*. Joseph LeDoux of the Center for Neural Science at New York University has contributed most to our understanding of how emotions – particularly fear – are represented in the brain. His accessible and excellently written book, *The Emotional Brain* (London, Weidenfeld & Nicolson, 1998), tells the fascinating story of his scientific work.

p. 172 . . . *of years ago*. This anecdote about Darwin is reported in LeDoux's book, p. 112.

p. 173 . . . *the clever cortex*. Amaral, D.G., *et al.*, 'Anatomical organization of the primate amygdaloid complex, in Aggleton, J.P. (ed), *The Amygdala: Neurobiological Aspects of Emotion, Memory and Mental Dysfunction*, New York, Wiley-Liss, 1992.

p. 177 . . . *they appeared subliminally*. Morris, J.S., *et al.*, 'Conscious and unconscious emotional learning in the human amygdala', *Nature*, 393,

1998, pp. 467–70.

p. 177 . . . *with the angry faces.* Shin, L.M., *et al.*, 'Visual imagery and perception in posttraumatic stress disorder: a PET investigation', *Archives of General Psychiatry*, 54, 1997, pp. 233–41.

p. 177 . . . *are being persuaded.* Bornstein, R.F., 'Subliminal mere exposure effects', in Bornstein, R.F., and Pittman, T.S. (eds), *Perception without Awareness: Cognitive, Clinical and Social Perspectives*, New York, Guildford, 1992, pp. 191–210.

p. 179 . . . *by the experience.* Claparede, E., 'Recognition and "me-ness"', in Rapaport, D., *et al.*, *Organization and Pathology of Thought*, New York, Columbia University Press, 1911.

p. 179 . . . *and danger involved.* 'Face processing impairments after encephalitis: amygdala damage and recognition of fear', *Neuropsychologia*, 36, 1998, pp. 59–70.

p. 179 . . . *much less readily.* Angrilli, A., *et al.*, 'Startle reflex and emotion modulation impairment after a right amygdala lesion', *Brain*, 119, 1996, pp. 1991–2000.

p. 179 . . . *some innocuous stimulus.* LaBar, K.S., *et al.*, 'Impaired fear conditioning following unilateral temporal lobectomy in humans', *Journal of Neuroscience*, 15, 1995, pp. 6846–55.

p. 180 . . . *in a normal way.* Hare, R. D., 'Psychopathy and physiological activity during anticipation of aversive stimulus in a distraction paradigm', *Psychophysiology*, 19, 1982, pp. 266–71.

p. 185 . . . *tends not to happen.* LeDoux, J.E., *et al.*, 'Indelibility of sub-cortical emotional memories', *Journal of Cognitive Neuroscience*, 1, 1989, pp. 238–43.

p. 186 . . . *package of treatment.* Solomon, S.D., *et al.*, 'Efficacy of treatments of posttraumatic stress disorder', *Journal of the American Medical Association*, 268, 1992, pp. 633–8.

p. 187 . . . *the 'caudate nucleus'.* Baxter, L.R., 'PET studies of cerebral function in major depression and obsessive-compulsive disorder. The emerging prefrontal cortex concensus', *Annals of Clinical Psychiatry*, 3, 1991, pp. 103–9.

p. 190 . . . *post-traumatic stress disorder.* Pynoos, R.S., *et al.*, 'Issues in the developmental neurobiology of traumatic stress', *Annals of the New York Academy of Sciences*, 821, 1997, pp. 176–92.

p. 190 ... *hypervigilance and edginess.* Southwick, S.M., *et al.,* 'Noradrenergic alterations in posttraumatic stress disorder', *Annals of the New York Academy of Sciences,* 821, 1997, pp. 125–41.

p. 191 ... *shown in this case.* Markowitsch, J.J., *et al.,* 'Psychic trauma causing grossly reduced brain metabolism and cognitive deterioration', *Neuropsychologia,* 36, 1998, pp. 77–82.

p. 193 ... *to their normal size.* McEwen, B.S., 'Paradoxical effects of adrenal steroids on the brain: Protection versus degeneration', *Biological Psychiatry,* 31, 1992, pp. 177–99.

p. 193 ... *with physical abuse.* Teicher, M.H., *et al.,* 'Preliminary evidence for abnormal cortical development in physically and sexually abused children using EEG coherence and MRI', *Annals of the New York Academy of Sciences,* 821, 1997, pp. 160–74.

p. 195 ... *in the frontal lobes.* Baker, S.C., *et al.,* 'The interaction between mood and cognitive function studied with PET', *Psychological Medicine,* 27, 1997, pp. 565–78.

p. 195 ... *film solved it!* Isen, A.M., *et al.,* 'Positive affect facilitates creative problem solving', *Journal of Personality and Social Psychology,* 52, 1987, pp. 1122–31.

p. 195 ... *feel more positive.* Schiff, B.B., and Lamon, M., 'Inducing emotion by unilateral contraction of hand muscles', *Cortex,* 30, 1994, pp. 247–54.

p. 196 ... *are less inhibited.* Davidson, R.J., 'Anterior cerebral assymmetry and the nature of emotion', *Brain and Cognition,* 20, 1992, pp. 125–51.

p. 196 ... *fit your expression.* Larsen, R.J., *et al.,* 'Facilitating the furrowed brow: An unobtrusive test of the facial feedback hypothesis applied to unpleasant affect', *Cognition and Emotion,* 6, 1992, pp. 321–38.

p. 196 ... *peppered with 'ü's.* Zajonc, R.B., *et al.,* 'Feeling and facial efference: Implications of the vascular theory of emotion, *Psychological Review,* 96, 1989, pp. 395–416.

p. 198 ... *a gloomy roommate.* Hokanson, J.E., *et al.,* 'Interpersonal perceptions by depressed college students', *Cognitive Therapy and Research,* 15, 1991, pp. 443–57.

Chapter 10

p. 202 . . . *general intellectual abilities.* Winocur, G., and Moscovitch, M., 'A comparison of cognitive function in institutionalised and community dwelling old people of normal intelligence', *Canadian Journal of Psychology*, 44, 1990, pp. 435–44.

p. 202 . . . *lives and destinies.* Albert, M., *et al.*, 'Predictors of cognitive change in older persons: MacArthur studies of successful aging', *Psychology and Aging*, 10, 1995, pp. 578–89.

p. 203 . . . *vulnerable to disease.* Irwin, M., *et al.*, 'Life events, depressive symptoms and immune function', *American Journal of Psychiatry*, 144, 1987, pp. 437–41.

p. 206 . . . *one study has shown.* Cohn, J.F., *et al.*, 'Face-to-face inter-actions of postpartum depressed and nondepressed mother–infant pairs at 2 months', *Developmental Psychology*, 26, 1990, pp. 15–23.

p. 206 . . . *to other people.* Field, T., *et al.*, 'Infants of depressed mothers show "depressed" behaviour even with non-depressed adults', *Child Development*, 59, 1988, pp. 1569–79.

p. 208 . . . *might not be desirable.* Taylor, G.J., *et al.*, 'The alexithymia construct: a potential program for psychosomatic medicine', *Psychosomatics*, 32, 1991, pp. 153–64.

p. 208 . . . *songs or rhymes.* Shoda, Y., Mischel, W. and Peake, P.K., 'Predicting adolescent cognitive and self-regulatory competencies from preschool delay of gratification: Identifying diagnostic con-ditions', *Developmental Psychology*, 26, 1990, pp. 978–86.

p. 213 . . . *on the increase.* Achenbach, T., and Howell, C., 'Are America's children's problems getting worse? A 13-year comparison', *Journal of the American Academy of Child and Adolescent Psychiatry*, 32, 1993, pp. 1145–54.

p. 214 . . . *taken into consideration.* Smith, J.R., and Brooks-Gunn, J., 'Correlates and consequences of harsh discipline for young children', *Archives of Pediatrics & Adolescent Medicine*, vol. 151, 1997, pp. 777–86.

p. 215 . . . *an adult stranger.* Dunn, J., *et al.*, 'Family talk about feeling states and children's later understanding of others' emotions', *Developmental Psychology*, 27, 1991, pp. 448–55.

p. 216 . . . *by parental death.* Rutter, M., 'Parent–child separation: psychological effects on the children', *Journal of Child Psychology and*

Psychiatry, 12, 1971, pp. 233–60.

Cowan, P.A., and Hetherington, E.M. (eds), *Family Transitions*, Hillsdale, NJ, Erlbaum, 1991.

p. 217 . . . *had not split up.* Richards, M., *et al.*, 'The effects of divorce and separation on mental health in a national UK birth cohort', *Psychological Medicine*, 27, 1997, pp. 1121–8.

Richards, M., 'The international year of the family – family research', *Psychologist*, 8, 1995, pp. 17–20.

p. 217 . . . *to an abnormal degree.* Malatesa, C.Z., and Haviland, J.M., 'Learning display rules: the socialization of emotion expression in infancy', *Child Development*, 53, 1982, pp. 991–1003.

p. 217 . . . *to be aggressive themselves.* Grych, J., and Fincham, F., 'Marital conflict and children's adjustment: a cognitive contextual framework', *Psychological Bulletin*, 101, 1992, pp. 267–90.

p. 217 . . . *angry verbal argument.* Cummings, E.M., 'Coping with background anger in early childhood', *Child Development*, 58, 1987, pp. 976–84.

p. 217 . . . *babies were born.* Belsky, J., *et al.*, 'Continuity and discontinuity in infant negative and positive emotionality: Family antecedents and attachment consequences', *Developmental Psychology*, 27, 1991, pp. 421–31.

p. 217 . . . *children had seen one.* Richters, J.E., and Martinez, P., 'The NIMH Community Violence Project: I. Children as victims and witnesses of violence', *Psychiatry: Interpersonal and Biological Processes*, 56, 1993, pp. 7–21.

p. 219 . . . *towards their spouses.* Huesmann, L.R., *et al.*, 'Stability of aggression over time and generations', *Developmental Psychology*, 20, 1984, pp. 1120–34.

p. 220 . . . *happened in the family.* Beck, R., and Fernandez, E., 'Cognitive-behavioral therapy in the treatment of anger: a meta-analysis', *Cognitive Research and Therapy*, 22, 1998, pp. 63–74.

p. 220 . . . *stimuli than normal.* Blair, R.J.R., *et al.*, 'The psychopathic individual: A lack of responsiveness to distress cues?' *Psychophysiology*, 34, 1997, pp. 192–8.

p. 222 . . . *better brain functioning.* Kolb, B., and Gibb, R., 'Neuroplasticity and recovery of function following brain injury', in Stuss,

D.T., Winocur, G., and Robertson I.H. (eds), *Cognitive Neuro-rehabilitation*, New York, Cambridge University Press, 1999.

p. 222 ... *that are stunted.* This evidence comes from an as yet unpublished study by Professor Harry T. Chugani of the Department of Radiology, Wayne State University School of Medicine, Detroit, USA.

p. 223 ... *course of their stay.* Tizard, J., and Hodges, J., 'The effects of early institutional rearing on the development of eight-year-old children', *Journal of Child Psychology and Psychiatry*, 19, 1978, pp. 99–118.

p. 223 ... *were psychiatrically ill.* Quinton, D., *et al.*, 'Institutional rearing, parental difficulties and marital suppport', *Psychological Medicine*, 14, 1984, pp. 107–24.

p. 224 ... *almost total isolation.* Koluchova, J., 'Severe deprivation in twins: a case study', *Journal of Child Psychology and Psychiatry*, 13, 1972, pp. 107–14.

Koluchova, J., 'The further development of twins after severe and prolonged deprivation: a second report', *Journal of Child Psychology and Psychiatry*, 17, 1976, pp. 181–8.

p. 225 ... *with their mothers.* Main, J., and Solomon, J., 'Procedures for identifying infants as disorganized/disoriented during the Ainsworth Strange Situation', in Greenberg, M., *et al.* (eds), *Attachment in the Preschool Years*, Chicago, University of Chicago Press, 1990.

Carlson, V. *et al.*, 'Disorganized/disoriented attachment relationships in maltreated infants', *Developmental Psychology*, 23, 1989, pp. 525–31.

p. 225 ... *their infant children.* Lyons-Ruth, K., *et al.*, 'Infants at social risk: Maternal depression and family support services as mediators of infant development and security of attachment', *Child Development*, 61, 1990, pp. 85–98.

p. 227 ... *an unhappy marriage.* Weissman, M.M., 'Advances in psychiatric epidemiology: rates and risks for major depression', *American Journal of Public Health*, 77, 1987, pp. 444–51.

Index

genitals and phantom limbs 52, 54
genius and mental development 153–6
geography analogy 53
'glue ear' (otitis media) *see* otitis media
golfing analogy 102
'good-neighbours' function 72, 75–6
Gould, Glenn 41
grammar 146
'gut feeling' 171

Hale, Sheila 88–9
Hale, Sir John 88–90, 90
hate 181–3
Head Start project (USA) 152
headhunters analogy 35
hearing 63–4, 145
    see also deafness
Hebb, Donald 10
Hebbian learning 10, 13, 16, 18
    and complexity of neural network 69–70
    fear and danger 174, 186
    and phantom limbs 60
    reconnection of cells 94
    and rehabilitation 103
    and RSI 31
hemispheres of brain
    competition between 95–6
    damage to 79–80, 93
    help and hindrance in 78–80
    living with half brain 81–3
    right vs. left activity 42, 57, 74, 93, 98–9,
        195–6
hippocampus area of brain 2, 192–3
homes, broken 216–17
hormones, steroid stress 192
Huntingdon's disease 109, 230
hurdling analogy 25–6, 40
hyperalertness and terror 189–91

identity, personal 227–8
IGF2R (gene) 150–1
illiteracy 133–6
    see also education
imagining physical movement 36–41
independence 202–3
infarction, cerebral 72–3
inhibition
    as constraint 91, 109
    and ignoring distraction 114–15
input, importance of 91, 102
intelligence 69, 144, 148, 230
    emotional 166
    fluid vs. crystallized 115

see also education
inter-connectedness of webs 228
IQ (intelligence quotient) in children
    148–51, 154
ivory-tower scholars analogy 60–1

job, brain shaped by 31–3, 121–3
John (medical student case study) 210–12
Jordan, Michael 41

Kerrigan, Nancy 41
Killy, Jean-Claude 41

language 32, 74, 79, 81–3
    brain's response to 91
    children and impairment of 105–6
    development in children 105–7, 139–40,
        152, 205–6
    dyslexia 160–5
    dysphasia 89
    feedback to children 142–4
    phonics 161–3
    see also speaking
learning 10–11, 28, 47, 105
    and age 113
    before birth 142, 206
    in a different way 108
    and importance of feedback 156–7
    see also education
lifestyle and ageing 119
limbic system 171
literacy *see* illiteracy
locus coeruleus part of brain 189, 190
logical reasoning 127
long-term potentiation (LTP) 10
love
    and brain growth 221–4
    healing power of 226–7
    problems of relationships 224–6
LTP (long-term potentiation) 10
Lucy (parenting study) 200, 206

map of the body, brain's 54–7, 62
Mark (parenting study) 201–2, 218, 219–20
marketing *see* advertising
marshmallow experiment with pre-school
    children 208–9
Mastermind television programme 122
medulla 14
memory 83, 86
    effect of stress 192–3
    long-term 14
    for numbers 154–5
    for source of knowledge 113–14